A HISTORY OF FINANCIAL TECHNOLOGY AND REGULATION

Using the lens of history, *A History of Financial Technology and Regulation* illuminates recent changes to the world of finance. With lucid prose and the help of concrete examples, Seth Oranburg helps readers understand the role of technology in finance today, including complex phenomena such as mutual funds, cryptocurrencies, and the stock market itself. Chapters begin with basic principles and historical analogy before describing complex digital-investment strategies and instruments. Readers will also gain an introduction to key concepts in financial regulation, learning how law and regulations prevented some financial crises while perpetuating others. Oranburg concludes with ideas about what's next for finance and how the law should respond. This book will appeal to specialists and nonspecialists alike who are interesting in learning more about business, economics, finance, law, and regulation.

Seth C. Oranburg is an award-winning scholar on Law & Entrepreneurship. His work on Securities Regulation is published in multiple languages and selected as some of the best articles in the field. His scholarship is praised as informative, interesting, and easily readable. He teaches Business Associations, Contracts, Financial Skills and Venture Capital Law at Duquesne University.

A History of Financial Technology and Regulation

FROM AMERICAN INCORPORATION TO CRYPTOCURRENCY AND CROWDFUNDING

SETH C. ORANBURG
Duquesne University

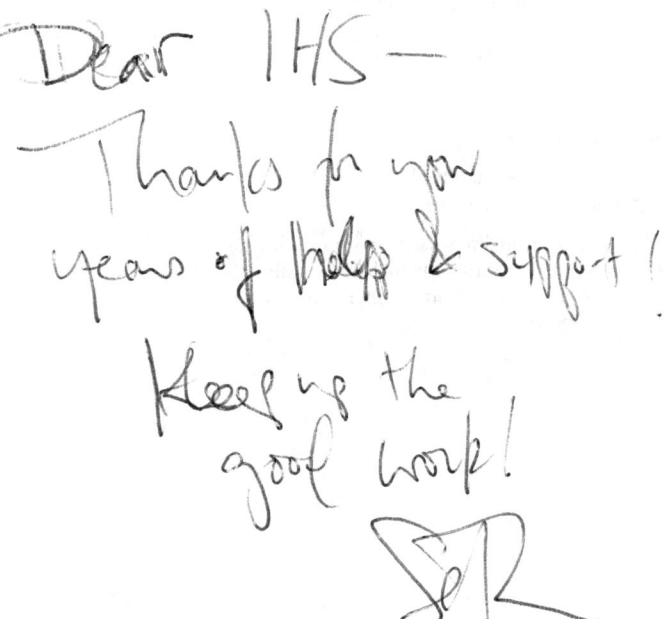

CAMBRIDGE
UNIVERSITY PRESS

University Printing House, Cambridge CB2 8BS, United Kingdom

One Liberty Plaza, 20th Floor, New York, NY 10006, USA

477 Williamstown Road, Port Melbourne, VIC 3207, Australia

314–321, 3rd Floor, Plot 3, Splendor Forum, Jasola District Centre, New Delhi – 110025, India

103 Penang Road, #05–06/07, Visioncrest Commercial, Singapore 238467

Cambridge University Press is part of the University of Cambridge.

It furthers the University's mission by disseminating knowledge in the pursuit of education, learning, and research at the highest international levels of excellence.

www.cambridge.org
Information on this title: www.cambridge.org/9781107153400
DOI: 10.1017/9781316597736

© Seth C. Oranburg 2022

This publication is in copyright. Subject to statutory exception and to the provisions of relevant collective licensing agreements, no reproduction of any part may take place without the written permission of Cambridge University Press.

First published 2022

A catalogue record for this publication is available from the British Library.

ISBN 978-1-107-15340-0 Hardback
ISBN 978-1-316-60730-5 Paperback

Cambridge University Press has no responsibility for the persistence or accuracy of URLs for external or third-party internet websites referred to in this publication and does not guarantee that any content on such websites is, or will remain, accurate or appropriate.

What has been will be again, what has been done will be done again; there is nothing new under the sun.

Ecclesiastes 1:9

Contents

List of Figures	*page* xi
Acknowledgments	xii
Introduction	1

THE FIRST ERA: THE WILD WEST

1	**Under a Buttonwood Tree**	7
	The Nature of Corporations	8
	Corporate Limited Liability	8
	Corporate Investors	9
	Corporate Risk and Reward	10
	Corporate Fraud	11
	Origins of the New York Stock Exchange	13
	Free Incorporation	16
	The Panic of 1837	17
	The Free Banking Era	19
	Return to National Banking	20
	Bibliography	22
2	**The Golden Spike**	24
	Financing the Railroads	26
	Preferred Stock	26
	Financial Preferences	28
	The Gold Standard	29
	Bibliography	30
3	**Roar and Crash**	31
	The Ticker	31
	Network Effects	33

	Self-Regulatory Organizations	34
	Bucket Shops	34
	Wash Sales	37
	Investment Fever	37
	Bibliography	39

THE SECOND ERA: ELECTRIC LIGHT

4	**A New Deal**	43
	Aftermath of the Crash	44
	Keynesian Economic Theory	45
	Brandeisian Regulatory Theory	46
	The New Deal Securities Regulations	47
	Bibliography	49

5	**Computational Asymmetry**	51
	Pre-regulation Investment Advice	52
	The Investment Company and Investment Company Act of 1940	52
	Mutual Funds	53
	Diversification	54
	Information Costs	56
	Transaction Costs	56
	Agency Costs and Misaligned Interests	56
	Computer Power	59
	The Index Fund	62
	Agency Costs in Index Funds	62
	Mistakes Have Been Made	63
	Regulation of Index Funds	63
	Conclusions on Computational Investing	64
	Bibliography	65

6	**Silicon Valley**	67
	The Start of Startups	68
	Early Origins of Venture Capital	69
	Evolution of Venture Capital	70
	Modern Venture Capital	75
	Reg. D: Private Financing's Safe Harbor	77
	Accredited Investors and Qualified Purchases	78
	Bibliography	84

THE THIRD ERA: SOCIAL MEDIA INVESTING

7	**The Dot-Com Bubble**	87
	NASDAQ: The Tech Stock Market	89
	Penny Stocks	89
	The Dot-Com Bubble	91
	The Sarbanes-Oxley Act of 2002	93
	Bibliography	94
8	**Social Media Activism**	96
	Direct Democratization of Corporate Governance	98
	Internet Shareholder Voting	98
	Regulation FD and Shareholder Collective Action	99
	Corporate Gadflies	103
	Influencers	104
	Meme Investing	108
	Bibliography	109
9	**Cryptographic Theory and Decentralized Finance**	112
	Origins of Cryptography	112
	Cypherpunks	113
	Bitcoin	115
	Satoshi Nakamoto: What's in a Name?	116
	Nakamoto's Emails	118
	Cryptocurrency: Private, Not Secret	119
	Digital Currency's Double-Spend Problem	121
	Blockchain Technology	123
	Investing in Cryptocurrency	123
	Bibliography	124
10	**Cryptocurrency Regulation**	129
	Who Regulates Digital Assets?	130
	SEC Regulation of Crypto-Securities	131
	Initial Coin Offerings	132
	Regulation of Cryptocurrencies	136
	Cryptocurrency Markets	142
	Constitutional Questions	144
	Bibliography	151

11	**Crowdfunding**	153
	Crowdfunding's Origins in the Dot-Com Era	153
	The JOBS Act	157
	Equity Crowdfunding in 2021	157
	Limited Fundraising	159
	Lack of Resale Options	160
	No Special Purpose Vehicles	162
	How Crowdfunding Could Work	162
	Why Should We Care about Crowdfunding?	169
	Bibliography	172
	Conclusion	174
Index		191

Figures

1.1	A private banknote issued by Allentown Business College Bank in 1874	page 20
2.1	Replica of the Golden Spike	25
3.1	Western Union Ticker Model 3-A	32
3.2	Cover of *Fame and Fortune Weekly*, May 6, 1921, titled "After a Golden State or Breaking a 'Bucket Shop' Combine"	35
4.1	Unemployed men queued outside a depression soup kitchen opened in Chicago by Al Capone	45
5.1	A female "computer" at Langley	59
5.2	Logarithmic increase in processing power, according with Moore's law	61
6.1	The garage in Palo Alto, California where the Hewlett-Packard (HP) corporation began – and where some say Silicon Valley was born	69
6.2	The traditional startup financing timeline	74
8.1	The Kodak price spike	97
9.1	Market share of the top fifteen cryptocurrencies in February 2021	115
9.2	Illustration of public and private cryptographic keys	120
10.1	Regulation of Digital Assets	130
12.1	Financial crises, regulations, and the IPO market from 1973 to 2020	188

Acknowledgments

Thanks to my research assistants, Christian E. Hakim, Joseph R. Stead, and Sarah D. Shumate-Connor, and to the Duquesne law librarians, Julie Tedjeske, Amy Lovell, Chuck Sprowls, and Tsegaye Beru, for your invaluable contributions to this book, and to Duquesne University for providing the resources to employ you in this work. Thanks to the Classical Liberal Institute at New York University for sponsoring my research and especially to its codirector Richard A. Epstein for his mentorship and support. Thanks to my colleagues at Duquesne and elsewhere who read and commented on my drafts, including Lisa Bernstein, Pablo Echeverri, Richard Heppner, Robert Miller, Wesley Oliver, and Ann Marie Schiavone. Above all, thanks to my wife, Talia DeFrancesco Oranburg, and my mother, Penny Oranburg, both of whom not only supported me during the production of this book, but who also read drafts, made edits, and provided comments. I am so lucky to have you all in my life. Thank you.

Introduction

The end is nigh for financial regulation. The financial revolution will not be televised; rather, it will be liked, shared, tweeted, and direct messaged. Data technology, such as "apps" for cellular phones, may prove to be as transformative for investing as the telegraph or even the Internet. But few people understand how these technologies impact investing. This book explores the legal dynamics and ramifications of financial regulations in the digital age and offers readers a detailed, but digestible, account of corporate finance history. It pairs lively narrative with brief applications of economic theory. This provides readers with the historical context and theoretical framework needed to understand the true nature of finance today – and where finance is trending.

This book focuses on the impact of technology on investing in regulated markets. It identifies how legal regulation is lagging behind technology, leaving ordinary investors and main street entrepreneurs without safe and profitable financial options. The current regulatory apparatus is vastly expensive and causes huge wealth disparities. Instead of providing for a land of equal financial opportunity, the system protects entrenched interests at the expense of newcomers. These problems demand that scholars and policymakers study our distended financial regulatory system and work to reform it.

Our story of U.S. corporate finance unfolds in three eras. The first era began with the ratification of the Constitution in the 1790s and ended with the Great Depression in the 1930s. The second era began with the Securities Act of 1933 and ended with the Great Recession of 2007–2008. The third era began with the emergence of Bitcoin in 2008 and continues to this day. We are living in the third era of corporate finance.

With this timeline in mind, we can see qualities that are particular to each of these eras. The first era is characterized by unbridled capitalism, rugged individualism, and western expansion. In the first era, there were many financial markets across the young nation, but they were relatively disconnected. Then, technological advances, including the railway and the telegraph, inexorably intertwined the nation of states into an economic union. By the time that the last continental territory, Arizona, was admitted as a state on February 14, 1912, a vast network of roads, rail, telephone lines, and power grids knit the United States together as a single economic entity. Unfortunately, that interconnectedness also meant that any financial crisis would be of national proportions.

The second era was characterized by a centralized command-and-control approach to securities regulation. This began when this nation fell into the Great Depression, which provided the impetus for sweeping political and economic change. This international economic crisis created political instability across the globe. Americans looked to Uncle Sam for help in this desperate time as socialism and communism swept across Europe. The U.S. federal government responded by dramatically increasing in size and scope. President Franklin Delano Roosevelt created a plethora of new federal agencies, including the Securities and Exchange Commission (the SEC). To pay for this growing federal bureaucracy, the maximum federal income tax was increased from about 3 percent in 1932 to over 50 percent by 1944.

As Washington, DC, increasingly became America's political center, New York City increasingly became the locus of financial activity in the United States. Yet amid this period of centralization and consolidation, an intrepid group of risk-seekers began developing its own self-regulated band of venture capital investing – an investors' club limited to the affluent. The New York Stock Exchange rose in the East as Silicon Valley rose in the West. Meanwhile the middle of America did reasonably well. For a time, corporate profits seemed to flow to a rising middle class. But by the 1990s, investment had changed. Most public stock were owned by large firms, not people. The dot-com era was the last hurrah for public stock markets. After its excesses crashed in Y2K, regulators once again tightened the screws on domestic stock markets.

In the third era, however, geographic limitations fall away as the Internet increasingly makes financial markets ubiquitous and accessible to all. Rising social consciousness about wealth inequality and popular notions of Startup Nation and Silicon Valley have brought about a renewed interest in democratizing entrepreneurship and investment, while a growing distrust of federal regulators and centralized banks has brought "cypherpunk" culture – which combines cryptography and anarchy – into the mainstream. Now, anyone can participate in exotic, unregulated financial products, like cryptocurrencies, initial coin offerings, and decentralized autonomous organizations. The recent rise of "metaverses," which are persistent online worlds that have their own societies and economies, is further hastening the demise of any efforts to centrally control finance.

In our third era, financial law has fallen far behind financial technology. Federal laws that regulated communications about investment opportunities that were drafted during the Great Depression no longer make sense in the digital age. For example, the legislative history of the Securities Act prohibits fraudulent advertising, but these concepts do not easily map onto a social media world where "influencers" promote companies through "buzz" and "likes." Further, new technologies allow us to write self-enforcing contracts that eliminate the need for courts of law and lawyers. Judges continuously and emphatically struggle to fit the square peg of modern communication into the round hole of traditional advertising and business practices.

How do we further the dual goals of regulation – encouraging the generation of capital while protecting investors? What legal regime would fit with the flexible and varied nature of investment and in the Third Era economy? How do we balance the benefits of less regulation with the potential costs of fraud and corruption? Is there an efficient amount of regulation, and, if so, how do we calculate it?

By studying the history, theory, and reality of corporate finance, this book finds that, in general, the costs associated with overregulation are vastly underestimated. But the solution is not random deregulation. While reverting to an era of deregulation may seem appealing, the truth is, some regulations are more necessary than others. The question becomes, which regulations should be increased, and which should be diminished?

When this question is presented to regulators and policy makers, history shows that very wealthy investors and long-established companies have an oversized impact on the regulatory process. The result are financial policies that perpetuate and even increase wealth inequalities, without preventing financial crises that are devastating for ordinary investors and small businesses. This untenable problem causes Americans to lose faith in capitalism – even if our current system is really bureaucratic cronyism masquerading as free-market capitalism. The solution requires a reevaluation of financial technology and its regulation.

The First Era

The Wild West

1

Under a Buttonwood Tree

In 1792, a handful of would-be stock traders gathered underneath a buttonwood tree on Wall Street in New York City. They signed an agreement, known as the Buttonwood Agreement, that would one day grow into the New York Stock Exchange, which is by far the world's largest stock exchange today. But, in those days, information travelled slowly, so markets were regional. The federal government was small, and it lacked the resources to police financial practices in the vast and growing new nation. Citizens were mainly left to fend for themselves. In this Wild West of rugged individualism, expansion, and industrialization, many stock markets came and went. Small and often shady operations, known pejoratively as bucket shops, let people bet on stock prices without actually selling the stock itself.

> It might be demonstrated that the most productive system of finance will always be the least burdensome.
>
> – Alexander Hamilton, Federalist Paper No. 35

Most students of American history know that our Constitution is based on a strong belief in protecting personal liberty. Indeed, the original Thirteen Colonies that formed the United States of America declared their independence from England on July 4, 1776, to secure their inalienable rights to "Life, Liberty, and the pursuit of Happiness." Capitalism is a form of personal economic liberty, and the Constitution contemplates a capitalist society. To protect capitalism from social control by the states, the commerce clause was ensconced in the Constitution.

But the wealthy, landowning Founders surely thought differently about capitalism and corporations than we do today. In early America, corporations could only be organized by introducing a private bill in the state legislature, which needed to be passed and signed into law by the governor. Accordingly, there were only six for-profit incorporations in colonial America by 1789. Indeed, the lucky few who successfully lobbied the legislature to grant a corporate charter received an effective monopoly. For this reason, early corporate charters were also known as "patents." Today, a patent refers to the exclusive right granted by a sovereign state to commercialize a certain product or to employ a certain process. In colonial days, obtaining the state's permission to create a corporation was tantamount to an exclusive right to conduct that line of business under the corporate form.

THE NATURE OF CORPORATIONS

Modern corporations can be freely formed by filing some simple forms. But why do people form corporations? And why do governments permit it? The answer to this fundamental question requires a little discussion on the nature of the corporate form. The following sections provide a brief review of key corporate concepts.

CORPORATE LIMITED LIABILITY

Corporations are entities that exist separately from the people who form them and the governments who charter them. Some have even gone so far as to say that corporations are people, but that is not precisely true. However, corporations do have certain rights of their own, rights which are not derived from the individual rights of their progenitors. Corporations may own property and even have limited rights to free speech. And, since they have an existence that is separate and independent from any particular human being, they can effectively exist forever. These characteristics make corporations powerful vehicles for the agglomeration of great wealth. As states increasingly allowed individuals to form corporations at will, the corporate form drove economic development in early America.

The key reason people choose to concentrate wealth in corporations is because investors in corporations cannot lose more money than they invest. This is a concept called limited liability, and it does not exist when a person pursues a trade without a corporate form. For example, imagine that Bob, a builder, spends $200 in materials to build a storage shed for Carry, who pays Bob $300 for his work and materials. Now Bob has an additional $100 thanks to his work. But what if the shed collapses due to a defect in Bob's work, destroying Carry's goods stored there, worth $500? Carry can sue Bob for $300 to rebuild the shed plus $500 to replace the goods. Bob is now $700 worse off than before he started because he has unlimited liability for injuries caused by his work.

What if Bob formed a corporation instead? Imagine that Bob invests $200 in Bob Corp., and Bob Corp. spends $200 in materials and pays Bob $100 in salary to build a shed for Carry. Bob receives the same $100 that he would have received if he did the work for Carry directly, but the result for Carry is quite different. When the shed collapses, Carry sues Bob Corp. for $800, but, after paying for materials and Bob's salary, Bob Corp. is broke. Carry cannot recover anything from Bob Corp., and Bob is not personally liable for the injuries caused by Bob Corp. Carry cannot recover from Bob for the injuries caused by Bob Corp. because Bob, an investor, has limited liability.

If this result seems unfair, consider a third scenario where Irina, who is not at all involved in the operations of Bob Corp. and knows nothing about building sheds, invests $200 in Bob Corp. Should Irina be personally liable for Bob's shoddy work? What if Carry's shed is destroyed by a foreseeable natural disaster, like a heavy snowfall in Boston in February, or an unforeseeable event, like an earthquake in Washington, DC? If you are still not sure, take this hypothetical to its extreme example: suppose 20,000 people each invest $0.01 in Bob Corp. Should all 20,000 of those investors be personally liable to Carry for her $800 claim?

This simple example highlights several fundamental issues with corporations that will run throughout this book. First, limited liability is necessary to attract outside investors to a business enterprise. If investing $0.01 in a single share of Bob Corp. made you personally liable for their entire debt, would you risk losing tens of thousands of dollars for the opportunity to make a few cents? Of course, you would not. When you buy Bob Corp. stock, you only risk losing your penny investment, because investors in corporations have limited liability.

Second, limited liability externalizes the risk of corporate failure onto other people. This is the part of the equation that seems unfair to Carry. But some concerns about externalizing risks may be mitigated when you think more critically about the entire situation. First, Carry is aware that Bob Corp. is a limited liability entity because it has "Corp." in the name. Indeed, corporations are required to include a suffix like corporation, incorporation, or company to signal to consumers that they are limited liability entities. Second, with this knowledge, Carry can negotiate for a lower price or for other protections. For example, Carry can demand that Bob Corp. obtains insurance before doing the work, or she can hire someone else who will do the work for more money but will not have limited liability. But these solutions can be limited, especially when a corporation is a monopoly, such that Carry has no alternative choice. And, sometimes, these so-called corporate externalities spill over onto society in general. What if Carry's shed fell not on her property but instead toppled onto and damaged the house of Ned, her neighbor? Ned will have no recovery against the broke Bob Corp. after the fact, and Ned may have no opportunity to protect himself before the fact (although financial products like insurance can mitigate some of these risks). As we will see throughout this book, the issue of limited liabilities versus corporate externalities is at the heart of many struggles regarding corporate finance and securities regulation.

CORPORATE INVESTORS

Many people assume that corporate investors are ordinary people like themselves. But nothing could be further from the truth. Over 80 percent of investors in public stock markets (like the New York Stock Exchange and the NASDAQ) are massive institutional investors who might control large blocks of stock and have powerful voting rights. In private markets, more than 99 percent of funding comes from wealthy accredited investors, including angels and venture capitalists.

In theory, corporations attract investors in part because of their structure, which separates ownership and control. The investors who buy stock, called stockholders, technically own the corporation, but the board of directors (who are appointed by the stockholders) has authority and controls the corporation's actions. Shareholders have limited rights under corporate law to control a corporation that they own, but shareholders can negotiate for contract rights of control. Contractual control rights (like the right of shareholders to prevent the company from issuing more stock, to obtain financial information about the corporation, to prevent other shareholders from selling the corporation's stock, or to have a representative on the board of directors) are often found in private stock purchase agreements. For public companies, shareholders have to find other ways to corral management, perhaps by manipulating public opinion.

In practice, investors throughout the ages have found it useful or necessary to maintain some control over corporate management.

CORPORATE RISK AND REWARD

Setting aside for a moment the debate on limited liability versus corporate externalities, we can next examine what people receive when they invest money into a corporation. People generally do not simply give their money to corporations, expecting nothing in return. In return for their investment, people receive a "security." In Part III, The Third Era, we will discuss some of the new and exotic forms of securities and investment contracts, but, for now, we will start with the most familiar security: common stock. Stock, at its most basic, just reflects a percent of ownership – a "share" – of a corporation. Investors buy stock because stock value increases as the worth of the company increases. For example, Alexander Hamilton founded the Bank of New York (BNY) (today, BNY Mellon) in 1792, and he raised money by initially selling 500 shares of BNY stock to investors. Imagine that BNY sold 125 shares of its common stock to its founder, Hamilton, for one dollar per share, totaling $125. Then, Mr. Hamilton would own 25 percent of BNY. Today, BNY is worth about $54 billion, so Mr. Hamilton's 25 percent would be worth about $13.5 billion. Even accounting for inflation, that is a 4,500,000 percent return on investment. Mr. Hamilton's investment in BNY turned out to be quite good.

Of course, things do not always go so well. Most corporations fail, and 25 percent of $0 is zero. Sometimes businesses are profitable, and sometimes they go bust. But that is the nature of risk, and, as they say, no risk, no reward.

A corporation can fail for many reasons, but one particularly troublesome reason is because the corporate managers commit fraud. Consider the Enron Corporation. In early 2001, its managers – whose pay is based on revenues – claimed the corporation had annual revenues of nearly $101 billion. But, in December 2001, it was revealed that the number was basically fabricated. The stock price tumbled from $90 per share to $0, and Enron declared bankruptcy. Shareholders lost their entire investment, and 20,000 people lost their jobs. The risk of fraud is a particularly troublesome risk for investors, but fraud also creates social harm that justifies its regulation. Briefly reviewing a theory of social utility is helpful in understanding why.

CORPORATE FRAUD

Society must permit some amount of risk in order to obtain some rewards. But as we will see the law protects people from the risk of fraud more than from other business risks. Why? Because fraud, unlike other business risks, always produces a negative effect on social utility or welfare. Social utility is an economics concept that roughly equates to worth or value. In fact, economics uses the concept of utility to predict (or "model") how people will act based on their expected value from a set of choices. Generally, people are assumed to make choices that will increase their own value, or utility. In other words, economics applies an intrinsic utility function as a mathematical mechanism to model how people will behave when presented with a choice. Moreover, if we can determine how people will generally act given a set of choices, law can constrain those choices or change the relative costs and benefits of those choices to produce a socially desirable result.

For example, imagine that Jill is cold, and she would increase her utility (her own value) by one if she burns old newspapers in her fireplace. But the smoke from the fire is noxious to her neighbor Kyle, whose utility will decrease by ten if Jill burns the newspapers. If left to her own preferences, Jill will burn the newspapers, because that will increase her utility, even though the net effect on the utility of this tiny society of Jill and Kyle is overall decreased by nine. This presents an economic problem called a negative externality. A negative externality or "external cost" is an economic activity that imposes a negative effect on an unrelated third party. Internal costs and benefits plus external costs and benefits combine to equal the total social cost or benefit from an activity. This is also known as social utility or social welfare. When external costs exceed internal benefits, laws may be required to prevent this economic activity from taking place and causing a net loss to social welfare.

We see laws designed to increase social welfare in many contexts. For example, water pollution laws that prohibit a textile factory from discharging toxic dyes into a public lake are intended to curb negative externalities from clothing production. Taxes on cigarettes that discourage people from smoking are designed to reduce negative externalities from tobacco consumption. Applied intelligently, laws could be used to ensure that people willingly engage in economic activity only when there is an expected net benefit to social utility.

Fraud, however, does not produce any net social value. Rather, it serves only to transfer wealth from one person to another. Moreover, the fraudster will spend some effort in conducting the fraud. This is bound to reduce social welfare. Recall that social welfare is the total value that society has. The smallest possible society would consist of just two people. Let's say that Harry and Sally comprise all of society for purposes of this illustration. Harry has $10 and Sally has $100, so the total social welfare is $110.

Consider the fraud situation first. Harry spends his entire net wealth of $10 on bottling and marketing a fake health tonic, which he sells to Sally for her entire new wealth of $100. Prior to the fraud, Harry had $10, and Sally had $100, so our little society had $110 in social welfare. After the fraud, Harry has $100 and Sally has zero (she now has no money and no cure, just a worthless bottle of fake health tonic), for a total of $100. While Harry has gained $90, Sally has lost $100. Society is thus $10 worse off in this fraud scenario.

The consequences of fraud are even worse when you consider what else Harry might have done with his time and money if he were not working on defrauding Sally. Perhaps Harry could have spent his $10 developing a cure for Sally's disease instead of scamming her. If Sally values the cure to be worth $200, and she pays Harry $100 for it, then she would end up with a welfare or value of $200 (which is how much she values the cure she now has). Harry would have used his $10 in wealth and effort to end up with $100. In this scenario, the total social welfare is Harry's $90 plus Sally's $200, for a total of $290. Society is thus $190 better off in this scenario.

The little society illustrates an important concept called opportunity cost, which is the loss of potential gains for alternative action that were not pursued. If you simply compare the fraud scenario to the status quo, that is, the situation before the fraud, you will estimate a $10 reduction in social welfare. But when you consider what else Harry might have done with his time, such as creating a cure for Sally's illness, you add the opportunity cost to this equation and find that Harry's fraud made society $200 worse off as compared to the alternative situation.

Corporate fraud falls into the textbook definition of an economic concept called "rent-seeking." Fraud is akin to theft. Fraudsters seek to increase their share of wealth, or "rents," without creating any new wealth for society. Rather, they waste some of their value to effectuate a wealth transfer from others to themselves. They are social-value leeches who cause total social welfare to go down not only by spending time and money on defrauding others but also from the opportunity cost of not spending that time and money on things society needs and wants. But fraudsters are not irrational. Rather, rent-seeking behavior, although selfish, is rational.

Fraud is not the only wasteful behavior in financial markets. In regulated markets, obtaining regulations that benefit oneself is a result worth pursuing through rent-seeking, even if this results in a regulation that is a net negative for society at large. Lobbying is a classic example of rent-seeking behavior, where a business will lobby for grants, favors, subsidies, or international protection.

The theoretical notion of rent-seeking was developed conceptually by the "father of economics," Adam Smith. He wrote a qualitative analysis in 1776, which was explicated by Gordon Tullock's definitive 1967 paper, *The Welfare Costs of Tariffs, Monopolies, and Theft*. Simply put, rent-seeking behavior lowers social welfare because the actors who engage in rent-seeking divert their energies to pursue transfers of already realized resources instead of creating new ones. Fraud is likewise an economic "waste" of efforts. Fraud diverts wealth but it does not create wealth. Moreover, the fraudster destroyed wealth insofar as his efforts could have been put to productive use, creating wealth for society.

Rent-seeking theory focuses on the opportunity costs of engaging in activities that produce a "zero-sum" game (or in some cases, a negative-sum game), rather than a positive-sum game. Corporate fraud is a classic example of rent-seeking. Although fraud is usually illegal, people commit fraud to increase their own personal wealth. This requires efforts by fraudsters to commit and perfect their craft, rather than devoting time to activities that contribute to society. Corporate actors who engage in theft divert realized resources or assets to increase their own wealth, rather than, for example, investing that time and energy in securing more funding, developing a new product, or focusing on the growth of the company. When corporate actors engage in fraud, they simply seek to increase their personal share of wealth, or "rents," without creating any new wealth.

We can readily relate these concepts to financial activity. Now, Harry is a partner at Harry Investment Company. Instead of searching for investment opportunities, he spends his time creating fake reports, so his client Sally does not notice him syphoning part of the profits into his own personal account. Society is worse off because of Harry's actions because society must commit to mitigating these actions in the future, not to mention the opportunity cost of Harry actually doing his job and finding good opportunities for Sally to invest in.

For these reasons, fraud is not a risk that investors should bear. Protecting investors against securities fraud is one of the primary responsibilities of securities regulators, and it is especially important where fraud can have negative externalities to society at large.

Unfortunately, as we will see, securities regulators have gotten themselves into the business of "protecting" investors but also against *normal* business risks, which has caused many problems in financial markets. Indeed, sometimes regulation has the unintended consequence of harming the people it was designed to help.

ORIGINS OF THE NEW YORK STOCK EXCHANGE

Since it can be difficult to evaluate business risk, many people hire specialists called brokers to help them invest in corporations. This creates a demand for professional organization and institutions who deal in the trade of stock. The story of self-regulated organized stock markets in America begins on May 17, 1792, when twenty-four brokers and merchants met under a tall buttonwood tree on Wall Street in Lower Manhattan. There, they signed a short document, now known as the Buttonwood Agreement, in which they agreed to terms for buying and selling stock:

> We the Subscribers, Brokers for the Purchase and Sale of Public Stock, do hereby solemnly promise and pledge ourselves to each other, that we will not buy or sell from this day for any person whatsoever, any kind of Public Stock, at a less rate than one quarter per cent Commission on the Specie value and that we will give a preference to each other in our Negotiations. In Testimony whereof we have set our hands this 17th day of May at New York. 1792.

Note that this simple document is actually a form of securities regulation, in that the Buttonwood Agreement governs how people can buy or sell stock. But the Buttonwood Agreement is a private contract, not a law passed by Congress or a regulation promulgated by a governmental agency. How can a private contract be a securities regulation? It can because organizations can self-regulate, and thus potentially obviate the need for governmental regulation. Such self-regulatory organizations (or SROs) are discussed in more detail in Chapter 3, but, for present purposes, it is enough to recognize that the New York Stock Exchange originated as a self-regulated organization.

Astute observers might also notice that the terms of this self-regulation benefit the traders who signed the Buttonwood Agreement, at the expense of those who are not a part of this small investors' club.[1] We would expect an agreement such as this to increase the average price that an investor would pay a stockbroker in commissions, which in turn would have the effect of decreasing the number of trades that are ordered and limiting the number of people who can afford to participate in the stock market. Of course, the signatories would counterargue that such an agreement is necessary to maintain quality and stability in this emerging stock market. We see throughout financial history these arguments for economic inclusion versus counterarguments for market quality. Generally, the arguments for quality and safety have prevailed, but the unintended consequence of such regulations is that the people who are excluded from the regulated market find alternative ways to participate in unregulated and often unsafe markets. More troubling, it is usually the poor and uninformed who are lured to the danger of unregulated markets when they are shut out from over-regulated ones.

The Buttonwood Agreement introduced another key theme: economic crises prompt financial regulation. The Buttonwood Agreement was signed just months after the Financial Panic of 1792, a financial crisis caused in large part by easy-lending policies of the fledgling Bank of the United States. This trope – financial innovation, boom, bust, then regulation – repeats throughout the eras of corporate finance.

---

[1] The Buttonwood Agreement would most likely be illegal today because it forms a cartel whose members agreed on minimum prices, which violates the Sherman Antitrust Act of 1890.

In those early days, very few corporations existed. The only stocks available were for insurance companies and banks, including the Bank of the United States, the Bank of New York, and the Philadelphia Contributionship for the insuring of Houses from Loss by Fire. But the New York Stock Exchange (today known as the "NYSE") was primed to become the largest stock market in the world, thanks to a massive increase in the number and type of corporations in America early in the first era of corporate finance.

Rise of Corporations in America

In the colonial period, the right to form a corporation was only granted in special instances via a complex process that included lobbying the state legislature. As a result, there were only six for-profit corporations chartered in America by 1790.[2]

Despite the massive hurdles required to form a corporation in the early years of the United States, a few lasting corporations were founded in this period. Many of them were banking corporations. Such banking corporations can create systemic risks that impact many people beyond the corporation's shareholders. For this reason, even today, banking corporations are treated quite differently from regulation corporations.

It is perhaps informative that banking corporations in the early United States were formed by some of the most powerful men of that era. Their competing commercial interests fueled political rivalries, and occasionally turned deadly. A famous incident in history illustrates how tightly banking corporations and politics were intertwined in this early era.

On July 11, 1804, Alexander Hamilton set out from Manhattan before dawn. He rowed through the morning mist across the Hudson River to meet Aaron Burr in Weehawken, where the two were to have a duel. Hamilton was the first Secretary of the Treasury and founder of the Bank of New York, who famously said that "the debt of the United States . . . was the price of liberty." Burr was the third Vice President of the United States and founder of the Bank of the Manhattan Company, which is JPMorgan Chase today. Hamilton and Burr warred about politics, business, and finance, but public insults made the rivalry personal. Observers disputed who shot first, but, when the smoke cleared, the forty-seven-year-old Hamilton lay mortally wounded. This deadly display of machismo between two founding fathers of

---

2   "During the days of colonial government there were in all but six of these of strictly American origin or character. They came in this order: (1) The New York Company for 'Settling a Fishery in these parts,' 1675; (2) The Free Society of Traders, in Pennsylvania, 1682; (3) The New London Society United for Trade and Commerce, in Connecticut, 1732; (4) The Union Wharf Company in New Haven, 1760; (5) The Philadelphia Contributionship for the insuring of Houses from Loss by Fire, 1768; (6) The Proprietors of Boston Pier, or the Long Wharf in the Town of Boston in New England, 1772."

Simeon E. Baldwin. *American Business Corporations before 1798*, 8 THE AMERICAN HISTORICAL REVIEW 448, 450 (1903).

Democratic capitalism captures the rugged individualism of this early period of American expansion and investment, the first era of corporate finance.

FREE INCORPORATION

In the 1830s, state law began to "democratize" corporations, making their formation available to an increasingly broad swath of the population. Several states began to allow a much wider range of American entrepreneurs to incorporate through standardized processes, which diversified the corporate form. By 1850, the United States chartered at least 13,000 corporations. This expansion continued to modern times. In 2011, over 5.8 million active corporations filed tax returns with the Internal Revenue Service.

As corporations increased in number, so did corporate finance increase in importance to the United States. Governments, like people, invest money in various assets. In the early 1800s, France did not own any corporate stocks, England invested 3 percent of its total assets in corporate stocks, and the United States had about 10 percent of its total assets in corporate stocks. By 1850, the United States increased its corporate stock holdings to 18 percent of its total assets.

The national inclination to invest in business corporations was likely a result of the Federalist-capitalist perspectives, as expressed by founding fathers, including Alexander Hamilton, John Adams, James Madison, John Jay, and many others. The Federalist party formally organized in 1792 and dissolved in 1824, but in that brief period it made a lasting impression on American democracy and the economy.

But the founders' ideals of individual liberty through free markets and limited government were constantly attacked by those who wanted the government to actively advance the rights of the common man against a corrupt aristocracy. Initially, the anti-Federalists, including Patrick Henry, Samuel Adams, and George Clinton, opposed ratification of the Constitution in order to preserve states' rights against the threat of an imperial presidency. While the anti-Federalists failed to defeat the Constitution, they succeeded in passing the Bill of Rights, which limited the powers of the newly formed United States central government.

The debate between centralized versus decentralized power unfolded in other dimensions as well. In particular, the Federalists tended to be bankers and merchants, whereas the anti-Federalists tended to be landowners and farmers, who were generally in favor of landed interests over moneyed interests. These differences in philosophy and allegiance were evident when Andrew Jackson, the first President who openly rejected Federalist policies, was elected on March 4, 1829. Subsequently, he removed all federal funds from the Bank of the United States, and he permitted the nation's first bank charter to expire in 1836, thus ending America's first central banking experiment.

Privately owned bank corporations, however, quickly expanded in number and size during this early period of liberalized incorporation. From 1790 to 1835, the number of state-chartered banks increased from 3 to 584, and the total lending power of the American banks rose from $3 million to $308 million. Although the federal government no longer had its own bank after 1836, Uncle Sam owned an enormous amount of stock in private banks. Indeed, most of the stocks owned by the United States government during this period were bank stocks. These banks used the invested funds to lend money – that is the function and purpose of banks, after all – but what were the uses of these loans? It appears that some of the loans were used to charter yet more new banks. These new banks, in turn, issued more loans, potentially for investment in even more banks. Banks were thereby engaging in a leveraged investing.

THE PANIC OF 1837

Leveraged investing has been accused of causing financial crisis throughout history. To understand the merits of these accusations, one must first understand what leverage means in the context of corporate finance. Investments that are purchased with borrowed money are "leveraged." Investors who purchase stocks using borrowed money can obtain a higher return on capital, but the practice exposes the leveraged investors to greater risk.

Think of leveraged investment in the following way. You can use your own money to buy one share of stock for $100. If the stock value goes up to $110, you gain $10. If the stock value goes down to $90, you lose $10. But what happens if you invest using borrowed money, also called trading on margin? If you have a 50 percent margin, you can invest $100 of your own money and $100 of borrowed money to buy two shares of stock. If the stock goes up to $150, you gain $100, because you gained $50 times two shares (minus interest payments for the loan). If the stock falls to $50, however, you lose your entire $100 investment, and you still have to pay interest to the bank. Even worse, if the stock goes down to $0, you lose your entire investment, and you owe the bank $100, plus interest. Before the stock price goes that low, the bank will demand that you make a margin call, meaning you must put up more cash. With margin trading, investors can lose more than their entire investment, and banks take some of the risk.

Margin investing was extremely prevalent in the early nineteenth century. As a result, seemingly profitable investments could be wiped away overnight. And that is precisely what happened during the banking boom of this time. In hindsight, the banking boom of the 1830s was a bubble – akin to the great real estate bubble of 2007–2008.

Upon his reelection in 1933, Jackson began removing federal funds from the Bank of the United States to state banks. This began the decentralization of the U.S. banking system. Jackson also began paying down the national debt in an effort to further limit bankers' power over the country. When the federal accounts were tallied on January 1, 1835, the nation was no longer in debt. As the economy continued to improve, and as Jackson increased the rate at which the federal government sold off its land, the federal Treasury had a surplus going into 1836.

How could paying off the national debt lead to a financial crisis? It may seem counterintuitive, but a surplus can be as harmful as debt, given the wrong policies. The administration's anti-Federalist policy led them to deposit that federal surplus in a number of state banks. The federal government had little control over these state banks, who used the deposits to make new loans. Meanwhile, the federal Treasury prepared to distribute much of the surplus back to the citizenry. Jackson sponsored the Distribution Act of 1836, which authorized the Treasury to lend the surplus to state government for capital improvement projects. Jacksonian Democrats advanced financial policies that made land available easily and cheaply. This policy could fairly be characterized as populist: common people – farmers, mechanics, and laborers – favored the notion of easy access to capital.

These policies resulted in easy loans and cheap money, but instead of helping the common people in the long run, this led to a depression that hit common people the hardest. State officials boosted impossibly ambitious canal and railroad projects. The loans were never repaid. As unsound projects went bust, banks quickly reigned in lending, but it was already too late. Many of the 584 state banks were impossibly overextended. Not only did they lend money at low rates to state and local governments that seemed increasingly unlikely to ever repay these loans, but the banks had also inadvertently overexposed themselves to the stock market and to systemic risks. Easy lending policies made it possible to use one bank's notes as investment into other banks' even more speculative ventures. The high rate of leverage meant that banks were overexposed to significant stock market risk.

When the Bank of New York realized it was overextended, it tried to correct by raising interest rates and scaling back lending. Investors, however, were no longer able to borrow money to pay for margin calls when stock prices declined, forcing them to sell at a loss, which drove stock prices down even lower. The downward spiral continued until the Panic of May 10, 1837, when banks in New York City stopped making payments. A sustained period of unemployment and deflation persisted until 1944. President Martin Van Buren, Jackson's successor as the leader of the (Jacksonian) Democratic party and anti-Federalist politician, lost his 1840 reelection bid to William Henry Harrison of the Whig party, which was built on remnants of the Federalists.

Although history keeps showing that populist financial policies may be economically unsustainable, promises of easy loans and cheap cash remain attractive to many people, and we will see how these policies have led to more recent financial disasters. Apparently, we have not learned from this crisis that government policies designed to encourage easy lending practices can result in financial catastrophes. When governments encourage lending to particular sectors, this creates distortions that amplify the effects of financial crisis. Whether the intention is to improve American infrastructure or to encourage American home ownership, using fiscal policy as a tool for social change often creates perverse incentives that lead to unintended consequences.

In the Panic of 1837, banks were highly leveraged in speculative investments, the political party in power lost control of the White House, and ordinary citizens – most of whom were not invested in these banks – lost their jobs and their savings. Banks and wealthy investors externalized risks onto society at large. As banks failed, people and corporations who depended on banks – such as farmers who borrowed money to buy seed and repay the loan from profits of the resulting harvest – lost access to the capital they needed to survive. Many plantations went bankrupt, which in turn reduced the food supply and raised food prices. Higher food prices affected almost every American, especially the least wealthy. In the end, financial engineering most seriously harmed the people it was intended to help. And the populist backlash against the corporate form was fierce.

Although Jackson and the anti-Federalists lost power in the 1840 election, they struck a critical blow against central banking before leaving office. Their policy changes impacted how the nation recovered from the Panic of 1837. While Jackson's financial policy failed miserably, his political policy of decentralizing banking power had succeeded. Jackson first crippled the Bank of the United States, then he killed it. Meanwhile, public opinion of banks and bankers was at an all-time low. This opened the door to a new era of free banking that would last until the Civil War.

THE FREE BANKING ERA

The period from 1837 to 1863 has come to be known as the "free banking era" in the history of American banking, although the era began its end with the Panic of 1857. This era is probably the most notable period in terms of currency in the United States. Two attempts at establishing a central bank for the country had failed. Prior to the Panic of 1837, incorporation or chartering a new bank required an act of state congress. This not only limited the number of new banks that could be formed, but also ensured that lucrative banking privileges would only go to well-connected people who could influence state legislatures. The Panic engendered public skepticism of this crony capitalism.

States responded to bank failures and the credit crunch by passing new laws that allowed banks to be automatically chartered. Michigan was the first state to allow free bank incorporation. Michigan's Act to Organize and Regulate Banking of 1837 allowed state banks to operate with very little oversight. New York and Georgia passed free banking statutes in 1838. Alabama passed a similar statute in 1849, and New Jersey did the same in 1850. Illinois, Massachusetts, Ohio, and Vermont followed suit in 1851, as did Connecticut, Indiana, Tennessee, and Wisconsin in 1852. Some states imposed reserve requirements, interest rate limits, maximum debt to equity ratios, and other requirements, but this period was primarily characterized

FIGURE 1.1 A private banknote issued by Allentown Business College Bank in 1874. Such banknotes are a type of private currency – similar to cryptocurrencies like Bitcoin today. Public domain work.

by loose regulations and little oversight. These banks reflected the Wild West character of this first era of corporate finance in America.

Article I, Section 8 of the Constitution reserves the right to coin money to the federal government. States cannot mint their own coin and other "hard currency." But private entities such as banks can effectively create "soft money" by issuing banknotes. Banknotes were probably the earliest form of paper money. In the eleventh century, the Song Dynasty of China issued paper notes called "jiaozi" which promised that the bearer could reem the banknote at a later time in exchange for valuable coins. During the private banking era, American banks and even private corporations such as the Delaware Bridge Company issued banknotes, which the bearer could later exchange for government-issued currency.

Private banks issued their own banknotes against their deposits of gold and silver. Even drugstores, railroads, and insurance companies issued their own currency. As a result, various private currencies circulated during the free banking era. Some notes were not worth the paper on they were printed on. So-called "wildcat banks" were virtually free from federal regulation and only subject to control on the state level. But this does not mean banks were completely autonomous. Economic rules of supply and demand, social rules regarding reputational effects, and legal rules prohibiting fraud still applied. Although about half of the banks chartered during this period failed, the national economy prospered for much of this era. This shows that deregulation and decentralization can have a positive impact on the economy.

RETURN TO NATIONAL BANKING

The prosperity of the free banking era ended in 1857 as a series of unfortunate events unfolded. The Ohio Life Insurance and Trust Company, one of the country's largest financial institutions, failed. That institution had invested heavily in agriculture by lending money to farmers. This was a good investment while the Crimean War raged in Europe from 1853 to 1856. Europeans purchased food from America while its population was fighting instead of farming. But when that war ended, and the soldiers returned home to their farms, European food production resumed as well. Global food prices fell. Many farms became unprofitable and unable to repay their loans. With so many bad loans on its books, Ohio Life was not receiving enough income from loan payments to pay its other obligations. This bank went bust, and suddenly its promises to pay others became worthless.

Five million dollars in private banknotes issued by Ohio Life lost their entire value. Worried investors ran to other banks and attempted to redeem paper banknotes for gold and silver "specie" currency. Then, the SS Central America sank while carrying $1.5 million in gold bullion. The Bank of Pennsylvania, unable to access hard money, suspended redemption of its notes. Other banks followed suit. Businesses were unable to redeem banknotes for hard cash and so had no way to pay employees but with more worthless banknotes.

The end of the Crimean War, which allowed European nations to access Russia's bountiful grain harvest, affected not just Ohio Life's investments but the entire American economy. The worldwide price of grain plummeted, which especially impacted farmers in the American west. As farms failed, railroads suffered for want of goods to ship back east. The flow of goods from east to west slowed, impacting regions from New England to Georgia. The lesson here is that the economy is intertwined in sometimes surprising ways. The forces that caused Ohio Life to fail also caused other banks to fail. The failure of these banks caused other firms to fail. Those failures caused even more failures to occur in industries that were not obviously connected to American agriculture.

It is hard to say whether this financial crisis, which magnified disparities between the agrarian south and the more industrialized north, was a factor leading to the Civil War. But financial crises do not generally help resolve social problems. And social tensions between north and south were rapidly escalating. The Confederate States of America, whose economy was significantly based on slavery, organized and voted to secede from the Union on December 20, 1860. Although the free banking era technically ended with the passage of the National Banking Act of 1863, which established a system of federal banks, the free banking era had unofficially ended already as the nation prepared for civil war.

The federal government desperately needed a way to fund the war and a universal currency by which to do it. In 1861, the federal government issued its first currency through the United States Department of the Treasury. The Legal Tender Act of 1862 permitted the government to issue "greenbacks," aptly named for their color, and distributed them directly into circulation among the American people allowing them to be used for public and private debts. The National Bank Act of 1863, also known as the National Currency Act, established a plan for a federal currency. The National Bank Act of 1864 established the new category of banks known as federally chartered national banks. It forbade the practice of printing private money and essentially ended wildcat banking in all but the most remote locations. By the time that Confederate General Robert E. Lee surrendered the last Confederate army to Union General Ulysses S. Grant at the Appomattox Courthouse on April 9, 1865, the American banking system was essentially a national system.

The trials and tribulations that the nation faced during the Civil War gave weight to the Federalist's argument that the federal government should govern the nation in its entirety, including the currency by which the nation paid its debts. But it would take several more decades before the federal government had power to domesticate the financial Wild West.

The government in the first era struggled with regulating the awesome economic power of the corporate form. Corporations are legal entities, formed under state law, which exist perpetually and grant limited liability to their investors. These features make corporations much more powerful economic entities than human beings can be; after all, humans cannot live forever. Corporations are a compelling reason why America quickly grew from a war-ravaged huddle of colonies to a world power.

However, corporations – and the nature of investment into them – are also why the Panic of 1837 affected not only bankers but also merchants, farmers, and ordinary people. Therefore, lawmakers must be careful when implementing financial policies, especially ones that encourage loose lending practices.

BIBLIOGRAPHY

Atack, Jeremy & Peter L. Rousseau, *Business Activity and the Boston Stock Market, 1835–1869*, 36 EXPLORATIONS IN ECON. HISTORY 144 (1999).

BOARDMAN, FON WYMAN, AMERICA AND THE JACKSONIAN ERA, 1825–1850 (H. Z. Walck eds., 1975).

CASKEY, JOHN P., THE EVOLUTION OF THE PHILADELPHIA STOCK EXCHANGE (2004).

CHAUDHURI, RANAJOY RAY, THE CHANGING FACE OF AMERICAN BANKING: DEREGULATION, REREGULATION, AND THE GLOBAL FINANCIAL SYSTEM (2014).

Desai, Mihir A., *A Better Way to Tax U.S. Businesses*, HARV. BUS. REV., July–August 2012.

Dwyer Jr., Gerald P., *Wildcat Banking, Banking Panics, and Free Banking in the United States*, 81 ECON. REV. – FEDERAL RESERVE BANK OF ATLANTA (1996).

FEDERAL RESERVE BANK OF PHILADELPHIA, THE FIRST AND SECOND BANKS OF THE UNITED STATES: THE HISTORICAL BASIS FOR A DECENTRALIZED FED (2009).

Hannah, Les, *Corporations in the US and Europe 1790–1860*, 56 BUS. HISTORY 865 (2014).

Khwaja, Asim Ijaz & Atif Mian, *Rent Seeking and Corruption in Financial Markets*, 3 ANN. REV. ECONS. 579 (2011).

Klapper, Leora et al., *Entry Regulation as a Barrier to Entrepreneurship*, 82 J. FIN. ECON. 591 (2006).

LANDES, WILLIAM M. & RICHARD A. POSNER, THE ECONOMIC STRUCTURE OF INTELLECTUAL PROPERTY LAW (2003).

LONG, KATHRYN THE REVIVAL OF 1857–58: INTERPRETING AN AMERICAN RELIGIOUS AWAKENING (1998).

Majaski, Christina, *Rent Seeking*, INVESTOPEDIA (August 28, 2019), https://perma.cc/7SBQ-BBGR.
Rowley, Charles K., *The Intellectual Legacy of Gordon Tullock*, 152 PUB. CHOICE 29 (2011).
Simeon, E. Baldwin, *American Business Corporations before 1789*, 8 AM. HIST. REV. 448 (1903).
SMITH, ADAM, AN INQUIRY INTO THE NATURE AND CAUSES OF THE WEALTH OF NATIONS (1776).
Sylla, Richard & Robert E. Wright, *Corporation Formation in the Antebellum United States in Comparative Context*, 55 BUS. HIST. 650 (2013).
Tollison, Robert D., *The Economic Theory of Rent Seeking*, 152 PUB. CHOICE 73 (2011).
Tullock, Gordon, *The Welfare Costs of Tariffs, Monopolies, and Theft*, 5 GORDON W. ECON. J. 224 (1967).
Willis, Hugh Evander, *Capitalism, The United States Constitution and the Supreme Court*, 22 KENTUCKY L. J. 343 (1933).
Wright, Robert E., *US Corporate Development 1790–1860*, MEAD (2015).

2

The Golden Spike

As American financial markets grew, so too grew the power and influence of the wealthy. In particular, the Great American Railroad turned millionaires into dynasties. In 1869, Leland Stanford (the namesake of Stanford University) placed a golden railroad spike to connect the Union Pacific and Central Pacific lines at Promontory Summit, in the Utah Territory, creating the first transcontinental railroad. This story is legend, but lesser told is the story of how this great infrastructure project was financed. The story of the railroads is also a story about an important financial innovation: preferred stock. Chapter two explores the political problems with this financial solution, which preludes challenges to come.

> The production of wealth is the result of agreement between labor and capital, between employer and employed. Its distribution, therefore, will follow the law of its creation, or great injustice will be done.
>
> – Leland Stanford

Despite the Depression of 1837 to 1843 that followed the Panic of 1837, the nation's economy continued to chug along, thanks at least in part to a new technology. The railroad connected people, products, and information across the country. The railroad is so significant to the development of America that historians have referred to the mid-1800s as "The Railroad Era."

While rail cars of one sort or another had existed since ancient Greeks drove wheeled vehicles along grooves in limestone streets, modern railways were not possible until iron replaced wood, and steam engines replaced horsepower. Richard Trevithick built the first steam-powered locomotive in 1804 in Wales, but it was Colonel John Stevens who brought this technology to the United States in 1826. In 1857, George Pullman invented the Pullman Sleeping Car, which made long-haul passenger travel much more convenient.

But a rail car is useless without a rail line on which it can travel. It is not rail cars, but rail lines that are the subject of this chapter because rail lines turn out to be the vastly more expensive part of the transportation equation. The greatest railway project of that era was the Transcontinental Railroad, which at the time cost over

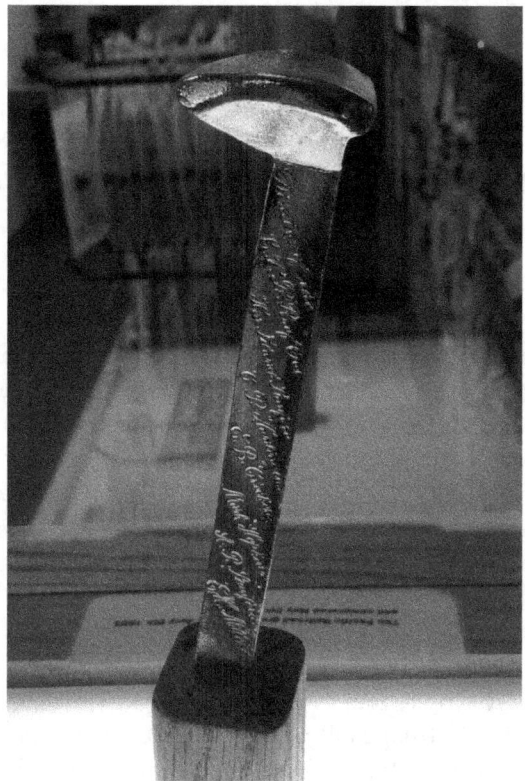

FIGURE 2.1 Replica of the Golden Spike. Credit Lucas Hugie, Park Ranger, Golden Spike National Historic Park.

$100 million.[1] To put that figure in perspective, that amount of money in 1865 would be worth about $1.5 billion today. In contrast, a new boxcar today costs about $135,000, which amounts to less than $10,000 in 1865 dollars. In fact, the Transcontinental Railroad may have been one of the most ambitious financial projects of that era.

The entire project was so expensive that its consummation was celebrated by driving the last railroad spike, a spike made of solid 17.6 karat gold, into the ground.[2]

[1] Congressman Oakes Ames (R-MA 1863–73) testified that the Union Pacific line, which stretched from Council Bluffs, Iowa to Promontory Summit, Utah, cost $60 million. Estimates of the cost of the Central Pacific Line, which ran from the San Francisco Bay to meet the Union Pacific at Promontory Summit, range from $36 to $51.5 million. These conjoined lines were called the Transcontinental Railroad, despite the fact that the eastern terminus was over 1,300 miles from New York City and the East Coast.

[2] The Golden Spike symbolized the completion of the transcontinental railroad. Leland Stanford, chief financier of the transcontinental railroad and founder of Stanford University, ceremoniously placed this spike into the final railroad tie on May 10, 1869. The golden spike now resides at the Cantor Arts Center at Stanford. According to that museum, the spike was never "hammered ... into anything," rather it was "gently nudged into a pre-drilled hole[.]" Further, it was immediately removed and put on

But even shorter rail line construction projects required massive investments. To pay the great expense of rail line construction, a new sort of financing needed to be developed. In fact, a theme recurring throughout the eras of corporate finance is that technological innovation often requires financial innovation. This is especially true with large infrastructure projects. Here, we see how the barons of the railroad industry invented a new type of security – preferred stock – to incentivize investment in the great railway projects of the 1800s.

FINANCING THE RAILROADS

In 1834, the Baltimore and Ohio Railroad (B&O) ran from Baltimore, Maryland, to Harper's Ferry, West Virginia. The next year, B&O extended its line from Baltimore to Washington, DC, and began lobbying the Maryland legislature for funds to complete an additional line to Pittsburgh, Pennsylvania. Meanwhile, the Chesapeake & Ohio Canal Company (C&O), which was then unprofitable (perhaps due to its lack of access to Pennsylvania's rich coal fields), the Eastern Shore Railroad Co., the Maryland Canal Co., and the Annapolis and Potomac Canal Co. also asked Maryland for capital-improvement funds.

The Maryland Assembly heard a bill on March 9, 1836, which proposed to use public funds to purchase $8,000,000 of capital stocks of the five private railroad and canal companies. This is the equivalent of approximately $208 million today. The Maryland Assembly rejected the bill, but the financiers were undeterred. They just needed to find a way to make this stock subscription more enticing to the legislature. This called for a little imagination and resulted in a critical financial innovation: preferred stock.

PREFERRED STOCK

The financiers introduced a second bill, which called for a stock subscription to B&O provided that the company guarantee a 6 percent annual dividend to the state. This was a financial innovation. By combining financial features of equity and debt securities into a new instrument, the railroad promoters created the first "preferred stock." This financial product might seem obvious today, but at the time, this combination was novel.

We can see this in how the definition of "dividend" has evolved. In Webster's Dictionary of 1828, a "dividend" was defined as "the share of the interest or profit of stock." In other words, the 1828 definition of dividend was purely an equity concept. Now, however, we understand "dividend" to mean a sum of money that a corporation

>display at the museum at Stanford University (now the Cantor Arts Center). Interestingly, the spike is only 73 percent gold. A replicate of the Golden Spike was taken into space on a Space Shuttle mission in 1990 and now resides in the Golden Spike National Park, http://cantorcollections.stanford.edu /objects-1/info/3852; www.roadsideamerica.com/story/64772.

pays regularly to its stockholders. To put it another way, the definition of "dividend" shifted from a portion of the profits to a set percentage like the interest of a debt.

The fact that the common understanding of "dividend" now means a set mandatory percentage of investment as opposed to a pro rata share of profits is a direct result of the financial innovation of preferred stock. To understand preferred stock – which is today described as a debt-like type of stock – it is helpful to first understand debt and common stock.

Recall from Chapter 1 that corporations can finance their operations by issuing stock to investors or issuing debt to lenders. Lenders who hold debt are entitled to regular interest payments for a set period of time, then a return of the principal at the end of the term. For example, C&O could have financed its operations by issuing a 6 percent ten-year bond, which is a type of debt. If you purchased such a bond for $1000, what would you be entitled to receive?

Assuming simple annual interest (although there are more complex interest terms), you would receive 6 percent of $1000, or $60, each year for ten years. At the conclusion of the ten-year term, you would then receive your initial $1000 deposit back. All in, you would earn $600 on this loan. This is calculable in advance because debt earnings are fixed. You will not earn more than $600 on a 6 percent ten-year $1000 loan under any circumstances.

However, what happens if C&O goes bankrupt before you are fully repaid? Then, you become a creditor. C&O will have a liquidation sale – where C&O sells its boxcars, steel rail lines, intellectual property, and other assets – to pay its creditors in their order of priority. Unfortunately for creditors, things like steel rail lines are worth much less when take from the ground and smelted down than it cost to install them as railroad lines. In other words, the liquidation value of the assets of C&O paled in comparison to its operational value. Thus, a debt investor runs the risk of losing its principal and some of the interest payments if the debtor goes belly up. A smart lender will account for this by adjusting the interest rate (and other terms) depending on the risk of nonrepayment. The lender's decision whether to issue the loan requires in part a calculation of C&O's bankruptcy risk.

Stock earnings, on the other hand, are unlimited, but even more uncertain. Stockholders own a piece of the company, so they are entitled to their share of the profits (if any are distributed) and a portion of the residual if the company is sold. There is no concept of "interest" with regard to common stock. As a common stockholder, you do not expect to get paid regularly.

In fact, many common stockholders are never paid at all. For example, Berkshire Hathaway is an investment company founded in 1929 in Omaha – only miles from the eastern terminus of the Transcontinental Railroad – whose common stock now costs almost $300,000 per share. But Berkshire Hathaway has never paid its stockholders a penny! In fact, there are many corporations that have never issued a dividend. Shareholders are not entitled to demand dividends. The board of directors of the corporation decides whether to issue dividends to common stockholders, and some choose never to do so.

Why would anyone pay $300,000 for a share of stock that will never issue a dividend? Because common stock has fundamental rights to the value of the entire corporation as a going concern. In fact, the price of all the stock is the same as the operational value of the business. If the corporation is sold, the stockholders receive the residual payment. If Warren Buffett – who is the chairman and CEO of Berkshire Hathaway and by far its largest stockholder – decides to sell Berkshire Hathaway, each stockholder will receive the same price per share as Mr. Buffett. There are 750 million shares outstanding, so if someone else values the entire company at $75 billion, each share will be paid $1,000. For the same reason, another investor might be willing to pay you $300 for your share today, in the hopes it will be worth $1,000 someday. The value of common stock is tied directly to the value of the company as a going concern, although the stock has little value if the company fails and goes bankrupt. Each common stock share is therefore worth its percentage share of the entire business value, called the "residual." People buy common stock because they estimate that its value will go up, usually because the company as a whole improves. For these reasons, stock is a good investment vehicle for companies whose operating value exceeds their liquidation value.

Preferred stock is thus a mix of both debt and common stock. The proposed B&O "preferred" stock subscription offered Maryland its percentage share of the entire company value, plus a guaranteed amount annually. This is like getting the residual plus interest. In other words, preferred stock has all the benefits of common stock plus some of the benefits of debt. Debt, however, has benefits that preferred stock does not: debt is paid before stock in a bankruptcy, and the corporation must pay its debtholder their principal back at the end of the term before paying any stockholders. This particular combination of financial terms had not existed before. Therefore, preferred stock was a financial innovation.[3]

FINANCIAL PREFERENCES

B&O's preferred stock proposal initially failed in the legislature, but the idea began to take hold in the popular consciousness. Local newspapers reported that the bill "giving a preference to the state in the Baltimore and Ohio Rail Company, was lost." Constituents began to demand that the Maryland Assembly obtain this

---

[3] The Corporation of Georgetown, a substantial common stockholder of B&O, published an editorial in the Baltimore American & Commercial Daily Advertiser that demonstrates how novel and unusual this proposed preference was: "It is to the unreasonable and anomalous character of the loan that Georgetown objects. Upon what principle of justice does Maryland claim to receive a certain stipulated dividend, or interest, if you please, to the exclusion of all other stockholders, and at the same time to have equal rights with those excluded stockholders in controlling by her vote, the interests and work of the company?" Note that Georgetown considered the dividend equivalent to an interest payment. BALTIMORE AMERICAN & COMMERCIAL DAILY ADVERTISER, June 2, 1836.

"preference," and the Maryland Assembly demanded additional rights from B&O. For instance, Maryland negotiated for the right to appoint one director for every 5,000 shares of stock it might hold, a provision designed to give Maryland control over one third of the B&O board of directors. When B&O conceded, the bill passed, and preferred stock was born.

Today, preferred stock has a number of other "preferences," which are discussed more thoroughly in Chapter 8. Financiers are constantly innovating their offerings to make them more appealing to investors, and concepts such as "dividends," "participation," "multiples," and more have been introduced as needed to make the finances of preferred stock attractive to venture capitalists.

The key lesson from the Golden Spike is that financial innovation is necessary to advance technological innovation. Novel inventions and different circumstances present new challenges and opportunities for fundraising and investment. It is critical that our financial regulations permit the right amount of financial innovation.

THE GOLD STANDARD

While the private markets created innovations in corporate finance, the federal government continued to evolve its approach to currency markets. As discussed in Chapter 1, political thinkers and politicians in the early United States had different views about the role of the federal government. The Federalists supported a stronger central government, while the anti-Federalists would cede more power to state and local governments. The Federalists originally had the upper hand regarding financial policy, but anti-Federalist President Andrew Jackson quashed the National Bank of the United States in 1836 and ushered in the free banking era. Then, the Civil War (1861–1865) necessitated a return to a central financial structure. Although there was some fiscal decentralization during Reconstruction (1863–1877), financial policy generally continued to trend toward a strong central government.

The Constitution gives the federal government the exclusive right to mint coins, and it had been doing so pursuant to the Mint Act of 1792 and its successor, the Mint Act of 1837. Both statutes permitted minting of gold and silver, but they were replaced again by the Mint Act of 1873, which permitted minting only of gold bullion. The Gold Standard Act of 1900 confirmed the United States' commitment to the so-called "gold standard," which fixes the international value of currency to the market price of gold. The Act effectively assigned value to the federal paper money ("greenbacks") first created in 1861, with a guarantee to the public that a certain amount of paper money was worth, and could be redeemed at will, for a certain amount of gold.

The problem with this standard was that it handcuffed the government in terms of influencing monetary policy. Gold is a scarce resource. Gold is finite. If a certain amount of money is to equal a certain amount of gold, then the amount of paper currency the government can issue must be directly correlated to the government's deposits of gold. Ergo, paper currency was also finite when it was backed by gold. After an additional economic downturn and two world wars, the monetary system in the second era needed an overhaul, in the United States and globally, which prompted a departure from the gold standard. Perhaps ironically, in the third era, a nongovernmental cryptocurrency would take the world by storm precisely because it mimicked the limitation of the supply of gold. But, for now, government money was as good as gold.

BIBLIOGRAPHY

Dornbusch et. al., Rudiger, *The Gold Standard: Historical Facts and Future Prospects*, 1 BROOKINGS PAPERS ON ECON. ACTIVITY 1 (1982).

Evans, Jr., G. H., *Early Industrial Preferred Stocks in the United States*, 40 J. POL. ECON. (1932).

Evans, Jr., George Heberton, *The Early History of Preferred Stock in the United States*, 19 AM. ECON. REV. (1929).

Hansmann, Henry and Mariana Pargendler, *The Evolution of Shareholder Voting Rights: Separation of Ownership and Consumption*, 123 YALE L. J. 948 (2014).

Hochfelder, David, *"Where the Common People Could Speculate": The Ticker, Bucket Shops, and the Origins of Popular Participation in Financial Markets, 1880–1920*, 93 J. AM. HIST. (2006).

Kiby et. al., Doug, *The Golden Spike (In Transition)*, https://perma.cc/Z82E-UNME.

Stanford University, *The Last Spike*, https://perma.cc/7XPK-4H9Z.

VELETSIANOS, GEORGE, LEARNING ONLINE: THE STUDENT EXPERIENCE (2020).

White, Richard, *For Tech Giants, a Cautionary Tale from 19th Century Railroads on the Limits of Competition*, THE CONVERSATION, *available at* https://perma.cc/SJ9E-BT3M.

3

Roar and Crash

A *zeitgeist of rugged individualism, freedom, and excess characterized the early Roaring Twenties. America largely avoided the destruction of World War I, which decimated Europe and especially Germany. But these United States were not immune to the turmoil. As the old nation-states of Europe decayed into history, new ideas about government – Communism and Socialism – enticed those disenfranchised by Capitalism. On September 16, 1920, at 12:01 pm, a group of anarchists detonated a bomb in Manhattan's Financial District that killed 38, injured 143, and troubled many more. The Wall Street Bombing was not the last time that an anarchist group would strike against a central locus of capitalism. Meanwhile, Capitalism went to war with itself. On October 29, 1929, the Great Crash began. On this Black Tuesday, the Dow Jones Industrial Average (DJIA) lost 13 percent of its value. The Great Crash ushered in the Great Depression – and a newfound political appetite for economic statism, a political system where the government exercises significant control over corporate finance.*

> The Sultan asked Solomon for a Signet motto, that should hold good for Adversity or Prosperity. Solomon gave him, "this too shall pass away."
> – Edward Fitzgerald, Polonius: A Collection of Wise Saws and Modern Instances (1862)

Just as railroad technology bound America together through its network of steel, another technology emerged that forever changed how America shares information, in particular, financial information. The modern telegraph was developed in 1832 and subsequently commercialized by Samuel Morse. Morse – the namesake of Morse code – invented a communications device that conveyed electrical signals via a wire, and it recorded what it received via dots and dashes on a moving paper tape. This paper tape would eventually become the eponymous "ticker" that captured America's hearts – and wallets.

THE TICKER

The New York and Mississippi Valley Printing Telegraph Company – known today as Western Union – incorporated in 1851. Their business model was to demonite the

FIGURE 3.1 Western Union Ticker Model 3-A. WU first introduced its popular stock ticker in 1866. The Universal Model 3-A ticker was designed by Thomas A. Edison in 1873 and sold through about 1900. Credit Don DeBold, licensed under CC0-1.0.

new market for communication of information. Through an aggressive policy of acquiring smaller competitors, Western Union quickly came to dominate the market for telegraph lines. In 1861, Western Union built the first transcontinental telegraph.

Such rapid expansion was expensive. Western Union financed its growth through many rounds of stock issuances. By 1876, America's centennial, Western Union had sold $41 million in stock, which equates to a market capitalization of almost $1 billion today.

Western Union also developed innovative telegraph technology that would change finance forever. In 1866, Western Union introduced the world's first widespread stock ticker. The Hughes Telegraph was the first machine capable of printing text (not just dots and dashes) on the ticker tape. The machine printed a series of ticker symbols (e.g., "GE" for General Electric Corporation) along with information such as the current price at which corporate stock was being bought and sold.

Thanks to the technological innovation of the stock ticker, people across America could now gain timely and reliable access to information that was previously only available to stockbrokers located inside the New York Stock Exchange (NYSE). The ticker's tangible embodiment and widespread availability of otherwise esoteric financial information had a huge impact on the democratization of finance. Indeed, the stock ticker seemed to capture the public's popular imagination, as an entire generation learned to "watch the ticker."

Ticker technology also encouraged the centralization of stock exchanges. While it became easier to "watch the ticker" from almost anywhere in America, it became correspondingly harder to watch multiple tickers. Western Union sold access to ticker information on a per-exchange basis, so it cost double to get access to two exchanges instead of one.

Watching two tickers takes twice as much time as watching one. If the incremental benefits of that second ticker are not worth its costs, people will only watch one ticker. If one stock exchange is better than another, people will tend to focus their efforts on the better one. As more people focus on a single exchange, that exchange becomes even better because it has input from more people. This feature of stock exchanges is called a "network effect," and industries that have strong network effects tend to see consolidation toward one network.

NETWORK EFFECTS

As people begin to focus efforts on one ticker and thereby one exchange, the trading volume on that exchange increases. This creates a vicious cycle, where the increased trading volume makes that exchange more valuable, and thus continues to drive people to watch that exchange's ticker to the exclusion of others. Therefore, the innovation of the telegraph and ticker tape technology simultaneously drove the democratization of access to stock exchange information and the centralization and consolidation of stock trading onto one exchange, the NYSE. To put this another way, ticker technology gave a much broader range of Americans access to stock market information, but it had the opposite impact on stock markets themselves.

Ticker technology, however, did not completely obviate the demand for alterative stock exchanges. One reason for this is historical. Prior to the telegraph, stock markets were regional, sheltered from national competition. Buying and selling stock was limited to people within a geographic region around the market, so each region required its own stock market.

The Philadelphia Stock Exchange (PHLX) was founded in 1790 as the Board of Brokers, making it the oldest stock exchange in America. In 1834, this successful group moved trading out of coffee shops and into the Merchants Exchange building at 3rd and Dock Streets.

That same year, thirteen people formed the Broker's Board in Boston, which would become the Boston Stock Exchange (BSE), the third oldest stock market in America. Underscoring the regional character of these pre-telegraph exchanges, corporations listed on the BSE were primarily incorporated in Massachusetts.

Moreover, this localization did not seem to hurt the exchanges. Over the period 1835 to 1869, scholars found that the BSE outperformed the NYSE. As prominent economic professor John P. Casey observed, "relatively high communication costs enabled the regional exchanges to compete in the first half of the [nineteenth] century." During this pre-telegraph period, multiple regional stock exchanges developed, and such large entities tend to persist.

However, the telegraph and the ticker greatly reduced communication costs, so stock exchanges could compete nationally. By the 1860s, New York was clearly the center of America's economic activity. In 1865, the NYSE relocated to its present location at 11 Wall Street, which anchored the NYSE on Wall Street as the premier stock exchange of choice for brokers, investors, and corporations alike. However, the Philadelphia and Boston exchanges did not simply disappear overnight. Moreover, other exchanges have since been established. Why would there be multiple stock markets when interconnected technology makes it possible for there to be only one?

SELF-REGULATORY ORGANIZATIONS

One reason alternative stock exchanges remained viable is because of self-regulation. Self-regulation is where an industry creates, monitors, and enforces its own adherence to standards. The NYSE, for instance, had rules regarding which companies could list on the exchange and which people could trade on it. Even today, the NYSE is listed as a "self-regulatory organization" (or "SRO") in the Federal Register. NYSE self-regulations pertain to admission of members, listing and delisting of companies, off-hours trading, arbitration of disputes, broker conduct, and disciplinary rules.

Not all firms or brokers were able to meet the NYSE's stringent rules. Many of those firms and brokers elected to trade on the PHLX or BSE – exchanges with less demanding rules – instead. Even today there are "alternative" stock exchanges, such as the Canadian Securities Exchange (CSE), which compete by offering simplified reporting requirements and reduced listing requirements.

Moreover, thanks to ticker technology, an entire industry emerged purportedly to serve the "Main Street" investor who could not afford a "Wall Street" stockbroker. The rise and fall of these so called "Bucket Shops" thus illustrates the unintended consequence of overregulation.

BUCKET SHOPS

The proliferation of the ticker through American society raised public awareness about investing and stock markets. To some extent, this drove more Americans to invest in corporations, which is generally helpful for economic development. Moreover, as more people participate in stock markets, the information they produce about price and value of corporations becomes more accurate. But the ticker

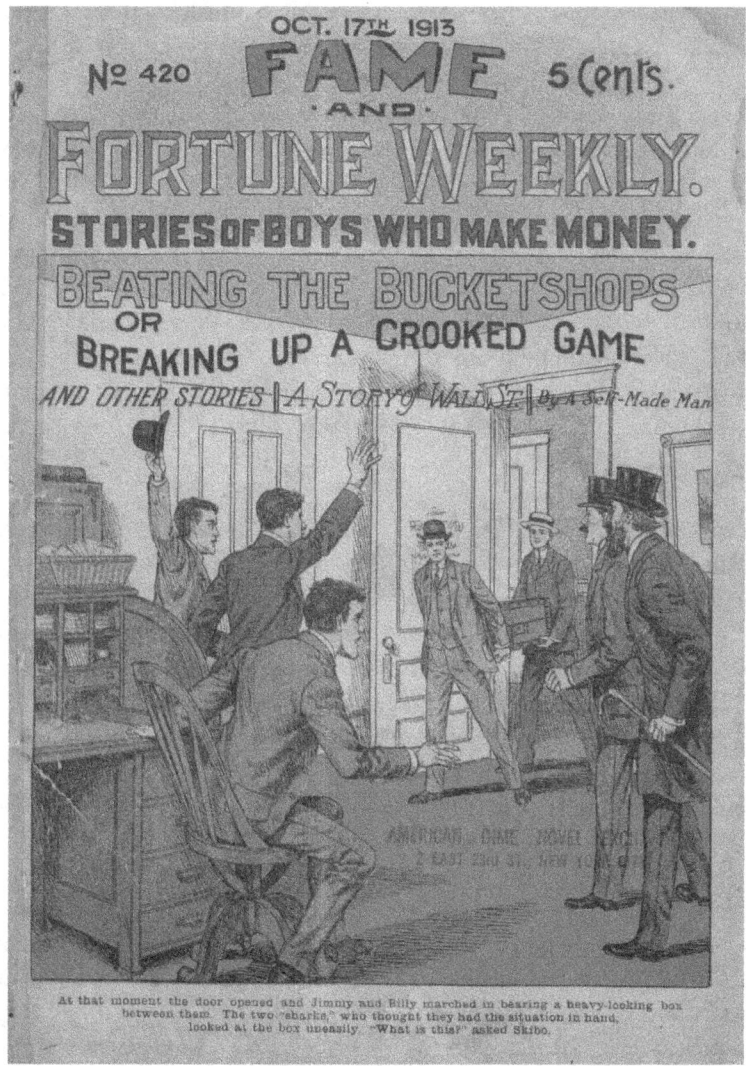

FIGURE 3.2 Cover of *Fame and Fortune Weekly*, May 6, 1921, titled "After a Golden State or Breaking a 'Bucket Shop' Combine." Credit Northern Illinois University Nickels and Dimes Collection.

also facilitated a certain type of gambling that proved quite problematic. This gambling on stock markets occurred in bucket shops that popped up across America in the latter half of the nineteenth century, causing problems for "investors" and broader problems for society in general.

A bucket shop is a physical location, typically in an office building, designed to look like a high-end brokerage firm. These shops existed far beyond Manhattan;

indeed, bucket shops promised to give a typical Main Street investor access to Wall Street investment opportunities. There would typically be a board, on which current stock prices were written, and, of course, a ticker machine, the source of this data. But, while this gave the look and feel of authentic stock brokerage operations, there are clear differences between genuine stockbrokers and bucket shop operators.

First and foremost, a bucket shop does not actually buy or sell stock, so the bucket shop customer never becomes a shareholder. Bucket shop operators are not licensed stockbrokers, so they cannot themselves trade stock. Indeed, neither the bucket shop operator nor the client has any expectation of actually receiving the stock. Instead, the client simply expects to be paid out if the stock price goes up, or to lose the "investment" if the stock price goes down. Since no stock purchase or sale actually takes place in a bucket shop, no trade based on this information ever occurs. Therefore, the "investment" does not actually go to finance corporations, and the information about value does not directly impact the prices on the stock market.

This creates two direct problems. First, the information is wasted in the sense that that client's decision to "buy" or "sell" a stock does not enter the exchange and become reflected in the overall stock price. Therefore, the price of a stock does not really reflect how people truly feel about its value. Second, and more problematically, this divorces the operator's interest from the client's interests. Since no stock is ever bought or sold, any payment to a client comes at the expense of the operator. For reasons that may quickly become obvious, this divergent interest in how a stock will move creates motivation for mayhem.

A traditional stockbroker is a person who buys or sells a stock on the client's behalf. Such a stockbroker is generally paid in two ways: a fee to execute a trade, and a percentage of profits from that trade. While this payment structure creates a conflict of interest with regard to "churning," which is the incentive for a stockbroker to make a lot of trades in order to generate trading fees, it aligns the stockbroker's interest with the client regarding the value of stock. Both stockbroker and client want the stock value to go up because both of them profit in that case.

In a bucket shop, on the other hand, the operator's interests are completely opposite from the client's interests. If the client makes a bet that the stock price will go up, the bucket shop only earns money if the stock price goes down. In economic terms, when the interests of the client and the operators are so sharply opposite, the client bears a substantial "agency cost." To put it another way, the bucket shop's interests are directly adverse to the interest of its "client." This misalignment of incentives means that clients need to be wary of bucket shops, who would like to take advantage of them, and who are well equipped to take advantage by manipulating information about stock prices or even attempting to manipulate the stock price itself.

Thus, the second problem with bucket shops is that fraud was rampant. Some bucket shop frauds could be passed off as mere negligence, like failing to keep enough cash on hand to pay patrons for their winning bets. Other frauds were petty, like writing numbers on the board that did not accurately reflect the ticker. Some frauds, however, had a much wider and more insidious impact on the entire market. Large bucket shops could employ a technique called a "wash sale" to manipulate actual stock prices, cheating the bucket shop client and harming the legitimate market as a whole. While petty frauds that harm individual "investors" are bad enough, these wash sales had a negative impact on society in general. Some contemporary commentators tried to draw attention to the vice of bucket shops, which were illustrated as crooked institutions to be broken up in early twentieth-century nickel and dime publications such as *Fame and Fortune Weekly*.

WASH SALES

To understand how a wash sale works, first you need to understand how stock market prices go up and down. In simple terms, stock price goes up when more people want to buy it, and it goes down when more people want to sell it. Think about a classic supply-and-demand graph. The demand curve slopes downward, signifying that fewer people will buy something the more that it costs. The supply curve slopes upward, signifying that more people will sell something the more it costs. The market price is where the supply and demand curves meet. If the demand for something increases, the demand curve shifts to the right, so supply and demand now meet at a higher price. If the supply of something increases, the supply curve shifts to the right, and the curves now meet at a lower price. Stock works the same way. If more people want to buy a stock, that increase in demand relative to supply causes the price goes up. If more people want to sell, that increases supply, and the price goes down.

In a wash sale, a bucket shop will notice that a lot of its clients are betting that a particular stock will go up. To prevent their clients from winning this bet, the operator will offer to sell a lot of shares of that stock. The sudden increase in supply of that stock causes its price to go down. Once its price falls far enough for the clients to lose their bets, the bucket shop operator repurchases the stock while it is offered at an artificially low price. This increased demand for buying generally brings the stock back to its market price (although the rapid and unexpected change can also cause unexpected events, known as second-order effects, to follow the initial action as a sort of ripple effect).

INVESTMENT FEVER

Given this bucket shop's clients are subject to fraud and not entitled to shareholder protections, why would anyone patronize a bucket shop? The answer to this question is more complicated because it implicates human psychology as well as economic rationality. The short answer is that NYSE regulations prevented ordinary people from truly investing in stock exchanges. With only about 1000 seats available on the NYSE until the 1900s, authentic brokers paid dearly for such seats. For example, in 1869, a seat on the NYSE cost about $5000, equivalent to about $90,000 today.[1] With so few brokers, demand for broker's time was high. Since brokers' pay was based on volume of trades executed, brokers (who could be choosy with their client) naturally preferred to work with larger investors who instead of smaller ones. Few brokers made time for small deals.

Brokers of that era typically required a $1000 minimum investment from their client, equating to almost $18,000 today. Ordinary people simply could not pay such high minimum investments. Moreover, NYSE rules required margins of at least 10 percent and trades of at least 100 shares. As a prominent financial historian Brendan Sapien pointed out, "These financial requirements effectively prevented the common citizen from playing a part in the stock market, allowing only the wealthy to partake in the business of investing and speculating."

Thus, authentic brokers were out of reach for most working-class Americans in this period. The appeal of becoming an overnight millionaire was not lost on the members of the working class. Cut off from authentic stock trading, but wishing to profit from corporate success, an ordinary American would be lured into the bucket shop, where a minimum "trade" could be $15 or less. As Sapien put it in his article *Financial Weapons of Mass Destruction: From Bucket Shots to Credit Default Swaps*, "to overcome this financial barrier, an illegitimate financial institution began to emerge, which offered average citizens an affordable opportunity to seemingly play the market as any wealthy investors would."

For investors, the tale of bucket shops is a reminder that "if it seems too good to be true, then it probably is." Many bucket shop clients were duped and bamboozled because they did not understand the economics behind a get-rich-quick scheme. Unsurprisingly, investors make similar mistakes today. Indeed, some of the new investment opportunities today make investors prone to the same problems faced by bucket shop clients of yesteryear. As we will explore in Chapter 9, many startups now offer crypto-currency trading platforms. On these platforms, people can buy and sell Bitcoin, Ethereum, Litecoin, and other novel financial products. But, lately, the crypto-currency trading platforms have been accused of manipulating prices, just as bucket shops did via wash sales.

The bucket shop illustrates America's investment craze at the beginning of the twentieth century. People were so eager to profit from stock markets that they mistook investing for gambling – although, as the next chapter points out, the distinction between gambling, speculating, and investing has never been clear.

---

[1] Purchasing a seat on the NYSE was itself an investment. Seat prices fluctuated wildly, but generally increased over time. In 2006, the NYSE sold its last seat for $3.575 million.

BIBLIOGRAPHY

Banner,Stuart, Speculation: A History of the Fine Line Between Gambling and Investing (2017).

Caskey, John P., *The Evolution of the Philadelphia Stock Exchange*, Fed. Rsrv. Bank Philadelphia Bus. Rev. (2004).

Hannah, Leslie, *A Global Corporate Census: Publicly Traded and Close Companies in 1910*, 68 Econ. Hist. Rev. 548 (2015).

Neal, Larry & Eugene White Lance E. Davis, *The Highest Price Ever: The Great NYSE Seat Sale of 1928–1929 and Capacity Constraints*, 67 J. Econ. Hist. 705.

O'Reilly v. Morse, 56 U.S. 62.

Sapien, Brendan, *Financial Weapons of Mass Destruction: From Bucket Shops to Credit Default Swaps*, 19 S. California Interdisc. L. J. 411 (2010).

The Second Era

Electric Light

4

A New Deal

President Franklin Delano Roosevelt (FDR) championed the theory, rhetoric, and politics known as the New Deal. The New Deal included new regulation of American business. Under FDR, the U.S. Congress passed the 1933 Securities Act (requiring the registration of sales of securities), the 1934 Securities Exchange Act (imposing fraud liability on securities offerings), the 1935 National Labor Relations Acts (allowing the federal government to regulate workers' hours and wages), the 1940 Investment Company Act (regulating mutual funds), and the 1940 Investment Advisers Act (regulating anyone who gives advice about trading securities). FDR thereby created the federal government's new financial police force, the Securities and Exchange Commission (SEC). Federal securities regulation is based on Brandeisian thinking, popularized in the Supreme Court Justice Louis Brandeis's book, Other People's Money and How the Bankers Use It.

> Sunlight is the best disinfectant; electric light the most efficient policeman.
> – Justice Louis Brandeis

The national economy was riding high during the period after the First World War known as the Roaring Twenties. In February 1929, the New York Stock Exchange (NYSE) increased its membership, known as seats, for the first time since 1879. Even though the NYSE increased the number of seats by 25 percent, the resale price of these seats reached their highest price ever (in terms of inflation adjusted real value) in 1929. But before that year ended, the prosperity created by stock markets would suddenly come to a crashing end.

A cacophonous scene erupted on the trading floor of the NYSE on October 24, 1929 as the Dows Jones Industrial Average (DIJA) lost 11 percent of its value. There was a brief rally on the Friday as a consortium of investment bankers led by Richard Whitney purchased large blocks of shares at above-market prices. But this only halted the slide before the weekend. When the markets reopened on October 28, many investors were trading on margin – meaning they were using borrowed money to buy stock. These margin investors owed interest payments for every day that they held shares bought on margin, making it costly to keep those shares, especially as the market value of those shares declined. Some margin traders who could not afford these interest payments decided to sell their shares, which drove the market price down further, and which in turn forced other margin traders to sell. This drove the price down further, and even investors who owned their stock outright began to panic and to sell. This pushed stock prices down further still. The DJIA closed on "Black Monday" at a record loss of 13 percent and an additional 12 percent loss on "Black Tuesday." The market lost a staggering $30 billion dollars in just two days. The Great Depression began on so-called Black Tuesday, October 29, 1929, a day that shall live in financial infamy.

AFTERMATH OF THE CRASH

The Wall Street Crash of 1929 played a major role in ushering in the worldwide Great Depression that would last for years, and its impact was felt for decades. The magnitude of this financial disaster was unprecedented. All in all, the DJIA fell from a high of 5,557 in August 1929 to a low of 796.22 in 1932. Indeed, it would not be until May 1959 that the market would fully recover from this loss, when the market finally hit 5,611.27.

One might argue that the stock market crash led in some ways to World War II and, ultimately, to the Pearl Harbor bombing on December 7, 1941, the day that shall truly live in infamy. The political economy of Germany was in serious trouble as the Great Depression spread worldwide. There, Adolph Hitler rose to power by promising to make Germany great again. The causes of World War II are beyond the scope of this book. But it is worth reflecting briefly on why Germany was in such trouble, as we should learn from the past to consider how to avoid a similar disaster in the future. In addition to a worldwide crisis, Germany was repaying reparations from World War I. If you lost a war in that era, you paid reparations. Germany's territory was carved up, they were under the thumb of these reparations, and then the entire global economy crashed. This led to the meltdown of German society and thus to World War II.

Even in America, able young men could not find work. They were standing in bread lines instead of assembly lines. The mobster Al Capone opened a soup kitchen, and people were so desperate for food that they ate out of Al Capone's hands. When the mobsters are society's safety net, the world is truly upside down.

The impact of the crash was not merely economic but political and legal as well. American citizens were unemployed and angry. Incumbent President Herbert Hoover, who presided during the Crash, lost the 1932 presidential election in a landslide victory for Franklin Delano Roosevelt (FDR). FDR, for his part, won that 1932 election after a campaign promising traditional economic policies including a balanced budget. A sweeping change in American politics was about to take place. By FDR's 1936 reelection campaign, he had completely changed his tune

FIGURE 4.1 Unemployed men queued outside a depression soup kitchen opened in Chicago by Al Capone. Credit National Archives, photo no. 306-NT-165319 c.

about balancing the budget and fiscal responsibility and instead adopted (his version of) Keynesian economic theory and Brandeisian regulatory theory.

KEYNESIAN ECONOMIC THEORY

Keynesian economics – the brainchild of John Maynard Keynes, who published *The General Theory of Employment, Interest, and Money* in 1936 – essentially posits that, in the short run, governments can lessen the severity of recessions and depressions by spending. In simplified Keynesian terms, recessions are periods when aggregate demand is low. Government investment in infrastructure and similar government expenditures can increase demand by injecting cash directly into the economy, which can create jobs and increase output. Sometimes, a small investment by the government can create a large economic improvement, and when this occurs, it is called a multiplier factor. This stimulation can lessen, or even reverse, the harsh effects of unemployment and decreased demand during a period of economic downturn. Keynes also advocated for the Federal Reserve to reduce interest rates to promote private borrowing and spending and to discourage excessive saving. It is critical to note that Keynesian economics puts the federal government in a much more active role vis-à-vis the economy as compared with classical economic theory (which generally prescribed a laissez-faire role of government).

Keynes met FDR on May 28, 1934 and explained his theories to the President in considerable technical detail. After their meeting, Keynes met with the Secretary of Labor, Frances Perkins, and clarified the multiplier effect in oversimplified terms. He explained that a dollar spent by the government on a public work's project is like a dollar given to a grocer, who in turn spends that dollar on supplies from the wholesaler, who in turn spends that dollar on supplies from the farmer, essentially creating four dollars' worth of output from a one-dollar investment. Perkins later noted that Keynes may have overestimated FDR's understanding of the underlying mathematical principles behind his ideas and that the meeting may have been more productive if Keynes had explained his theories in layman's terms, as he had done with Perkins.

Although their initial meeting was brief, Keynes made a profound impact on the president, who was then a vocal opponent of the classical laissez-faire role of the government. Inspired by Keynes's theories, FDR's New Deal set about an unprecedented expansion of the federal government that FDR enacted between 1933 and 1938. It included the creation of the Civilian Conservation Corps, the Public Works Administration, the Works Progress Administration, the Resettlement Administration, the Rural Electrification Administration, the Civil Works Administration, the Farm Security Administration, the Federal Crop Insurance Corporation, the Social Security Administration, and other government agencies and programs.

BRANDEISIAN REGULATORY THEORY

On the regulatory front, FDR was inspired by another leading thinker of the day, Justice Louis Dembitz Brandeis. Brandeis was an American Jew born to immigrant parents from Bohemia who raised him in a secular home. Despite these humble beginnings, Brandeis graduated Harvard Law School at age twenty and founded a law firm in Boston. Perhaps because of his background, Brandeis became well recognized as the "People's Lawyer" through his leadership for progressive social causes.

Brandeis was notably anti-corporate. He denounced "cutthroat competition" and, ironically, also denounced the evils of monopoly:

> We learned long ago that liberty could be preserved only by limiting in some way the freedom of action of individuals; that otherwise liberty would necessarily yield to absolutism; and in the same way we have learned that unless there is regulation of

competition, [capitalism's] excesses will lead to the destruction of competition, and monopoly will take its place.

In 1914, Brandeis published the book *Other People's Money and How the Bankers Use It*, which attacked investment funds and called for a breakup of the so-called Money Trust – the cabal of investment bankers who had abused the public trust and taken control of numerous industries. He also coined a phrase which would become the watchwords of the New Deal regulatory regime: "Publicity is justly commended as a remedy for social and industrial diseases. Sunlight is said to be the best of disinfectants; electric light the most efficient policeman."

In 1916, President Woodrow Wilson nominated Brandeis to the Supreme Court, to which he was confirmed on June 1 of that year. During his subsequent twenty-three years of service on the bench, Brandeis became one of the most influential members of that high court. Jacket Library Publishers reprinted Brandeis's polemic essays in 1933, resurrecting the attack on investment funds reflected in popular opinion at the time. American sentiment favored expansive New Deal regulations. *Other People's Money* supported the breakup of the Money Trust. Its more famous passages are often quoted in support of New Deal-era securities regulations.

THE NEW DEAL SECURITIES REGULATIONS

Amid this zeitgeist, the government was galvanized to prevent another market crash with federal securities regulations. The New Deal included four major pieces of federal securities regulations, which created the Securities and Exchange Commission and established a federal governance over investments.

Securities Act of 1933

The Securities Act of 1933 regulates the sale and initial offering of "securities." Securities is defined broadly to include sales of stock and other "investment contracts," which are the "investment of money in a common enterprise with profits to come solely from the efforts of others." The Securities Act requires investments to be registered with the Securities and Exchange Commission, unless they are exempt. Therefore, stock should always be analyzed with the Securities Act registration requirements (and exemptions to these requirements) in mind.

Securities Exchange Act of 1934

In addition to requiring initial registration, the Securities Exchange Act of 1934 created a continuing obligation to provide financial information. The "periodic reporting" required registered companies to regularly disseminate financial information that ostensibly allowed investors to check in and evaluate whether to hold or sell their investments, stretching accountability over the duration of the investment. These reforms mandated more information about the investments themselves.

Unfortunately, despite these reforms, many still considered the marketplace to be a bacchanal of fiduciary abuse. There was still a lack of transparency surrounding the companies who supervised financial investments and a lack of legal assurances that companies were doing so responsibly. Congress reached this conclusion after a multiyear investigation that examined the industry in "fastidious and convincing detail," involving working papers, court documents, and other technical memoranda.

Investment Advisers Act and Investment Company Act of 1940

The Investment Advisers Act of 1940 allowed the SEC to keep track of who investment advisers were. Its companion Act, The Investment Company Act of 1940 did the same thing, only with investment companies. The Investment Advisers Act of 1940 required the registration of all investment advisers. The Act draws a distinction between investment professionals and other professionals who give financial advice incidentally, such as "lawyers and accountants."

Sunlight Is the Best Disinfectant

The primary motivation behind the Securities Regulations was to compel disclosure. Investors were presented with standardized information, and then from there could make an informed decision about whether to entrust their wealth to an adviser or a specific investment. Companies now had to provide a baseline level of information, but the client still had the burden of evaluating their adviser or their investment opportunity. Initially, the Investment Advisers Act "lacked enforcement power." In fact, the SEC was not even authorized to conduct inspections until 1960.

Over time, the Courts filled in the blanks in this legislation, emphasizing the importance of the duty to disclose and ruling that the need to divulge conflicts of interest could never be waived. The Courts imputed a fiduciary duty on the part of investment managers and companies, even though it was unwritten in the legislation itself.

The anti-fraud provisions were litigated heavily. Section 10(b) of The Securities Exchange Act of 1934 is the provision which guards against fraud Rule 10(b) disallows "the use of any device, scheme, or artifice to defraud."[1]

---

[1] "Fraud" is defined as "deliberately deceiving someone else with the intent of causing damage." The Courts have held that 10(b) creates a private cause of action against market participants, and have commonly applied a 6-part test to prove an allegation of fraud: (1) An omission or misrepresentation that is material; (2) committed with scienter (ill intention); (3) a connection with the purchase or sale of a security; (4) reliance (5) economic loss; and (6) loss causation.

The primary remedies for fraud are rescission (return of ill-gotten money) and damages (payments for harm caused), depending on whether the Plaintiff possesses the security when the fraud complaint is filed. If the Plaintiff still owns the security, rescission entitles the Plaintiff to a refund of the security purchase price (plus interest), and in return the Plaintiff returns the security to the Defendant. If the Plaintiff does not own the security anymore, the Plaintiff may recover damages. The lie or the omission must have been reasonably clear to the Defendant. If the reduction in the security's value was caused by a fact other than the material omission or representation, damages may be adjusted accordingly.

On other topics, the securities laws are open ended, so guidance can be "scattered" and standards "unclear." Furthermore, securities laws regulate a diverse set of financial instruments – from high-risk hedge funds to temperate fixed-income securities. The general rule is: disclose everything.

Such disclosure rules made have been good policy in the 1930s, but, over time, this resulted in an information overload. It quickly became impossible for any human being to keep fully informed about market indicators and to act quickly upon that information. As the next chapter discusses, computer technology provided a solution to this information problem – but not everyone gained equal access to computing power, creating an asymmetry in access to computational power resulted in asymmetries in financial power, too.

BIBLIOGRAPHY

Blue Chip Stamps v. *Manor Drug Stores*, 421 U.S. 723 (1975).
BRANDEIS, LOUIS D., OTHER PEOPLE'S MONEY AND HOW THE BANKERS USE IT (1914).
BRANDEIS, LOUIS D., THE REGULATION OF COMPETITION VERSUS THE REGULATION OF MONOPOLY, (1912), https://perma.cc/B3VZ-PYPF.
Brown v. *Bullock*, 194 F. Supp. 217 (S.D.N.Y. 1961).
Carlson, David, *Fraud*, CORNELL U. (May 2020), *available at* https://perma.cc/G7GD-YHZM.
Carney, Caelainn, *Robo-Advisers and the Suitability Requirement: How They Fit in The Regulatory Framework*, 2018 COLUM. BUS. L. REV. 586 (2018).
Dura Pharms., Inc. v. *Broudo*, 544 U.S. 336 (2005).
Ernst & Ernst v. *Hochfelder*, 425 U.S. 185 (1976).
Fed. Hous. Fin. Agency v. *Nomura Holding Am., Inc.*, 873 F.3d 85 (2017).
Glass, Andrew, *Wilson Nominates Brandeis to Supreme Court, Jan. 28, 1916*, POLITICO (January 28, 2019 12:00 AM), https://perma.cc/B2Z7-BJQ5.
Herman, Edward S., *Lobell on the Wharton School Study of Mutual Funds: A Rebuttal*, VA. L. REV. 938 (1963).
History.com Editors, *Civilian Conservation Corps*, A&E Television Networks (May 11, 2010 (updated October 17, 2018)), https://perma.cc/LUZ8-G6QM.
Ji, Megan, *Are Robots Good Fiduciaries? Regulating Robo-Advisors under the Investment Advisers Act of 1940*, 117 COLUM. L. REV. 1543 (2017).
Kardon v. *Nat'l Gypsum Co.*, 69 F. Supp. 512 (E.D. Pa. 1946).
Kohn v. *Am. Metal Climax*, 458 F.2d 255 (1972).
Lentell v. *Merrill Lynch & Co.*, 396 F.3d 161 (2005).

Lin, Tom C. W., *Reasonable Investor(s)*, 95 B.U.L. REV. 461 (2015).
Lindsay v. Morgan Stanley, 592 F.3d 347 (2010).
Novak, Matt. Yes, Adolf Hitler Really Said He Would 'Make Germany Great Again.' Gizmodo (Nov. 22, 2016) [https://perma.cc/45UN-ZGH7] (citing Green Bay Press-Gazette, January 4, 1934 ("Adolf Hitler...told people that he would make Germany 'great' again."); St. Louis Star and Times, Feb. 24, 1940 ("Nationalism and Socialism...would make Germany great again.")
SEC v. Capital Gains Research Bureau, Inc., 375 U.S. 180 (1963).
Securities Act of 1933, amend. 15 USCS § 77a
Sharp v. Coopers & Lybrand, 649 F.2d 175 (1981).
Strategic Diversity, Inc. v. Alchemix Corp., 666 F.3d 1197 (2012).
The Investment Advisers Act of 1940, amend. 15 U.S.C. § 80b-1 §§ §§ 80b-1–80b–21.
The Investment Company Act of 1940, amend. 15 U.S.C. § 80a-1 §§ §§ 80a-1–80a–64.
Timeline: The Evolution of the CCC, WGBH https://perma.cc/XNR2-R2GB.

5

Computational Asymmetry

After World War II abated, American economic prosperity emerged in its wake. Technologies developed for war – including plastics, synthetic rubber and oil, and penicillin – trickled into consumer products. Nylons, radial tires, and the polio vaccine gave Americans a new confidence in Capitalism. The newly minted Middle Class hoped to become wealthy through investments, and, thanks to massive advances in computer power, a stock market innovation for the Everyman was invented. The Index Fund made profiting from Dow Jones returns easy. Computers managed and balanced funds in a way that only Investment Advisers could previously do. But computer power is not created equal, and some benefitted from computational financial innovations more than others did. This "computational asymmetry" benefits investment funds with T-1 lines and MIT programmers running custom formulas. As "trickle-down economics" began to fail, public opinion against corporations began to turn sour.

    Greed, for lack of a better word, is good.
       – Gordon Gekko, Wall Street (Directed by Oliver Stone, 1987)

After the Great Depression and the implementation of federal securities regulations, two distinctly different financial ecosystems began to develop separately in the East and in the West. In the East, which is the subject of this chapter, trading centralized in lower Manhattan in New York City, where the New York Stock Exchange was located. This ecosystem focused on publicly traded stocks which were registered under and regulated strictly by federal securities regulations. This chapter explains how this eastern terminus of American finance implemented computer technology to innovate and create new financial products through the twentieth century.

    Meanwhile, out West, a different market was growing far from the watchful eye of federal regulators. The next chapter tells the story of Silicon Valley, the western terminus of American finance, where technology startups grew from humble beginnings to corporations of immense size and power. Since these two different stories occurred at the same time, this book takes a necessary detour from its chronological narrative by first looking at what happened in the East, and then exploring events out

West over the same period. These parallel tracks converge again at the turn of the millennium, when the Western startups listed on the Eastern stock exchanges in a frenzy of financial activity that we now know as the Dot-Com Bubble and which is the subject of Chapter 7.

PRE-REGULATION INVESTMENT ADVICE

At the beginning of the twentieth century, investing was closer to an art than it was to a science. The criteria for evaluating wealth management were simpler – and more subjective. While good wealth managers may have intuitively understood market fundamentals, they were more prized for staying levelheaded through periods of market turbulence than for being good at math. Investing was known as "speculation," and investors were often forced to do just that: speculate. Standardized accounting statements were often unavailable. Even if financial snapshots were furnished to investors, many would lack the wherewithal to interpret them because the academic discipline of economics had not developed the core of methodologies for systematically evaluating and comparing securities. As a result, many people took investment advice at face value. The opacity of investment advice in general made schemes and frauds easier to perpetrate. The federal government sought to solve these problems with a set of new laws called securities regulations.

As discussed in the previous chapter, the federal government instituted the Securities Regulations in the 1930s in an effort to make investing less speculative and to make investment advising more objective. The primary mechanism for accomplishing this was disclosure regimes, whereby companies would have to regularly reveal their financial data in return for the privilege of seeking investments from the general public and listing on public stock exchanges. While the Securities Act of 1933 was primarily responsible for requiring disclosures about the securities themselves, the Investment Advisers Act of 1940 and the Investment Company Act of 1940 created a new disclosure regime for investment advisors.

THE INVESTMENT COMPANY AND INVESTMENT COMPANY ACT OF 1940

On August 22, 1940, just as the first German bombs fell within the London Civil Defense Region, the U.S. Congress passed the Investment Company and Investment Advisors Act into law. In its original form, Public Law 76–768 contained both the Investment Company Act (ICA) as its Title I and the Investment Advisers Act (IAA) as its Title II. Those laws are now codified in separate portions of the U.S. code, as they regulate different aspects of investing: the ICA primarily regulates what financial products may be offered, while the IAA regulates who can recommend financial products to clients.

In this period, two new financial products emerged that have remained highly relevant for financial markets. The first was the mutual fund, which first emerged in the Roaring Twenties and gained prominence after the Great Depression. These early mutual funds required substantial human involvement, but they paved the way for further financial innovations that automated investment in ways that were impossible in earlier times. Once computer technology developed to the point that computers could exceed human capacity for computation and mathematical analysis, a new financial instrument – the index fund – became possible. This development in turn paved the way for a new era of algorithmic trading.

But let's not get ahead of ourselves. To explain how we got to our present regulation situation, first, this Chapter will start with a discussion of the original mutual funds that the ICA sought to regulate. Notably, the original mutual funds were "actively" managed, meaning that human beings made decisions about when to buy and when to sell stocks in the fund. Second, this Chapter will describe the technological development of computers and the rapid increase in computing power created the new possibility of "passively" managed index funds, which were traded based on algorithms and not on human analysis and instinct.

MUTUAL FUNDS

The original mutual fund was established in 1924 by Massachusetts Investors Trust in Boston. This actively managed fund survived the Great Depression and can still be purchased today under the stock symbol MITTX. The fact that a mutual fund may have a stock symbol just as a publicly traded corporation does is an important clue in understanding the purpose and function of a mutual fund.

Mutual funds were a sort of platypus of the financial world in that they are hard to classify, as they have a novel combination of two features. On the one hand, shares in mutual funds can be bought and sold just like individual shares in corporate stock. On the other hand, mutual funds are not individual shares but rather a collection of a large number of shares of stock. The purchasers of a "share" in a mutual fund actually purchases a small percentage interest in a large number of other stocks. Mutual funds are therefore a sort of synthetic instrument in that they are an artificial bundle or construction of other instruments. They should have no independent value apart from the combined value of their constituent parts – although, as we will see, sometimes the whole has a greater value than the sum of its parts.

While a mutual fund can be bought and sold like corporate stock, a mutual fund is fundamentally different in that the fund itself is a collection of various corporate stocks. Often referred to as "investment pools," investors who purchase a share of a mutual fund are actually buying a collection of stock called a "stock portfolio." Mutual fund shareholders may not actually own stocks in the portfolio, but rather are simply entitled to gain or loss depending on whether the stock in the portfolio gains or loses value. This makes mutual funds somewhat similar to bucket shops: in both instances, the "investor" does not make an investment in and gain ownership of a corporation; rather, the "investor" makes a bet on whether the value of corporate stock (or a portfolio of stocks, in the case of a mutual fund) will go up or down.

However, mutual funds offer three great advantages for ordinary investors that bucket shops did not. First, mutual funds automatically diversify investments, thus lowering certain risks. Second, mutual funds are professionally managed, thus lowering information costs. Third, publicly traded mutual funds are highly liquid and convenient to buy and sell, thus lowering transaction costs. These three advantages make mutual funds a compelling value for investors.

DIVERSIFICATION

If you have ever been admonished not to put all your eggs in one basket, then you have some intuitive understanding about the importance of diversification. Diversification is quite simply allocating investments, opportunities, bets, or any other event subject to chance among multiple possibilities. Betting provides a rather straightforward illustration. If you go to Las Vegas and play roulette, you can make a bet on a game called roulette (French for "little wheel") that a little ball dropped onto a spinning wheel will land on one of thirty-eight spaces (numbered 1–36 plus 0 and 00). Your chance of winning this game is 1/38. (Note that the payout for winning straight-up roulette in Vegas is 35 times, making this by definition a bad investment as you are statistically guaranteed to lose money over time.) What if, instead of putting, say $100 on number 18, you put $50 on both 18 and 36? This will double your chance of winning $50 x 35, although it guarantees you will lose at least $50 on this spin (since the ball cannot fall into two slots on one spin).

Fortunately, the stock market is not exactly like Vegas, and investing in corporations is not exactly like dropping little white balls onto numbered spinning wheels. In Vegas, the casinos design the games so that statistically gamblers lose money over time. But it is possible to make money in the stock market through long-term investing. Additionally, more than one stock can increase in value during a given time, whereas there will never be two winning numbers in one game of roulette. The challenge with picking stocks is picking the right ones. For example, even when the stock market crashed in 1929, some stocks remained valuable. In fact, the Electric Boat Company survived the Great Depression and then returned 55,000 percent from 1932 to 1952. The Dow Jones Industrial Average (DJIA), which tracks the performance of the top stocks on the NYSE, only increased about 380 percent over that same period. Meanwhile, over 20,000 other companies went bankrupt in the wake of the Great Depression. While earning almost 150 times more than the DJIA returned seems like a great victory, there was little reason in 1929 to pick the Electric Boat Company instead of any one of the many companies that went bankrupt. While some people picked the right stock, doing so was little better than random chance.

Each company is unique and so it has unique risks that are technically known as idiosyncratic risks. Idiosyncratic or individual risk represents the chance that any one company will have a defect or be unlucky. For example, the CEO who led the company to success could suddenly die of a heart attack. A major supplier could fail to deliver a critical good. The novel technology that the company is developing might not pan out, or might be preempted by something newer. A regulatory agency might not permit production and sales to go forward. Someone might sue the firm and embroil it in years of expensive litigation. Fashions may change such that the company's products are not seasonable. The list of problems that can occur is almost limitless.

But as you invest in more and more companies, the risk of that unfortunate event happening to all of them goes down and down. While a single CEO might suddenly die of a heart attack, it is rather unlikely that ten CEOs would all suddenly die around the same time. Although a novel technology might not pan out, one of a dozen new technologies is likely to succeed. Even though fashions change, people still need to purchase products, so some of the firms in the clothing industry will prove fashionable in any given year.

Thus, diversification reduces (and may even eliminate) idiosyncratic risk. An investor who holds a well-diversified portfolio will not lose everything because a CEO happens to get sick, a technology happens to fail, a regulation happens to be imposed, or a fashion fails to develop. In fact, one company's struggles may be another company's opportunity. Picture two gas stations across the street from each other at a busy intersection in an otherwise remote location. If one station loses power and cannot make any more sales that day, many of its potential customers will divert to the other station, increasing its sales. This is an example of a zero-sum game, where one competitor's gain is always offset by the other's loss. Here, there is a certain amount of gas sales to be made at a given intersection on a given day, and one or the other competitor will capture those sales. While an investor who only has shares in the closed gas station will be upset at his unexpected loss, an investor who only has shares in the open station will be pleased at his surprise windfall. An investor who has shares in both gas stations will be indifferent as to which gets the larger share of the daily sales because he has diversified away the idiosyncratic risk that one or the other will close.

Although the investor in both gas stations has diversified away some idiosyncratic risk, he has not gotten rid of all of it. If people in that region switch from gas to electric cars, for example, or if people relocate away from that region or stop using that route would result in lost sales to both gas station. To diversify away the risk that drivers will switch from gas to electric cars, the gas station stockholder would also need to purchase stock in companies that supply electricity for vehicles. To diversify away the risk that people will leave the region, the investor will have to purchase stock in stations outside the region.

Even diversification by investing in several startups or even several industries and in various regions will not protect the investor if, say, a pandemic occurs and governments respond by issuing stay at home orders such that people drastically reduce their driving overall. To reduce this risk, the investor should buy stock in unrelated industries such as software and lumber. By investing in a wide range of industries and a number of companies within each of those industries, our investor may be able to diversify away almost all of the idiosyncratic risk he had when he just owned stock in one gas station.

INFORMATION COSTS

Diversification is a powerful way to minimize investment risk, but it takes time, efforts, and money to diversify holding. A smart investor researches each company before investing in it, so the amount of time spent on researching investments increases as the investor diversifies. The investor will also need to keep track of all his investments, which represents an ongoing time commitment that also increases with diversification.

TRANSACTION COSTS

To return to the basket analogy, one reason why putting all your eggs in one basket is a bad idea is because any single basket can break, and then everything will be lost. But if you use multiple baskets, it's less likely that all those baskets are defective, misplaced, or unlucky. The beauty of the stock market is that an investor can put eggs in multiple baskets, so to speak, at just a little additional cost. It is not totally free to diversify because an investor is wise to research any investment opportunity before investing, and this time spent on research is not free. Stockbrokers, who execute these trades, may charge for each transaction, so they can add transaction costs as well.

What if there was a way to get the benefits of diversification, which reduce or eliminate idiosyncratic risk, for little or no additional costs? Mutual funds, which are themselves baskets of multiple stocks, and the answer to the question of how to diversify cheaply and easily. By making one easy-to-track purchase, an investor in a mutual fund ends up with a diversified stock portfolio. To obtain the same level of diversification without using a mutual fund, that investor would have to research, purchase, track, and sell dozens or even hundreds of individual corporate securities. Mutual funds, however, create some new costs of their own.

AGENCY COSTS AND MISALIGNED INTERESTS

Despite the advantages of mutual funds to create cheap and easy diversification, mutual funds also present unique economic problems. Namely, there may be problems of misaligned interests among the entities involved in the fund. A mutual fund is usually organized such that investors put money into the fund but have no control over where the fund's money is allocated. The fund managers make the allocation decisions. In legal terms, the investors are the principals, and the fund manager is the agent. It is well known that such arrangements can go badly where the principal and the agent have different interests.

In the case of a mutual fund, the investors and the managers have different incentives. The investors want to maximize after-tax returns on investment. The fund managers want to maximize current assets under management, a pre-tax number that determines their compensation. When the goals of increasing money under management and maximizing returns per dollar invested conflict, the manager-agents have perverse incentives to take advantage of their investor-principals.

In a nutshell, Congress designed the ICA and IAA to deal with what is now known as the "agency cost" problem. An agent is a person who acts on behalf of another person called the principal. For a variety of reasons, agents may not always act for the principal's best interest, especially when the interests of the agent are in conflict with the interest of the principal. Consider an employee who is paid by the hour. While an employer would like the employee to work as much as possible for that wage, the employee would like to work as little as possible. The employee might prefer, for example, to take smoke breaks and chat with the other workers on the job, while the employer might prefer the employee to work diligently without rest or distraction. When employees work less diligently, this is called shirking.

Worse than shirking, an agent could use its position to steal from the principal. In a simple example, an employee could take cash from the register, pocket money from customers, or take company property and sell it on the side. Financial agents can likewise defraud clients. History is replete with examples such as Ponzi schemes, where the investment advisor pays one client with investments from another in order to make it look like advisor is making lucrative investment; pump-and-dump schemes, where the investment advisor buys low-priced stock for himself and then drives the price of that stock up by recommending it to clients before selling his own stock at an inflated price; advance-fee schemes, where the investment advisor recommends that the client put up a small, upfront payment to receive a large sum of money later; and many other schemes, scams, frauds, and deceptions.

Principals and agents may work to reduce agency costs in many ways as well. The agent may have to undergo a bonding process, where she completes a difficult task, such as getting a college degree in order to prove that she will work diligently in the future. The principal may monitor the agent to ensure he does not shirk or steal. The principal can incentivize the agent to work in the principal's interest by giving the agent a share of profits such that the interests of principal and agent are more closely aligned. Reputational effects may also be a powerful force to limit agency problems, as agents who get a reputation as bad actors are unlikely to be hired again while agents who do right by their principals may have increased opportunities for future employment.

These techniques to reduce agency cost are not free. Whether the cost is borne by the principal or the agent, someone has to pay for bonding, monitoring, incentivizing, and developing reputation. One might think of agency cost as a kind of "friction" in the mechanics of a mutual fund. Just as friction makes a machine inefficient by producing wasted heat energy, actively managed mutual funds tend to lose some efficiency as a result of agency costs.

Although the modern parlance of agency and transaction costs was not yet well established, lawmakers in the 1930s understood that fund managers could easily take advantage of clients and investors in myriad ways that range from relatively benign to forthrightly sinister. A relatively benign agency cost occurs when the fund manager spends time raising more funds instead of managing existing ones. This may result in lost opportunities for additional profits in existing funds, thus harming investors, while the manager increases the overall amount under management and thus increases the management fee. This is similar to when an elected official spends time campaigning for the next election instead of spending that time working on current legislation.

Law has established its own solution to the problem of agency cost – and these solutions are likewise not free either. It is costly to become an investment advisor, and this bonding process does not end with accreditation. Registered investment advisors need to keep up with continuing education and to produce regular disclosures. Clients pay at least part of these costs in the form of higher fees and commissions.

Aside from intentional wrongdoing, investors also lose money when fund managers make human errors in good faith. Investors generally cannot sue managers for good-faith errors in fund allocations. But fund managers, being human, are subject to the same cognitive challenges that all humans have. For example, finance scholars explained how "bounded rationality" (limited information limits rational decision making) results in fund-level decreasing returns to scale. In other words, as the fund gets bigger (remember that fund managers earn more by managing bigger funds, so managers try to maximize fund size), the fund manager is less able to remember, understand, and analyze all the fund's investment opportunities. As a result, all else being equal, the larger fund tends to earn a smaller return on investment. The emerging field of behavior finance continues to find new "behavioral costs" in which fund members' limited cognitive abilities make actively managed mutual funds inefficient.

As this section explained, mutual funds offer many benefits for investors. However, there are also significant agency costs that arise whenever one person actively makes decisions about another person's money. Even if a fund manager acts in good faith, the manager's latent biases and cognitive limitations result in hidden costs for investors.

Basically, the ICA and IAA attempt to reduce agency costs through a disclosure regime – although disclosure has its own costs – while doing very little to reduce behavioral costs. Based on the continued popularity of mutual funds, it appears that many investors believe the benefits of mutual funds outweigh their costs.

But what if there was a way to automate decisions about fund allocations? If funds were not actively managed by human intervention, then the human problem of agency cost may not arise. Although the mutual fund first emerged before passive management was technologically possible, computing power quickly grew to the point where computers could make investment decisions more efficiently than humans. Moreover, computers have no self-interest, so there is no problem of misalignment of interests between human principals and computer agents. The next section describes how the rise of computer power enabled passively managed funds and algorithmic trading.

COMPUTER POWER

The first "computers" were people, not machines. Organizations such as Langley Memorial Aeronautical Laboratory began hiring women to work as "computers," calculating mathematical equations by hand. From 1935 to 1970, hundreds of women, many of whom with degrees in mathematics, applied their computational skills to solve problems in statistical research, ballistics testing, and even aerospace engineering.

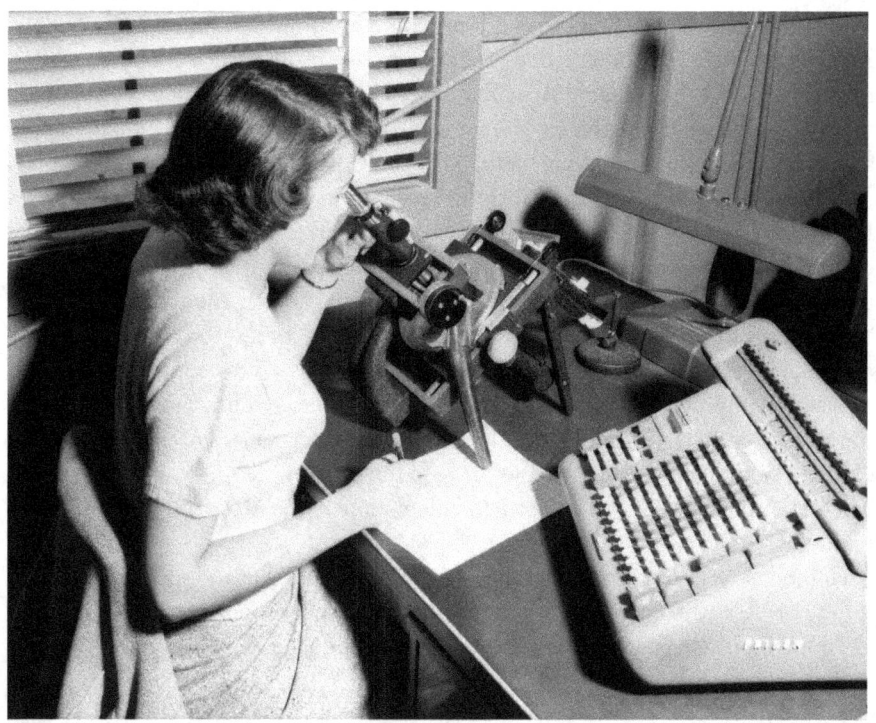

FIGURE 5.1 A female "computer" at Langley. Credit NASA, image no. L-74768.

Meanwhile, the World War II war effort led to government investment in the development of computer technology. Calculating reliable ballistic firing tables – which would tell soldiers in the field how to correct for wind, elevation, temperature, and other variables when firing long-distance projectiles at enemy combatants – required a great deal of computing power while demanding top secret treatment. These needs prompted the U.S. government to look for new technologies that could process vast quantities of data at all hours and without the need for security clearance. This led to the top-secret ENIAC Project.

Like the Manhattan Project – a secret research and development effort to produce atomic weapons that enlisted many of the world's top scientists including Robert Oppenheimer – the ENIAC Project was funded by the U.S. government. Building the ENIAC (Electronic Numerical Integrator and Computer) machine enlisted the top physicists and engineers at the University of Pennsylvania Moore School of Electrical Engineering. Work began in early 1943, and the ENIAC machine went online in 1945. Its first task connected directly to the Manhattan Project. Beginning on December 10, 1945, ENIAC spent six weeks computing thermonuclear calculations for the first hydrogen bomb. Notably, this calculation was rendered after Germany and Japan had surrendered and World War II had ended.

The University of Pennsylvania announced ENIAC to the world on February 15, 1946. At its unveiling, ENIAC could calculate a ballistic trajectory in thirty seconds. That same calculation required twenty human-computer hours to calculate. Moreover, ENIAC was designed in a modular format. Adding vacuum tubes, diodes, relays, resistors, and capacitors increased ENIAC's power and speed. But these vacuum tubes were volatile and inefficient, and ENIAC was nonfunctional for approximately half of its service lifetime.

When ENIAC was retired in 1955, Jack St. Clair Kilby – an engineer at Texas Instruments who would go on to win the Nobel Prize in Physics in 2000 – was developing a new technology that would revolutionize computing. Kilby produced the world's first functional integrated circuit in 1958, and he filed a patent for this "Miniaturized Electronic Circuits" technology on February 6, 1959.[1] Integrated circuits, or "ICs," are essentially a collection of tiny transistors connected together on a single chip. ICs proved far more reliable than vacuum tubes. Moreover, ICs are much smaller than vacuum tubes. Electronics move at a consistent speed (the speed of light), so the smaller distance they have to travel, the faster the computer will be. Therefore, the smaller ICs performed calculations faster than the larger vacuum tubes did.

Computer technology manufacturers raced to create smaller and smaller transistors, leading to ICs with more and more transistors per square inch. On April 19, 1965, Gordon Moore – the cofounder of Fairchild Semiconductor and CEO and co-founder

---

[1] Kilby's integrated circuit was awarded U.S. Patent No. 3,138,743. A copy of the patent, along with a description of its impact, is available here: https://inst.eecs.berkeley.edu/~ee40/su04/publications/3138743.pdf.

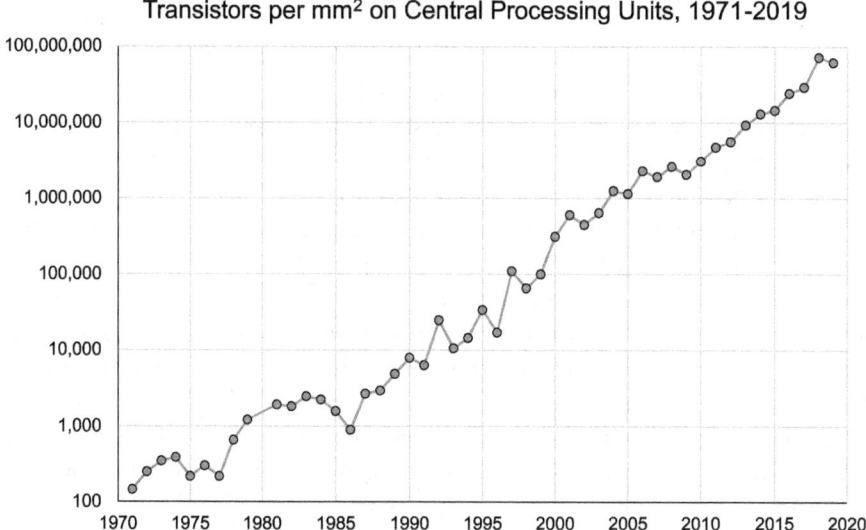

FIGURE 5.2 Logarithmic increase in processing power, according with Moore's law.

of Intel – published an article in Electronic Magazine in which he posited that the density of ICs will double approximately every year. In 1975, he revised this estimate and predicted a doubling of ICs and therefore of computer power every two years. His revised prediction proved remarkably prescient.[2]

By the mid-1970s, computer power was mature enough to enable technological innovation in financial markets. When the index fund was first revealed on December 31, 1975, however, it was not heralded with trumpets or revered for democratizing access to investment markets. Even though the financial industry's first index fund was designed as a low-cost way for individual investors to gain diversified exposure to the U.S. equity market, it was derived as a decidedly "un-American" invention. That first fund is known as the Vanguard 500 Index Fund (VFINX), which holds over $600 billion in securities today.

[2] Computing power (as measured by transistor density on ICs) has essentially doubled every year since then 1975. In 1976, RCA managed to squeeze 5,000 transistors on its 27 mm² "1802'chip. In 2019, AMD unveiled its "Ryzen 7 3700X" chip, which featured 9,890,000,000 transistors on a 273 mm² chip. From 1976 to 2019, transistor density increased from about 185 per mm² to over 36,227,106 per mm², representing an almost 200,000 times increase in computing power over these decades. For more on Moore's law, see Ilkka Tuomi, The Lives and Death of Moore's Law, 7 FIRST MONDAY (2002), available at https://doi.org/10.5210/fm.v7i11.1000. Moore's Law is currently thought to be at or near its theoretical limit; that is, it may not be physically possible to make transistors any smaller than they are today. The lower bound of transistor size is not only limited by the width of an atom but also by a quantum-mechanics issue called "electron tunneling," whereby an electron moves probabilistically and not linearly at tiny sizes. It is possible the quantum computers, which harness the probabilistic nature of electrons, will enable an entirely new kind of computing technology, which may in turn lead to heretofore unimagined financial innovations.

THE INDEX FUND

An index fund is a passively managed portfolio of investments that are bought and sold based on a static algorithm. To the extent they are pooled investments, index funds are a type of mutual fund. But passive management makes mutual funds fundamentally different from actively managed mutual funds, at least from the perspective of the economic costs and benefits. If a fund is actively managed, as opposed to passively managed, then the fund manager closely monitors the fund and usually intends to "beat the market" or provide a higher return than the overall market. This requires a great deal of human analysis and gut instinct, which are susceptive to cognitive biases, behavioral costs, and agency costs. An index fund, on the other hand, requires no human input, once deployed, to buy and sell securities. The index fund is a "fire and forget" financial weapon. This sharply reduces or even eliminates the costs described above. However, computer programs are only as good as their code, which today is still written by humans. Moreover, algorithms can hide deeply rooted biases and propagate errors at alarming rates.

AGENCY COSTS IN INDEX FUNDS

As described above, friction between mutual fund investors and mutual fund managers may reduce overall efficiency of actively managed funds. It may seem that removing the human element, the investment advisor, from the fund would also reduce agency costs to zero. While it is true that index funds do not employ humans to make day-to-day decisions, and therefore does not experience human agency cost on a day-to-day basis, index funds do not totally eliminate these costs.

It is possible to render bad advice, even in the context of passive investing. First, an index fund is only as diverse as it is programmed to be. There are broad-based index funds which are designed to track entire stock markets or even national economies, and there are narrow-based index funds which are designed to track specific industries or industry subsectors. Whenever a human advisor directs a client to a particular fund, there is a risk that human fund managers can direct investors to unsuitable index funds. For example, a fund agent could (improperly) recommend that a retiree invest 50 percent of savings in a volatile commodity index – such as an index fund for small-cap oil stocks, where that investor cannot afford to lose the amount of principal that is at risk is such a volatile narrow-based fund. On the other hand, a risk-averse advisor might recommend that a twenty-year-old millionaire invest only in broad-based funds that track the DJIA, but this would not give that millionaire enough exposure to high-risk, high-reward investment opportunities. To put it another way, index funds expose investors to a variety of benchmarks that vary in risk to suit a variety of risk-appetites. The human element of discretionary trading is largely removed from these investments, but that does not guarantee the suitability of an index fund for any given client.

As mentioned above, the law tries to reduce or eliminate agency costs through default and mandatory rules and regulations, which come with some costs in return for offering some protections. The landmark case of *Brown v. Bullock* held that fund managers must consider whether a product is feasible for a client. Additionally, investment advisers must disclose conflicts of interest that could bias their recommendations. Although regulations do not incentivize fund managers to unlock the hidden potential of fund stewardship, where fund managers are encouraged to make intelligent decisions that maximize the value of the fund, the hazards of index funds to investors appear managed within the SEC's current regulatory framework.

MISTAKES HAVE BEEN MADE

Just because a decision is made by a computer does not mean that decision is sound. Computer decisions are only as good as their base level programming. Sometimes a programmer does not consider a future situation that flummoxes the algorithm, sometimes with disastrous results.

On May 6, 2010, from 2:32 pm to 3:08 pm EDT, stock markets lost one trillion dollars. Why, on such a balmy day in Spring, did investors suddenly sell assets at the incredible rate of a half-billion dollars per second? The fault lies in part with trading algorithms and technical glitches. Although a British financial trader named Navinder Singh Sarao probably prompted the initial sell-off by using a "spoofing" algorithm (where buy orders are placed and then cancelled rapidly and automatically in order to manipulate stock process), other algorithms quickly followed suit. The initial spoof triggered a cascading sell-off. Without human intervention, computers ran amok, selling stock at incredible rates until humans physically shut them down. An SEC report on the Flash Crash found "a market so fragmented and fragile that a single large trade could send stocks into a sudden spiral."

REGULATION OF INDEX FUNDS

It seems that every crash, panic, downturn, crisis, and market failure leads to more regulations. The Flash Crash was no exception. As mentioned above, the ICA and IAA were designed to resolve agency problems that resulted from active human management of mutual funds. These statutes were not designed to handle the problems caused by passively managed index funds. In fact, these securities regulations are particularly inept at dealing with solo traders who are not managing anyone else's money. But it was precisely this sort of solo trader who crashed the entire stock market on May 6, 2010. Sarao was just a guy in an apartment with a personal computer who was able to create and deploy algorithms that would spoof the market so he might gain a financial advantage.

The SEC responded by promulgating Regulation NMS, which prohibits spoofing and other nefarious stock market activities such as "banging the close" and "layering."

Without getting into too much technical detail, these are effectively new types of scams that have been enabled by computerized trading. For example, a trader can quickly place and cancel orders that he never intends to fulfill by using a computer program to place and then quickly cancel trades. This fake order is called a "spoof." By placing a spoof bid to buy stock, for example, the trader artificially increases the price of the next trade on that stock by indicating there is more demand for it. This is easier to do when the market for that stock is thin, meaning, that stock is not frequently traded. While the price is artificially elevated, that same trader places a real bid to sell at the higher price. The trader then cancels the buy order, thus obtaining the stock at a lower-than-market price. Layering is a more complex and higher speed variant of this scam where the trader places multiple buy offers to drive the price even higher before fulfilling multiple sell orders and then finally cancelling the buy orders.

Spoofing, layering, and similar algorithmic schemes have been outlawed. But regulators have a hard time keeping ahead of the technology. As technology continues to increase the speed at which trading operates and the complexity of trading algorithms, fraudulent conduct becomes harder to detect. Moreover, the line between harmful high-frequency fraud and beneficial activities that quickly resolve price anomalies can be blurry. Regulating these technology-driven trading schemes and strategies is like playing a game of Whack-a-Mole at an accelerating pace. As Moore's Law predicted, computer speed has roughly doubled every two years, and algorithmic traders double their speed too as the processors get faster. In addition, innovations in communications technology like fiber optic internet access and 5G high-speed wireless networks allow traders to take quantum leaps forward. The result is a system where regulations are always behind, and regulators make constant efforts just to keep up. This marks the beginning of the end of the Second-Era model of regulation.

CONCLUSIONS ON COMPUTATIONAL INVESTING

The Flash Crash represents a turning point in the history of securities regulation. Regulations created at the beginning of the Second Era were primarily designed to prevent large institutions from taking advantage of ordinary investors. This goal was to be accomplished primarily by requiring disclosures from large firms on the one hand and prohibiting ordinary investors from participating in risky markets on the other. At least in the early and middle parts of the twentieth century, these regulations appeared to work reasonably well. Investment in mutual funds increased, and the stock market slowly climbed from the pits of the Great Depression to all-time highs in the 1980s.

Meanwhile, computational technology and computing power increased at an exponential rate. By the 1970s, technology had developed to the point where index funds became possible. These index funds can act like computer programs that trade based on their code and not on further human instructions. This reduces agency costs and human error, but such algorithmic trading also opened the market up to a new sort of risk. As computational power grew to the point where virtually anyone could implement a trading algorithm, computers created a new risk that did not exist before. High-frequency trading, enabled by massive computing power, enabled new ways to spoof, bang, layer, front-run and otherwise defraud and cheat the market at large. Meanwhile, individual human decision makers failed to keep pace with the rate of algorithmic trading.

As the twentieth century drew to a close, widespread fear about computers taking over impacted the American mindset. From movies like *The Terminator* – where an algorithmic system gains self-awareness and attempts to destroy humanity – to the Y2K problem – where people feared that society would collapse on January 1, 2000, because computers were not programed to handle four-digit dates – popular anxiety about the rise of the machines grew. While the 1950s promised that computers would handle the tedious tasks so humans could engage in more leisure time, the 1990s were laden with fear that humanity would become subverted by the almighty algorithm.

But history took a different turn. In the early part of the twenty-first century, web technology matured such that "Web 2.0" technologies emerged. The Internet shifted from a situs of information to a locus where people would connect with each other. Powerful new ways of using technology to tap into human decision-making, such as crowdsourcing, advanced finance, and the sciences. Technology became much more personal. Laptops, smartphones, Wi-Fi, and broadband access connected society. As the new millennium dawned, a new source of data and decision-making appeared: society itself. This ushered in the Third Era of corporate finance.

BIBLIOGRAPHY

Ackert v. Ausman, 198 F.Supp. 538 (1961).
Aldred Inv. Trust v. Securities and Exchange Commission, 151 F.2d 254 (1945).
Bounded Rationality, STANFORD ENCYCLOPEDIA OF PHILOSOPHY (November 30, 2018), https://perma.cc/4ZR9-NGG9.
Breswick & Co. v. Briggs, 135 F.Supp. 397 (S.D.N.Y. 1955).
Brown v. Bullock, 35 Misc.2d 370 (1962).
Chan, C. Peter, *Battle of Britain 10 Jul 1940–31 Oct 1940*, WORLD WAR II DATABASE.
Cohen, Alma, et al., *Index Fund Scholarship*, HARV. L. SCHOOL FORUM ON CORPORATE GOVERNANCE (2018).
Derman, Emanuel, *A Stylized History of Quantitative Finance*, COLUM. U. (2016).
Entel v. Allen, 270 F.Supp. 60 (1967).
Ferris, Stephen P. & Xuemin (Sterling) Yan, *Agency Conflicts in Delegated Portfolio Management: Evidence from Namesake Mutual Funds*, 30 J. FIN. RSCH. 473 (2007).
Gaskill v. Polhemus, 57 A. 1048 (1904).
Glazer Donald, W., *A Study of Mutual Fund Complexes*, 119 U. PENNSYLVANIA L. REV. (1970).
Glicken v. Bradford, 204 F.Supp. 300 (S.D.N.Y. 1962).

Herman, Edward S., *Lobell on the Wharton School Study of Mutual Funds: A Rebuttal Lobell on the Wharton School Study of Mutual Funds: A Rebuttal*, 49 VIRGINIA L. REV. (1963).
Iuliano, Jason & Keith E. Whittington, *The Nondelegation Doctrine: Alive and Well*, 93 NOTRE DAME L. REV. (2017).
Kilby, J. S., Miniaturized Electronic Circuits, U.S. Patent 3,138,743 (1959).
Korobkin, Russell B., *Behavioral Analysis and Legal Form: Rules vs. Standards Revisited*, 79 OREGON L. REV. (2000).
Korpela, A. E. & L. I. Reiser, A.L.R. 3d § 30 (originally published in 1970).
Lanigan v. Apollo Savings, 288 N.E.2d 445 (1972).
Lauricella, Tom, *How a Trading Algorithm Went Awry*, WSJ (October. 21, 2010), https://web.archive.org/web/20101021141951/http:/online.wsj.com/article/SB10001424052748704029304575526390131916792.html.
Lin, Tom C. W., *Reasonable Investor(s)*, 95 BOSTON U. L. REV. (2015).
LIVERMORE, JESSE L. & RICHARD SMITTEN , HOW TO TRADE IN STOCKS: HIS OWN WORDS: THE JESSE LIVERMORE SECRET TRADING FORMULA FOR UNDERSTANDING TIMING, MONEY MANAGEMENT AND EMOTIONAL CONTROL (1991).
Lobell, Nathan D., *Rights and Responsibilities in the Mutual Fund*, 70 YALE L.J. 1258 (1961).
Lutz v. Boas, 171 A.2d 381 (1961).
McMenomy v. Ryden, 148 N.W.2d 804 (1967).
Miers v. Columbia Mut. Building & Loan Ass'n, 157 F. 940 (1907.).
Mintz v. Allen, 254 F.Supp. 1012 (1966).
Moore, G. E., *Lithography and the Future of Moore's Law*, 11 IEEE SOLID-STATE CIRCUITS SOCIETY NEWSLETTER (2006).
Mott v. Western Savings & Loan Ass'n, 20 P.2d 236 (1933).
PBS, *Timeline: The Evolution of the CCC*, WGBH, https://web.archive.org/web/20161225041953/https://www.pbs.org/wgbh/americanexperience/features/timeline/ccc/.
Press Release, SEC, Release No.33–295 (1935).
Roberts, Neal P., *Ballistic Analysis of Firing Table Data for 155MM, M825 Smoke Projectile* (U.S. Army Laboratory Command ed., 1990).
Rome v. Archer, 197 A.2d 49 (1964).
Saminsky v. Abbott, 194 A.2d 549 (1963).
Teller v. Wilcoxen, 81 N.W. 772 (1900).
The Mutual Fund and Its Management Company: An Analysis of Business Incest, 71 Yale L. J. 137 (1961).
Tucker, Anne M., *The Long and the Short: Portfolio Turnover Ratios & Mutual Fund Investment Time Horizons*, 43 IOWA J. CORP. L. 581 (2018).
Tuomi, Ilkka, *The Lives and Death of Moore's Law*, 7 FIRST MONDAY (2002), https://perma.cc/R9Z3-ENRH.
White v. Ludwig, 32 Misc.2d 120 (1961).
White v. Wogaman, 54 P.2d 793 (1936).

6

Silicon Valley

The Internet evolved from a Department of Defense project into the center of the new economy. Companies rushed to develop e-commerce, and investors bought almost any stock that pertained to the internet. There was a flurry of initial public offerings (IPOs), as companies rushed to sell registered stock on public exchanges to capitalize on the sudden interest in everything digital. But the bubble burst. Scandal dogged public markets, and federal legislators once again were galvanized to pass statist and protectionist laws. The sub-prime mortgage crisis further fueled the drive to regulate securities. In particular, the Sarbanes-Oxley Act of 2002 and the Dodd-Frank Act of 2010 parallel the New Deal securities regulation in that both limited and conditioned the public sale of stock. As a result, being a public company became much more expensive and less beneficial, so fewer companies went public.

Software is eating the world.
   – Marc Andreessen, Founder of Netscape, Opsware and the Andreessen
   Horowitz Venture Capital Firm

Stanford University (founded by Leland Stanford, the same man who hammered the Golden Spike that completed the transcontinental railroad in 1869) has attracted pioneers in science and technology to its campus in Northern California for over a century. The computer technologies developed there were used to power the index funds and algorithmic trading discussed in the previous chapter. But the companies who developed such technology are interesting in their own right, especially for our story, because these Western pioneers also developed a different financial ecosystem that evolved to become distinct from the stock markets back East. To understand this parallel track in the evolution of financial markets, we must go back in time and to another place, where one could reasonably argue that the modern computer era began – and where the venture capital finance industry started up.

The story of computers could well begin with the invention of the abacus, a machine that used beads on wires to calculate math problems even before Arabic numerals were invented. But we will begin our discussion of the brief history of computers as relevant to the evolution of financial markets in 1913, when electrical engineer Harris Ryan installed a high-voltage laboratory on Stanford's campus. His work accelerated in the Roaring Twenties, when it expanded its capacity to handle two million volts in 1926. Frederick Terman joined the Stanford faculty after receiving his ScD in electrical engineering from MIT in 1924. His work on vacuum tubes paved the way for the first computers, which were initially used in the giant machines that calculated nuclear missile payloads and trajectories.

THE START OF STARTUPS

Terman's legacy exceeded electrical engineering. Terman also institutionalized a sense of entrepreneurship and innovation into the Stanford University culture that helped generate a new business model that we now know as the startup model. Throughout the 1930s, Terman encouraged his graduate students, including William Hewlett and David Packard, to create new businesses based on their research. These businesses had unique qualities of being very risky and rather expensive, but their success had the potential to change the world – and make a lot of money in the process. The term "venture" – meaning an undertaking involving uncertainty, risk, speculation, and the hope of profit – was applied to these nascent technology firms.

Terman even invested money in these projects. In this sense, Terman was what we today call an angel investor, which is someone who invests their own money in startups. Investing in risky business projects at early stages in their development can generate huge returns, but more often than not the investment could be a total loss. This type of high-risk, high-reward investing is not for the faint of heart, but, with an appropriate level of diversification, it can be an incredibly lucrative pursuit. Although Terman provided capital for his students' ventures, he was not really a venture capitalist as that term is used today. The distinction between an angel investor like Terman and a modern venture capitalist is that venture capitalists invest other people's money, whereas angel investors invest their own money.

With Terman's financial support, William and David founded Hewlett-Packard in 1939. William and David started work in a one-car garage in Palo Alto, but went on to create a tech empire that developed personal computers, inkjet printers, handheld touchscreen devices, optical character recognition software, digital cameras and photo services, medical devices, rewritable DVDs, enterprise security software, cloud computing solutions, and more. The HP Garage at 367 Addison Avenue is now designated at the "Birthplace of Silicon Valley" by the California Historical Association.

HP formally incorporated on August 18, 1947 and went public on November 6, 1957. Perhaps unintentionally, Hewlett and Packard thereby established a paradigm that would resonate throughout the second era of startup history. HP's success set up a paradigm that ventures continue to emulate today: generating a business plan based on inventing power but unproven technologies, developing prototypes of that

FIGURE 6.1 The garage in Palo Alto, California where the Hewlett-Packard (HP) corporation began – and where some say Silicon Valley was born. Credit raneko (Flickr), licensed under CC BY-ND 2.0.

technology on a shoestring budget, attracting local venture capital to turn prototypes into products and to scale up production, and then going public by registering with the SEC and selling stock on the NYSE when it came time to broadly expand production. But this approach – which is now known as the startup model – would not really come into its own until the SEC made it easier for entrepreneurs to navigate the complex set of security regulations that were established to protect society from another Great Depression.

EARLY ORIGINS OF VENTURE CAPITAL

Today, venture capital is a multibillion-dollar industry. But in the early days of Silicon Valley, raising money for technology projects like HP was not yet institutionalized. Entrepreneurs like Hewlett and Packard raised money informally from people they knew well, like Terman. In fact, the first organization to describe itself as a "venture capital firm" was the American Research & Development Corporation (ARDC), founded in 1946 by Harvard Business School professor Georges Doriot and others.

ARDC created opportunities for soldiers returning from World War II to invest in the emerging defense industry, which included many veteran-owned businesses. It was a unique type of investment company because it sought funds from sources other than wealthy families. Prior to ARDC, only wealthy families – such as Rockefeller, Whitney, Payson & Trask – formed funds to invest in startup ventures.

ARDC was also novel for an investment company because it registered its fund with the SEC and listed its stock on the New York Stock Exchange. ARDC's decision to list stock publicly was a direct response to the New Deal securities regulations that made it difficult for ordinary investors to invest in private companies. As a public company that invested in private companies, ARDC made it possible for ordinary investors, including many World War II veterans, to profit from risky startups. This blurred the lines between public and private investing.

Moreover, ARDC blurred the definition of a mutual fund. Most mutual funds at that time simply bundled together publicly traded stocks, which could be purchased separately by ordinary investors via the NYSE. But ARDC's portfolio of investments included stock in private companies that ordinary investors could not have separately purchased.

ARDC closed in 1971, however, when Doriot retired and several other founding members went on to create private venture capital firms in Silicon Valley, including Greylock Ventures, one of today's most prominent venture capital firms. This marked the beginning of the end of the early venture capital era. But each financial era's end is a new beginning. In this case, this was more than passing the baton from ARDC to Greylock. It was the beginning of the modern venture capital (VC) era.

EVOLUTION OF VENTURE CAPITAL

In the more than seventy-five years between ARDC's advent of VC fund, the VC industry has evolved from an oddball stock to a major force in the global economy. VC investments has resulted in technologies and innovations that themselves changed the relationship between investors and regulators. Later chapters will discuss how venture-backed startups changed public markets forever due to the so-called Dot-Com Bubble, and how the rise of financial technology (FinTech), much of which was supported by VC dollars, has propelled America into the Third Era of financial evolution, where traditional financial regulation is no longer possible.

Other books provide a more detailed historical record of all the key people and companies in Silicon Valley and elsewhere that are part of the rich story of venture capital's evolution. This book will focus on the details that matter from the perspective of the impact of regulation and that shed light on what to expect in the future. Therefore, we fast forward from 1945 to the 1970s, when venture capital became known as its own type of investment or "asset class." It is no mere coincidence that this period in the 1970s coincides precisely with the development of transistor-based computers and their steady growth since then. The VC industry out West (described in this chapter) and the computers that powered stock market transactions back East (described in the prior chapter) were running on two parallel but symbiotic tracks that would collide at the term of the millennium in what is now known as the Dot-Com Bubble (described in the next chapter).

Two of the most historically important VC firms were established in 1972: Kleiner Perkins Caufield & Byers and Sequoia Capital. Over the next decade, Kleiner Perkins raised funds that invested heavily in semiconductors, databases, and computers. Startups in their portfolio include Compaq Computers (personal computers), Electronic Arts (video games), Sun Microsystems (computer chips and programming software), Quantum Corporation (data disk storage), Qume (computer printers), Tandem Computers (industrial computers), Applied Materials (semiconductors), and other business that have since transformed the technology and computing industry. Kleiner's investments into these companies proved incredibly profitable.

Sequoia Capital is equally impressive in its foresight and investment strategy. Two of its early investments turned into world-changing technology firms: Apple (personal computers) and Oracle (database software and server hardware). After Apple's successful initial public offering, an initial public offering being a type of liquidity event that returns cash to investors and will be discussed in detail in the next chapter, Sequoia deployed the cash proceeds from that event to invest in the next generation of technology startups including Cisco Systems (networking hardware), Webvan (online groceries), and Google (internet search). Sequoia was also one of the first VC firms to expand operations to Israel, a country which has since earned the moniker "Startup Nation."

Kleiner Perkins and Sequoia established a staged investment model that is still generally followed today.

Early- or Seed-Stage Financing

VC firms develop relationships with startup founders at the first, "early" stage, when the company may not even have a product or any revenue. This "seed" financing is used for product development and market research. Other "startup" financing may be used in initial product commercialization and marketing efforts, which may help the company develop its first revenue streams and hopefully get to the point where the company is earning revenue that meet or exceeds its expenses. In other words, the early-stage funding, often termed "Series Seed" or "Series AA," helps a startup go from having a marketing idea to commercializing that idea and, ideally, breaking even with its revenues versus expenses.

"Seedfunding" is the beginning of the startup financing cycle. Startups need money to create products and services before they ever earn their first dollar. They use seedfunding to research, assess, and develop an initial concept. Who would invest in a completely nascent unproven concept? Friends, family, and fools (FFF) – fools referring to the high risk associated with investment in nascent startups – provide seedfunding to local entrepreneurs, while angel investors provide the seedfunding capital to high-growth startups. In 2019, angels invested about $8.8 billion in seed-stage startups, which accounted for 37 percent of all the angel capital invested that year.

VC firms are less likely to focus on such early-stage startups. Although the VC industry invested a total of $9.6 billion in seed-stage startups in 2019, that represents just over 7 percent of the total amount that VC firms invested that year. And while VC funds invested slightly more total dollars into seed-stage startups than angels did that year, those VC funds invested all that money in just 4,760 startups, while the angels spread a comparable amount in approximately 23,580 startups.

Moreover, 2019 was somewhat anomalous for the VC industry, which usually invests in far fewer seed-stage startups. In 2006, for example, angels invested in about 23,460 seed-stage startups, while VC funds only invested in 460 seed-stage deals. This trend is consistent over time. Therefore, angels are the leading source of capital for most seed-stage companies.

Once a startup receives seedfunding, the company begins operations and enters the "seed valley of death," where companies require significant capital inflows but have little or no revenue. Startups begin to leave the perilous seed valley of death when their revenue increases enough to cover all monthly fixed and variable costs. This is called the "breakeven." Startups who survive until breakeven can continue to grow organically, or they can expand more rapidly through an infusion of expansion stage financing.

Expansion Stage Financing

The second stage is designed for expansion. Startups are distinguishable from other small businesses in that startups generally have ambition to grow rapidly so that successful ones can return substantial capital back to investors, whereas small business owners may be quite content with just doing a bit better than breaking even after salaries (including their own) are paid. In other words, small businesses generally do not have an emphasis on this expansion phase, if they have an expansion phase at all, whereas the expansion phase is a critical aspect of high-growth startups.

Startups decidedly exit the seed valley of death when a venture capital firm makes its first early-stage investment, called "Series A." After this point, VCs frequently reinvest in the startup in Series B, C, D, and so on, so the startup can afford to invest in growth even if doing so causes net profits to become negative again.

Small venture capital firms may only make early-stage investments. Large VCs make "later stage" investments all the way up to the end of the startup financing cycle, when a startup ceases to be a startup.

Fortunate high-growth startups move quickly through the breakeven to the "early stage," where VC managers become substantially more interested in investing in startup. VC managers prefer to invest in companies in the expansion phase because that provides an ideal mix of risk (which is lower than at the early stage because the product has been developed and is proven to work and be sellable to some market) and reward (because the company still has incredible potential for growth). But startups entering this phase requiring capital may first turn to their early-stage investors for additional financial support. This is why VC managers develop an investment relationship with promising startups during the early stage, so they are more likely to get the first opportunity to fund that startup in the lucrative expansion phase. Investments in the expansion phase are usually characterized by names like "Series A" and "Series B."

Later Stage Financing

Some VC firms continue to make new investment in companies who have completed the phase of rapid expansion and are now in the third, "later stage" financing. Companies in this later stage typically have a positive cash flow, meaning they take in more cash each month than they put out. This means that later stage companies no longer need VC investment to survive – but they may desire it to grow even faster.

Liquidity Events

The goal of most startups is to eventually return cash to investors in what is called a liquidity event. The traditional gold standard for a startup liquidity event historically was an initial public offering (IPO), which is discussed in the next chapter. After the IPO, the company is public. It will be listed on a stock exchange and function much like the companies described in the prior chapter. An alternative liquidity event that is growing in popularity is the sale of the startup to a larger firm in what is called a merger and acquisition (M&A) event. The cycle ends badly when the startup goes broke and liquidates or sells the fledgling operations at a discount.

The entire VC industry has evolved substantially since this second wave of investments into startup companies in the late 1980s. In 1987, there were only 361 VC firms and 687 VC funds in existence, who raised $4.4 billion that year. By 2007, the VC industry nearly doubled to 946 firms and 1,586 funds. Meanwhile, the amount of capital raised per year increase eightfold to $35.1 billion in 2007 – which also means that the average size of a VC fund grew tremendously. In 2019, there were 1,328 firms with 2,211 funds who raised a total of $50.5 billion that year.

As the VC industry matured and VC firms and funds grew, the Kleiner-Sequoia model of staged investment has changed. As VC firms and their funds get larger, which is usually the result of being successful in past investments, these larger firms find it harder to invest in smaller startups at earlier stages in the startup financing cycle. The result of the growth of VC funds size is that VC firms make larger investment in later stage startups. In 1980, over half of VC funds were deployed as

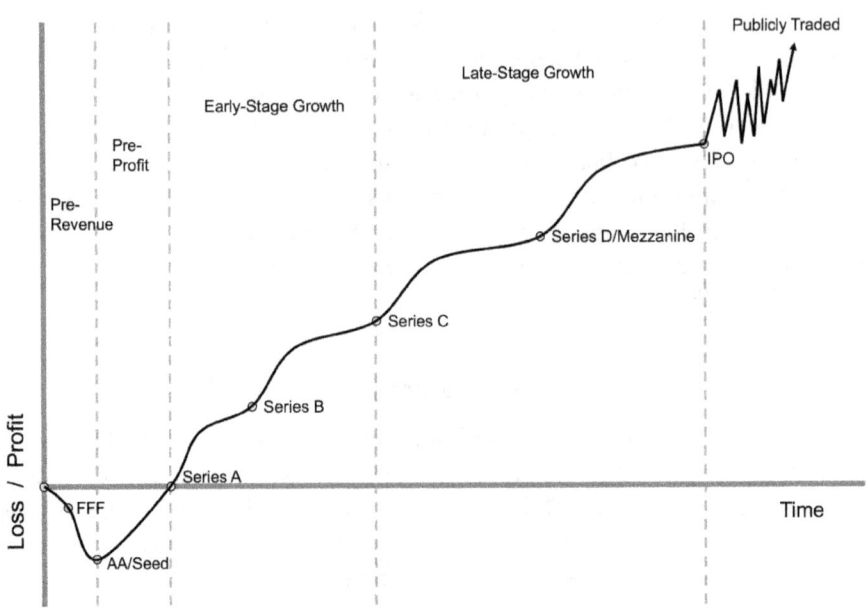

FIGURE 6.2 The traditional startup financing timeline.

investment into seed- and early-stage companies. By 2007, that trend had reversed, with almost 4/5ths of VC funds deployed into expansion- and later-stage companies. Through 2019, VC firms' preferences for investing into later-stage companies remained, with only 7 percent of total VC dollars invested that year into seed-stage companies.

A new group of investors called "angels" has picked up the slack in seed-stage financing. Angels, who are people who are not usually professional investors but rather are wealthy from other means and who invest their own money in startups, are discussed below. More recently, super angels, a term coined in the 2010s to describe wealthy people, who, like VC managers, and professional investors for whom investing is their full-time occupation, and who, like angels, invest their own money in startups.

Additionally, startups have begun to stay private for longer. The reasons why are discussed in the next chapter, but the effect is that it has become more common for additional investment rounds titled Series C, D, E, and even F to occur more frequently today than they did in the past. This stretches out the expansion phase of the startup financing cycle and thereby changes the nature of startups who fit in this model. In the 1980s, companies used to be valued in the tens of millions of dollars when receiving expansion phase financing. But a new concept has evolved of a "unicorn" company, which is a company that is valued at more than $1 billion in a private venture capital stock financing. In 1987, there were no unicorns. Today, almost 500 companies meet the definition of a "unicorn" by being very large private companies that still rely on VC investment even though they are valued at over $1 billion. In fact, new terms such as a "decacorn" (a venture-backed company worth $10 billion or more) and "hectocorn" (worth more than $100 billion) have been coined to describe these once-rare entities that now seem to be growing more and more common.

MODERN VENTURE CAPITAL

The modern VC industry is distinguishable from the ARDC's model in that it tends not to admit ordinary investors into its investment funds. Rather, venture capital today is predominately funded by extraordinarily wealthy intuitions and a few very wealthy people. The reason for this has to do with securities regulations, in particular the prohibitions against general solicitations and the limitations on sales to nonaccredited investors, which will be discussed in the next section. This section will convey the form and structure that is paradigmatic of the modern venture capital industry so you will more easily see how regulations caused this form to take its present share.

Venture capitalists create funds in which large institutional investors (such as pension funds and university endowments) invest. Typical investors in VC funds are pension funds, financial firms, insurance company, university endowments, and other large funds that want to allocate a small portion of their vast portfolios into high-risk, high-reward investment.

VC managers then "deploy" that capital primarily by purchasing stock in startup companies. The nature of venture capital firms is quite different from the nature of angel investors like Terman because VCs manage other people's money, whereas angels invest their own money. VC firms raise sums of money in funds that is far in excess of most angels' personal net wealth, and VCs have to deploy this money very quickly because the funds typically have eight to twelve-year lifespans. This limited lifespan of a VC fund is necessary for investors into that fund to receive their return on investment within a specified period. When the fund's life is over, the capital must be returned to investors. This create pressure on companies funded by VC funds to have a so-called liquidity event – where the startup's stock can be exchanged for cash – within the fund's lifespan.

As professional, institutional money managers, VC firms typically employ dozens of managers and hundreds of analysts and other support staff to help with sourcing deals, crunching numbers, drafting contracts and other transactional documents, and supporting startups after funding them. This is a small industry that has an outsized influence. Only a handful of top firms consistently raise the largest funds and have the greatest influence on the industry, on the startup market, and indeed on the entire American economy.

Most of the significant VC firms are located in California. In 2019, firms located in California raised 65 percent of the total amount of money raised by VC funds across all of America. Massachusetts was a distant second at 16 percent, and New York came in third at 10 percent. No other state received more than 2 percent of the total amount of VC funds. This further demonstrates that this industry is not as diverse as the simple number of firms might make it seem. In fact, the greatest concentration of VC firms anywhere in the world is on just one road a few miles from Stanford University: Sand Hill Road in Menlo Park, California.

Although popular culture and TV shows like Shark Tank make it seem that VC managers invest in very early-stage startups, the truth is that the modern VC industry typically invests at the later, growth stage of startup projects. It is axiomatic that earlier stage projects are riskier. But where there is risk there is also the opportunity for rewards. VC managers maximize their fund's risk-versus-reward calculation while optimizing their return on their time spent managing investments by investing an average of about $16.1 million dollars per company into companies that are valued at around $23 million; however, the average investment amount is a bit misleading because there have been a few so-called mega rounds, where VC invested more than $100 million into several early-stage biotech startups. Instead of considering the *average* Series A round size, the *median* Series A round size, which is $6.7 million per investment, is probably a better characterization of what most VC firms' initial investment into a company looks like.

VC managers do also invest smaller amounts into seed-stage startups that may have little more than a business plan or a prototype. They do this despite the incredible risks in order to form a relationship with that company that is calculated to lead to larger investment opportunities when and if that startup succeeds in its initial product development and marketing strategy. Usually, this happens where the founder of the startup is well-known for his prior successes in entrepreneurship. The VC manager may be betting that the founder will succeed again, regardless of the product. Similar to the real estate saying that one should invest in location, location, location, it seems that VC investors likewise invest in management, management, management.

It is a misperception that VC managers are risk-seeking. While it is true that VC funds invest millions of dollars into unproven startups, even thought that investment may be entirely lost, But VC managers have ways to mitigate the risks of investing in startups such that they can earn returns that outstrip the risks. In particular, VC managers diversify the investments of each fund. Funders Club Education Center reports that an average fund contains $135 million and invests in thirty to eighty companies. In addition, successful VC firms have multiple funds with different fund managers, which further diversifies the firm itself.

Complete diversification, however, is not plausible or desirable in the VC model. While VC funds diversify against the risk that any one company's technology or management team fails, VC funds are generally exposed to market risk for the tech industry and often exposed to additional risk in a specific subsector. VCs cannot completely avoid systemic risk because their fund managers tend to be specialists in a certain tech industry subsector. Such managers generally invest in their fields of expertise, where they can better evaluate technologies. Specializing in a tech area also helps VC managers become keenly aware of promising developments and pitfalls in that subsector. While this encouraged VC managers to invest more heavily in specific subsectors, the risk of portfolio imbalance is somewhat outweighed by the value add and synergies from focusing on a few types of companies.

VC managers also avoid some risk of failure by supporting the companies they fund. This support makes VC managers "more than money," meaning they provide benefits to startups beyond merely investing in them. Good VC managers are seen as partners with, or at least valuable advisors to, startups and their entrepreneurs. VC managers often sit on the board of directors of the corporations in which they invest. Today, larger VC firms like Andreessen Horowitz offer in-house logistics, marketing, sales, and strategy consultants to portfolio companies. But mega VC firms like Andreessen Horowitz did not take off into the financial scene until the SEC cleared a runway through the snarl of securities regulation. SEC Regulation D Rule 506(c), affectionately known as "Reg D" by those in the VC industry, is now the regulatory safe harbor through which trillions of dollars flow each year.

REG. D: PRIVATE FINANCING'S SAFE HARBOR

Prior to Reg D, the VC industry relied on Section 4(a)(2) of the Securities Act of 1933 to purchase startup stock without registering with the SEC. The Securities Act requires all securities (including private corporation stock sold to VCs) to be registered with the SEC – unless an exemption applied. Section 4(a)(2) provides the exemption VCs needed: the Securities Act's registration requirements "shall not apply to ... transactions by an issuer not with or through an underwriter and not involving any public offering."

This could include VC transactions, which do not typically require an underwriter. What, then, is a "public offering"? This term is nebulous and undefined in the Securities Act. The SEC first attempted to answer this question on January 24, 1935, when it published an opinion letter outlining four factors that would be considered in determining whether a public offering is involved in a given transaction:

1. The number of offerees and their relationship to each other and to the issuer
2. The number of units offered
3. The size of the offering
4. The manner of the offering

A four-factor test is relatively unhelpful at the beginning. This test is typical of a regulatory "standard." Standards are deliberately vague so that courts can consider each case on its own merits. This is great for achieving justice in each early case, but it makes it virtually impossible to evaluate what transactions will or will not be ruled invalid or illegal by a court. Early VCs and startups simply took the risk that the federal agencies in Washington might prosecute them for securities violations.

Under our common law system, however, standards develop contours over time. As courts make decisions in specific cases as to whether securities violations occurred or not, case law, or "precedent," defines what is and is not a securities violation. Over vast periods of time, common law systems regarding traditional doctrinal areas such as property and contracts develop into relatively clear rules. But this process takes time, perhaps centuries, to perfect. Meanwhile, the budding VC industry was impatient for clarity.

That clarity finally came in 1982, when the SEC promulgated Regulation D. The regulation is relatively complex, comprising six separate rules (501–506) in the Code of Federal Regulations. But the point is simple enough. Regulation D Rule 506(b) allows VCs to invest an unlimited amount of money in startups so long as there is no "general solicitation" (advertising the sale of stock to the general public) of the investment opportunity. VC firms – specialists in private stock financing – were perfectly poised to count on this easy-to-use safe harbor. The consequence, however, is that ordinary investors were generally not invited to participate in VC funds.

As a technical matter, Regulation D has other exemptions that allow startups to fundraise from ordinary investors, including friends and family, but in reality, these other exemptions are not often used. Over 99.9 percent of Regulation D financings fall under the Rule 506(b) exemption, which is only available to "accredited investors" as defined below.

ACCREDITED INVESTORS AND QUALIFIED PURCHASES

Until very recently, only "accredited investors" (AIs) could make unlimited investments in private startup corporations. Prior to August 2020, the only way to be classified as an AI, and thereby to gain access to invest in VC funds, was to demonstrate a sufficient amount of net wealth. The exact standards have changed over time, but, until recently, Regulation D Rule 501 deemed a natural person (human beings, not corporations or other legal entities) to be an AI if one has an annual income of at least $200,000 ($300,000 for joint income) or at least $1 million in net wealth (not including one's primary residence). A business entity is considered an AI if it has over $5 million in assets.

Then, on August 26, 2020, the SEC issued a press release stating that the agency will update the Rule 501(a) to permit natural persons (human beings) to qualify as accredited investors based on certain professional certifications, designations or credentials or other credentials issued by an accredited educational institution. This change could create entirely new classes of VC investors. It is too early to determine the impact of this change, which went into effect on December 8, 2020. It will be very interesting to see how this change in rules impacts the VC industry and especially how it impacts the number and nature of startups that receive money from VC funds.

But while the SEC has broadened the definition of who can invest directly in startups, there is another, higher standard required to invest in many VC funds. The general rule under the Investment Company Act (ICA) is that fund managers need to register as investment companies unless there is an exception from this registration requirement. Since registration is costly, time consuming, and risk generating, VC firms strongly prefer to avoid registration by finding an exception. There are two main exceptions that can be used for this purpose. First, under Section 3(c)(1) of the ICA, a VC firm is not an investment company if (1) it has not more than 100 investors, (2) the investors are all accredited investors, and (3) the fund did not "generally solicit" investors. General solicitation is a topic in its own right, but, in simple terms, the ban on general solicitation generally prohibits any public advertising of or notice about the fund that seeks the 3(c)(1) exception.

The problem with using the 3(c)(1) exemption, aside from the prohibition against general solicitation, is that it can be hard to count the number of investors. Many of these investors are themselves funds, corporations, trusts, and other entities. The VC firm is supposed to "look through" some of these entities to determine the number of ultimate beneficial owners (UBOs). This look through can be difficult to do, especially where some funds have signed confidentiality agreements with their clients, or where the fund views its client list as business confidential and proprietary information. In addition, the number of UBOs can change. For example, imagine that Adam is an accredited investor who forms an investment entity called Genesis Investments Limited. Genesis then becomes an investor in Sequoia Fund X. The ICA requires Sequoia to look through Genesis and count its owners; thus, Genesis counts as one UBO for Sequoia Fund X. Then Adam dies, and his children Abel, Cain, and Seth inherit Genesis Investments Limited. Now Sequoia Fund X has three UBOs through Genesis. If Sequoia Fund X had 99 investors before Adam died, it has 102 now, and it no longer qualifies for the exception. Disqualifying for the exception in this way can be incredibly costly and thus VC firms tend to avoid getting into this problem in the first place.

Fortunately for VC firms, there is another exception: ICA § 3(c)(7). Under the 3(c)(7) exception, more than 100 investors can participate in a private fund if all of them are "qualified purchasers" ("QP"). The wealth requirement of a QP is five times (5x) that of an AI; that is, a QP is a natural person with not less than $5 million in investment, or a business entity with not less than $25 million in investments.

As the landscape appears today, AIs have differentiated into two general types: angels and VCs. In the 2010s, a new investor class, termed super angels, emerged. The rise of super angels is described in the upcoming chapter on Social Media Investing.

Angels

Angels are professionals who invest their own money in startups. Traditionally, angels were hard to find. Throughout the late 1980s, these wealthy individuals connected with startups through informal and even secretive channels. In the early 1990s, angels began to form groups and publicize their activities. The first prominent angel investment group formed in 1994. Silicon Valley's "Band of Angels" began with twelve members and grew to 110 members by 1998. From then on, angel groups sprouted up throughout the United States. The number of registered angel groups has tripled since 1999. The Angel Capital Association estimates that there are between 10,000 and 15,000 angel groups operating in the United States today, with about 40 members per group. Many of these angel groups now have a prominent website that contains a contract form, public membership list, and even a list of portfolio companies.

Not all angels invest in groups. Some of the most popular angels continue to invest in the traditional, solitary, and secretive way. Many of these traditional angels – like Peter Thiel (one of the first investors in Facebook) and Naval Ravikant (who funded Twitter and Uber) – are famous for building groundbreaking startups or investing early in hugely successful ventures.

Not everyone can be an angel. Legally, an angel must be an "accredited investor," someone with at least $1 million in net wealth or $200,000 in annual income. The U.S. census counts household wealth, not individual wealth, so estimates for the number of potential angels varies, but 9.63 million American households had a net worth of $1 million or more in 2013, which is about 3 percent of the U.S. population. The Angel Capital Association estimates that about four million potential angels reside in the United States – although this number may be off because accredited status is determined by investors' self-reporting, and corporations often do little to verify whether such investors are actually accredited or not beyond merely asking the investors to certify their status.

Despite the large number of potential angels, only around 300,000 to 350,000 Americans make an angel investment each year. This is partially because an angel should have a solid understanding of business planning, corporate finance, preferred stock investment, and market conditions, plus a risk-seeking constitution. Angel investment is not for everyone.

Angel Groups

Angel investors have learned to flock together in groups called angel syndicates. In a syndicate, angels share the responsibility for sourcing opportunities to invest in startups, evaluating those opportunities, negotiating terms for financing the startups, and overseeing the startup's progress. Syndicates solve an economic problem called "rational apathy," which occurs when the time and effort spent on pursuing a financial opportunity exceeds how much profit that opportunity is expected to bring.

Investing in startups requires a lot of work and expense. First, the investors need to promote themselves, so entrepreneurs know to come to them looking for money, or investors need to attend events where entrepreneurs are seeking financing. Such events are also styled as "demo days," during which a variety of startups present their ideas and prototypes to a crowd of potential investors. Then the entrepreneurs and the potential investors usually have a meeting or series of meetings known as a "pitch," where the entrepreneurs share their ideas and explain what those ideas are likely to lead to lucrative businesses. No one cannot be an expert in all business areas, so simply understanding whether the pitch is plausible can be challenging for angels, especially when the idea regards new technology. The angels also need to evaluate whether the entrepreneurs seem reliable and honest.

If the business plan and the businesspeople pass muster, the investors will usually conduct a more thorough investigation in a process called "due diligence," in which confidential business documents are shared so the angels can evaluate more specific things like confirming the technology does not infringe on existing patents. The angels will also make sure the entrepreneurs' company was properly incorporated, that corporate actions were duly authorized, and that the company owns valid rights to essential technology. The angels will also need to review ancillary agreements like lease agreements (to confirm the corporation can continuing doing business at its location without great expense or disruption) and to make sure that no former founders or disgruntled employees will lay claims upon the company's property.

If the company passes diligence, then the angels usually pay for lawyers to negotiate the terms of the financing and to document the deal. Negotiating, documenting, and closing an early-stage angel financing deal can easily cost $10,000 or more. Even after the closing of the financial deal, angels still spend more time and incur more costs because they generally want to attend board meetings and review regular reports about the company's progress.

Keep in mind that angels, like VC funds, need to diversify their investment into at least thirty companies in order to minimize idiosyncratic risk. In 2019, 323,365 angels invested a collective $23.9 billion into 63,730 startups, which amounts to an average of $73,810 invested per angel investor. Angels usually do not create their entire diversified portfolio of thirty-plus companies in just one year, but even if a typical angel invests in four startups per year, this is less than $20,000 per angel per startup.

Given the relatively small amounts that most individual angels invest in each startup, it does not make sense for them to spend tens of thousands of dollars in transaction costs to identify, negotiate, and supervise these investments. In economic terms, angels should be rationally apathetic about doing so much work for a relatively small potential payoff. Moreover, if angels had to spend this much time, effort, and money on each financing transaction, that would further limit angels' ability to diversify their investments and to protect themselves from idiosyncratic risk.

The solution is angel syndicates. By collaborating, angels can share the work and the cost of financing startups, which makes smaller deals more profitable and allows angels to diversify enough to significantly reduce their investment portfolio's risk. In 2019, there was an average of 5.1 angels per investments. Angel groups have grown larger as technology has made it easier for them to organize. The rise of angel syndicate web platforms like Angel List are an important feature of twenty-first-century startup financing that is discussed in detail in the next part of this book on 'Social Media Investing'.

Venture Capitalists

To recapitulate the key points detailed above, VC firms create VC funds that are managed by VC managers. The VC industry is thus distinguishable from angel investing because angels invest their own money, whereas in the VC industry professionals manage the investments of large institutions known as qualified purchasers. VC managers first create VC funds, which are often structured as limited partnerships. The VC manager of a VC fund then solicits large institutional investors (such as pension funds and university endowments) to invest in these such funds. Once the VC fund is formed and capitalized, VC managers "deploy" that capital primarily by investment in startup companies. These investments are mainly in the form of purchases of preferred stock in those startups. Preferred stock is so called because it has various preferences that common stock does not have; for example, preferred stock is paid first upon a liquidation event, and this is known as the preferred stock liquidation preference.

The nature of VC investment is quite different from angel investment because, as mentioned above, VC managers manage other people's money, whereas angels invest their own money. VC funds raise sums of money far in excess of most angels' personal net wealth, and VC managers have to deploy this money very quickly because the funds typically have eight to twelve-year life spans. When the fund's life is over, the capital must be returned to the fund's investors. As a result, VC investment has evolved to occur in stages (early/seed, expansion, and late), while angels might only be able to afford investing in early-stage companies. By investing across multiple stages, VC managers mitigate some of the risk that startup investing typically entails.

The VC industry has grown tremendously over the last forty years, which has necessitated some changes in how VC managers invest VC funds. While the number of VC funds and the amount invested in those funds has increased dramatically, the number of VC fund managers has not. With a similar number of people managing a far larger amount of money, contemporary VC managers tend to make larger investments than VC managers made forty years ago. The result is that a very few companies get a lot of money from VC funds: in 2019, VC funds raised $51 billion of new money into just 272 funds. In that same year, VC managers invested $133 billion into 10,430 companies. But 44 percent of that entire amount was invested in just 237 "mega-deal" investments of over $100 million. In other words, less than 3 percent of venture-backed companies received almost half of the entire amount invested by VC funds that year.

The VC industry tends to specialize in investing in specific industries. This is partly because VC managers have expertise in just a few industrial sectors. Those VC managers have better abilities to determine which startups are good to invest in when they are looking in an industry in which they have great expertise. VC managers also add more value to the startup companies they invest into when those managers have relevant knowledge about the startup's business. In 2019, a third of all VC investment went into software companies. More than 10 percent went into pharmaceuticals and biotechnology, and another 10 percent was invested in commercial services. This trend has been consistent over time. Thus, over half of VC investment goes into just three industry sectors.

The VC industry tends to be localized. About 60 percent of all the U.S. venture capital invested into VC funds in 2019 went into funds located in California. Likewise, about half of all the capital that U.S. VC funds invested into startups went to startups located in California that year. All of the top ten VC funds are located in California, with many of them located on the same road, Sand Hill Road, just miles from Stanford University.

The startup financing lifecycle is a description of how VC funds invest into startups in stages – usually named Series A, B, C, and so on – that are described as lifecycle events. The average Series A fundraising round, which is typically defined as the first financing that a startup received from a VC fund, has grown larger over time. In 1980, the average first-round financing into a startup was just over $1 million. In 2019, the average first round grew to $4.14 million.

As VC firms succeed and grow larger, they tend to make larger investments, which has created a gap in the startup financing lifecycle at the earliest stage. Angels and, more recently, super angels moved in to fill that gap. While angels are individuals who invest their own money in startups, super angels are a new term to describe former angels who now organize funds. Super angel activities have been facilitated by the websites like Angel List that are dedicated to organizing investors and connecting them to startups, which in turn have only recently been both technology possible and legal thanks to changes under Regulation D as described above. Super angels invested around $500,000 in startups, which helps many early-stage firms cross the seed valley of death and grow into companies that become attractive investments for VC funds.

The modern startup lifecycle thus has distinct stages and distinct investors who participate more heavily at each stage. Angels invest small amounts at the earliest stage, sometimes before the startup even forms as a company when its first prototype is just an idea in the promoter's mind. Super angels have evolved to fill in the ever-widening gap, known as the seed valley of death, between when angels tend to invest and when VC managers tend to invest. VC funds invest in startups over stages, and increasing at later stages. The lifecycle ends well when the startup sells itself to another company in a merger or acquisition and returns a profit to investors. The lifecycle ends poorly when the startup goes broke and liquidates or sells the fledgling operations at a discount. The ultimate conclusion to a startup is when the startup goes public and accesses the public capital markets through an initial public offering.

The startup financing lifecycle has evolved since the modern VC business model was first developed by firms like Sequoia and Kleiner Perkins in the 1980s. Now it is going through another stage in its evolution. The original model concluded most successfully when a startup went public. The problem is that startups aren't going public as often anymore. Instead, they are becoming large private companies, a new beast in the wilds of private finance. The emergence and dominance of these large private companies, which were once called "Unicorns" for their rarity and now number over five hundred, seriously impacts not only the VC industry but also the public stock markets. The legal reasons why Unicorns became a destabilizing factor in the evolution of financial markets stems from reactions to a startup financing bubble, which we will discuss in the next chapter.

BIBLIOGRAPHY

CB Insights, *The Complete List of Unicorn Companies*, https://perma.cc/P9EP-AJY8.
Green, Alisha & Blanca Torres, *Not Venturing Far from Home: Why VCs Won't Leave Sand Hill Road*, SAN FRANCISCO BUS. TIMES (2017).
KARAHAN, FATIH ET AL., UNDERSTANDING THE 30-YEAR DECLINE IN THE STARTUP RATE: A GENERAL EQUILIBRIUM APPROACH (2015).
Manjoo, Farhad, *How "Super Angel" Investors Are Reinventing the Startup Economy*, FAST COMPANY (January 12, 2011).
National Venture Capital Association, *NVCA 2007 Activity Survey*, (2007).
National Venture Capital Association, *NVCA 2010 Yearbook*, (2010).
National Venture Capital Association, *NVCA 2011 Yearbook*, (2011).
National Venture Capital Association, *NVCA 2019 Yearbook*, (2019).
National Venture Capital Association, *NVCA 2020 Yearbook*, (2020).
National Venture Capital Association, *NVCA Yearbook 2008*, (2008).
Oranburg, Seth C., *Bridgefunding: Crowdfunding and the Market for Entrepreneurial Finance*, 25 CORNELL J. L. PUB. POL'Y 397 (2015).
Oranburg, Seth C., *Democratizing Startups*, 68 RUTGERS U. L. REV. (2017).
Press Release, SEC, Release No.33–295 (1935).
Rowley, Jason D., *There Are More VC Funds than Ever, but Capital Concentrates at the Top*, CRUNCHBASE NEWS (2019).
Bob Zider, Bob, *How Venture Capital Works*, HARV. BUS. REV. (1998).
Gompers, Paul A., *The Rise and Fall of Venture Capital*, 23 BUS. & ECON. HISTORY 1 (1994).

The Third Era
Social Media Investing

7

The Dot-Com Bubble

The emergence of the internet created at least two new opportunities for investors. First, many companies raced to dominate the new region of commercial cyberspace, and these "dot-com" companies needed billions of dollars of funds to do so, which they sought and received from the stock markets. Second, the internet created a new means of investing directly, without brokers. Ordinary investors could learn about stocks and even purchase them using new online platforms like Yahoo! Finance and e*Trade. While this democratized access to the stock market, it also created new challenges. Ordinary investors are generally less financially sophisticated and invest smaller amounts that large brokerage firms and institutional investors, making the ordinary investors less able and less willing to understand the risks involved with investing in "dot-com" companies. At some points it seemed that any company with "dot-com" in its name could raise millions or even billions of dollars, regardless of whether it actually made money. As investors piled into these technology stocks, a bubble formed, and when it burst, fortunes were lost. Angry citizens called upon the government to intervene, especially where losses could be blamed on loose regulations. Legislators answered the call by instituting new regulations that were meant to protect investors. But these protections went too far. Companies abandoned the public markets and instead sought funding from private sources, such as in Silicon Valley. Ordinary investors were left clambering for new investment opportunities, which they found in the forthcoming cryptocurrency marketplace, a marketplace that turned out to be far harder to regulate.

> I don't know technology, and I don't know finance and accounting.
> – *Bernard Ebbers, CEO of WorldCom, during his trial for accounting fraud*

The emerging dominance of large private companies (LPCs) – corporations that are not registered with the SEC yet are valued by shareholders at billions of dollars – undermines a fundamental assumption of securities regulation. Securities regulations are based on a sharp dichotomy between public and private companies. The public/private dichotomy is a hallmark of securities regulations. Securities regulations categorize a company as private if it has not registered its stock with the SEC.

Registration brings the obligation to make periodic disclosures to the public and the opportunity to raise money by selling stock in public markets. Startups traditionally sought to "go public" by registering and having an initial public offering within about seven years of formation because the venture capital funds that finance startups are established with a ten-year term. The invested money needs to be returned to the fund investors when the term expires. The ideal way for this money to be returned is when a startup has an IPO, which is regarded as the "gold standard" in venture capital success. The ten-year term limit on venture capital funds, established by HP's successful model, drove startups to go public within that time frame. The IPO was the crowning event at the culmination of a process known as the startup financing cycle.

It was once very rare for a privately funded startup to be worth more than one billion dollars and rare for a startup to stay private for long after being valued at more than one billion dollars. The startup worth more than one billion dollars was so rare it was called a "Unicorn." Startups, however, are not going public in an IPO or liquidating in an M&A event. Increasingly, they are staying private.

As of December 31, 2021, there were over 1,000 so-called Unicorns, with a cumulative value of over $3 trillion. The most valuable private U.S. companies – such as Ripple ($10.0 billion), Stripe ($95 billion), and JUUL Labs ($12.0 billion) – are so large they prompted the new coinage "Decacorn," a private startup valued at over $10 billion. Now there are even two hectocorns: Bytedance, a venture-backed startup now valued at over $140 billion, and SpaceX, worth over $100 billion, which have still not gone public.

To put this in context, consider how valuable an average publicly traded company is. Although it does not capture every public company in U.S., the Russell 3000 Index measure the performance of the largest 3,000 U.S. companies and represents about 98 percent of the investable U.S. public stock market. The median market capitalization of all the companies in the Russell 3000 Index, meaning the middle valuation of all 3000 of these companies, is just under $1.9 billion. In other words, about 1500 companies representing almost 50 percent of all publicly traded U.S. companies are worth less than $1.9 billion. Meanwhile, there are 216 private companies, each worth more than $1.9 billion. By the time you read this book, those high numbers will probably be even larger.

Large private companies are larger and thus more influential than many companies on stock exchanges, but they are not nearly as regulated. If companies can become so successful by deliberately avoiding public markets, that says a lot about how poorly markets are functioning for startups and their investors.

Startups staying private and growing extremely valuable is a new phenomenon that affects all startup stakeholders, including investors, employees, and society at large. This trend is the unintended consequence of the securities regulations and market factors, the result of which is a large and growing gap between large private financing rounds and initial public offerings. In other words, startups are now able to stay private, yet access plenty of capital. Staying private longer undermines many assumptions about private securities.

Why have unicorns – and now decacorns and even hectocorns – come onto the scene? Why aren't private companies going public anymore? The answer can be found by analyzing the impact of a set of federal regulations that were intended to protect the ordinary investors from the perceived excesses of the IPO markets. Those excesses are often referred to as the Dot-Com Bubble, a boom-and-bust cycle that was directly connected to the emergence of the public Internet.

NASDAQ: THE TECH STOCK MARKET

The Dot-Com Bubble, which burst in March 2000, might trace its origins all the way back to 1971. In that year, the National Association of Securities Dealers (NASD) founded a new stock market offering an innovation called "automated quotations" (AQ). Unlike the NYSE, which had a physically trading floor, the NASDAQ was a fully electronic system since its inception. A startup itself, the NASDAQ focused on offering more volatile growth-oriented securities. Its electronic AQ system, lower bid-ask spreads, and smaller commissions attracted technology companies.

As the NASDAQ grew in popularity, it added features including four-character stock symbols, whereas the NYSE was limited to three characters (e.g., MSFT versus CAT). The extra character multiplies the possibilities for naming and marketing stocks. In 2008, NASDAQ got even more flexible, allowing one-, two-, three-, or four-character symbols. Zillow (Z) because the first public company to offer a one-letter trading symbol. Perhaps the most impactful was the fact that NASDAQ could execute trades for as little as a penny per share. The NYSE, on the other hand, could not handle spreads below 1/8 of a dollar. Electronic trading made it possible for computers to execute thousands or even millions of trades per second, so the difference between $0.01 and $0.125 quickly added up to millions or even billions of dollars in savings on the spread. This paved the way for penny stock to enter the public markets.

PENNY STOCKS

Although the classic NYSE systems could not execute trades for less than 1/8 of a dollar, the NASDAQ's electronic system allowed trading for just a penny, which enabled the innovation electronically traded penny stocks. Prior to this financial innovation, penny stocks were mostly traded "over the counter" (OTC). OTC trades are one-off financial transactions.

There is no OTC market per se, at least not one that is centralized in any physical location. The absence of a central market, plus the variety of products sold, is what distinguishes an OTC market from a central marketplace. Without a market in which to sell, OTC companies originally got noticed by investors by being listed on a publication by the National Quotation Bureau (NQB), which changed its name to Pink Sheets LLC in 2000 and then the Pink OTC Markets in 2010. The moniker "pink sheets" comes from the color of the paper this publication was originally printed on. NQB would publish over 200 pages of daily quotations of bid and ask prices for stock that were generally much cheaper than those traded on exchanges like the NYSE. The only way to order one of these stocks was to telephone a broker – or get a call from one. The popular movies *Wolf of Wall Street* and *Boiler Room* show how brokers would aggressively sell these pink-sheet stocks, including stock in companies that were already bankrupt and others that never existed at all, to unsuspecting buyers. The promise of cheap stock and easy money have always proved alluring to the naïve and hopeful masses, especially those who feel otherwise deprived of the American Dream. In 1989, the *LA Times* reported that American investors were defrauded out of at least $2 billion a year by schemes involving penny stocks, and that many of these frauds were run by the mafia.

After the story broke, the federal government responded with the Penny Stock Reform Act of 1990, which imposed stricter regulators on OTC stocks sold for under $5 per share. This created an incentive for legitimate companies to list cheap stocks on an exchange. In economic terms, the pink sheets created a pooling equilibrium, in which it was hard to distinguish between legitimate and fraudulent OTC penny stocks. A solution to the pooling equilibrium problem is for one group to expend resources to send a signal that it is higher quality than the others in that pool.

Initially only the legitimate companies with the strongest finances spent the considerable resources to register with the SEC and list on an exchange, creating a semi-separating (or partial-pooling) equilibrium. But this made the pink sheet stocks even less attractive. Legitimate companies thereby found listing on the pink sheets less and less helpful and more and more legitimate companies abandoned the NQB.

The NASDAQ made registration and listing more attractive by presenting a cheaper and easier pathway than the NYSE. Today, the situation is reversed: the NASDAQ imposed the world's highest initial listing standards in 2005. Firms must have a market value of at least $45 million, and the minimum stock listing price is $4 per share. But it was and is cheaper to list on NASDAQ in part because there are three market tiers. At the lowest tier, listing on NASDAQ's capital market will cost about $80,000 for the initial listing and an additional $27,500 annually. In comparison, the NYSE initial listing fee would be about $300,000, with an additional $69,750 in annual fees.

Meanwhile, the growing internet was making it easier to get information about listed companies. This made it easier for investors and analysts to research small-cap companies. Moreover, investors could more easily share information. As America got connected to the internet, ordinary investors could trade from home. NASDAQ's digital features meant that, at least in theory, a trader in a home office in Cleveland had the same access to trades as a broker in New York. In the mid-1990s, the

NASDAQ appeared to be an affordable and equitable stock market, powered by the latest technology, that promised to give ordinary investors access to incredible opportunities to own a piece of the internet.

In practice, however, a digital divide was emerging, where high-speed internet connections would power algorithmic trading "bots" (automated software robots that execute stock trades) for the well-connected and technologically sophisticated, while others continued to get increasingly outdated data from traditional analog means.

THE DOT-COM BUBBLE

The internet grew organically from the need to connect the various computer networks that had been developing across the world. The Defense Advanced Research Projects Agency (DARPA) organization was especially interested in connecting military and research computer systems. DARPA awarded a contract to Bolt Beranek & Newman to build an Advanced Research Projects Agency Network (ARPANET) that connected UCLA and Stanford University. Other networks including PRNET and SATNET followed, but they all used different protocols and programming languages. DARPA and other organizations developed a universal Transmission Control Protocol and Internet Protocol (TCP/IP) in 1973 and published their findings in 1974. Their paper, known simply as FRC 675, contains the first use of the word "internet," as a shorthand for internetwork.

The early internet was slow and limited, but by the mid-1980s the National Science Foundation (NSF) had developed the hardware and software to send relatively highspeed messages across the country. NSFNET connected MIT in Cambridge, MA to Stanford University in Palo Alto, CA. Its decommissioning in 1995 was not the death knell for the internet but rather a harbinger of a shift from the internet as a military-industrial tool to a commercial product. While NSFNET was wrapping up, thousands of private internet service provider (ISP) companies were founded.

Although ISPs allowed ordinary people to access the internet, there was not much to see there in the early 1990s. The internet as we know it today did not yet exist, until Tim Berners-Lee developed the first web server and web browser in 1989 and 1990. Marc Andreessen, who would go on to found the Andreessen Horowitz (A16Z) venture firm, developed the Mosaic web browser in 1993, which he sold to Microsoft for use in its Internet Explorer. Both were surpassed by Netscape Navigator, the most popular browser of its time.

What made web browsers special is their graphical interface that everyone could use. The web employed a point-and-click interface that was much easier for non-technical people to use. Windows and Mac OS emerged around this time such that many computers could natively display colorful text, images, hyperlinks, and advertisements. Thus the modern internet was born as a user-friendly interface built on repurposed military technology that provided a user-friendly way to search for information and to shop online.

Internet shopping or e-commerce was one of the biggest trends of the 1990s. As consumer interest in the internet increased, virtually any company with dot-com in the name proved to be a hot investment, regardless of whether or not they were profitable. Pets.com became the poster child for this internet mania.

Pets.com launched their website in November 1998, incorporated in February 1999, obtained $10.5 million in venture financing in March 1999, went public for $11 per share in February 2000, purchased their biggest competitor Petscore.com in June 2000 for $10.6 million, and announced their failure and liquidation in November 2000. In its first fiscal year, Pets.com earned $619,000 in revenue and spent $11.8 million in advertising.

You do not have to be a financial analyst to understand that these numbers do not add up. Obviously, a company cannot survive long while spending fifty times more than it earns. But Pets.com represented a paradigm shift in thinking about investments and value. During the Dot-Com Bubble, companies went public before they made profits and, in some cases, before they realized much revenue. Financial analysis from respected publishers including the Wall Street Journal and CNBC suggested that investors should rethink fundamental theories in corporate financing. Some even suggested that traditional strategies, such as using profits-to-earnings ratios to assess whether a stock was over- or under-valued, no longer applied to internet stocks, whose price could seemingly go up forever even if the company never made any profits.

The Dot-Com Bubble did not last long. Dot-com spending may have reached its zenith in January 2000, when fourteen of the sixty-one ads shown during Super Bowl XXXIV were purchased by dot-com companies for about $2 million per thirty second video. Of these, only four of those companies remain in business today. And only three dot-com companies bought ad spots in January 2001 Super Bowl XXXV.

That year brought several disasters that probably contributed to the downfall of dot-com companies, including the September 11 attacks upon America's financial centers in New York and the Enron scandal in October 2001 that eroded confidence in public companies. But dot-com companies were already burning out. These events only accelerated their immolation. The WorldCom scandal in June 2002 and the Adelphia Communication Corporation scandal in July 2002 threw yet more fuel on the fire. Paper millionaires went up in smoke. When the flames finally burned themselves out, the stock market had lost $5 trillion.

One might think that we have learned from this conflagration. But the federal government responded the way it always seems to in the aftermath of a crisis: by presenting legislation so that past crises will never happen again. Unfortunately, this reactionary approach to legislation might have simply pushed investors headlong into an even more risky and unregulated market: cryptocurrencies. In any event, the regulatory response is correlated with a growing divide between a wealthy private investor class and the rest of America.

THE SARBANES-OXLEY ACT OF 2002

The Sarbanes-Oxley Act of 2002, sometimes called "SOX," is a rare thing by today's standards: it was a bipartisan financial bill. It quickly passed Congress with a vote of 423 in favor, 3 opposed, and 8 abstaining in the House and 99 in favor and 1 abstaining in the Senate. President George W. Bush signed it into law saying, "today I sign the most far-reaching reforms of American business practices since the time of Franklin Delano Roosevelt." He meant this as a positive, but history might prove otherwise.

The intentions of the law were quite clear and consistent with the original securities regulations that FDR signed into law in the 1930s. They were founded on the belief that higher disclosure requirements would eliminate fraud. The problem with Enron, WorldCom, and the rest of those scammers was simply that the requirements for audits were too easy to manipulate, investors were too naïve, and management too inept.

Never mind that Pets.com, WebVan.com, and Beauty.com all disclosed that they made almost zero revenue while spending millions, yet people purchased these stocks anyway. The blame was squarely laid on immoral managers and lazy auditors. "The auditors will be audited," President Bush went on. "The accountants will be held to account." But who will audit the audits of the auditors? Who will account for accounting for the accountants? And who will pay for all this?

Dr. Suess addressed this problem in his philosophical treatise, *Did I Ever Tell You How Lucky You Are?* The young protagonist, Duckie, travels to the fictional land of Hwatch-Hawtch, where there's a Hwatch-Hwatcher Bee-Watcher whose job is to watch the lazy town bee, who presumptively will work harder and produce more honey if he is watched. But monitoring the bee in this way did not result in increased honey output. The town blames the Bee-Watcher for being lazy and prescribes another Hwatch-Hawtcher to be a Bee-Watcher-Watcher. The story unfolds in an endless chain of useless oversight:

> The Bee-Watcher-Watcher watched the Bee-Watcher. *He* didn't watch well. So another Hawtch-Hawtcher had to come in as a Watch-Watcher-Watcher! And today all the Hatchers who live in Hawtch-Hawtch are watching on Watch-Watcher-Watching-Watch, Watch-Watching the Watcher who's watching the bee. *You're* not a Hawtch-Hawtcher. You're lucky, you see!

Instead of concentrating their efforts ensuring that the worker bee was not shirking his responsibilities, perhaps the Hawtch-Hawtchers would have been better served by diversifying their investments: investing in other industries would make the town less dependent on its bee's performance. Alternatively, they could have incentivized the bee to work harder by creating a profit-sharing or stock-option plan, where the bee was incentivized to work harder by earning a share of the profits from its honey. Instead, the Hawtch-Hawtchers imposed a costly strategy on their society. Likewise, the SOX offers limited protection at a premium price. Conservative estimates provide that companies spend about $10 billion each year on SOX compliance. Financial Executives International surveyed 200 public companies in 2006, four years after the enactment of SOX. At that time, only 22 percent of respondents believe that SOX's costs were worth its benefits.

SOX also has a hidden cost to society that its promotors might not have considered. Because SOX make it relatively expensive to be a public company, it encourages companies to stay private, where SOX and a myriad of other regulations do not apply. SOX focuses its regulatory efforts on public companies. In fact, one of its primary contributions was to create the Public Company Accounting Oversight Board. As the name implies, this board only oversees public companies. Private companies are spared the expensive, hassle, and potentially criminal liability for corporate financial officers. Berkeley Law Professor Randy Bartlett researched the impact of SOX on staying private. His 2009 paper found that not only did SOX have a significant impact on firms' decision to stay private, but SOX actually drove going-private transactions. In 2007, $329.7 billion in take-private deals were announced.

This take-private trend continues today. In August 2019, Bain Capital announced that the pendulum has swung in favor of private deals over public ones. It seems that going public is too expensive for most firms. The result is the government has even less oversight and control, and even fewer disclosures are required, than before SOX was passed. Although public companies might be safer thanks to SOX – and the jury is still out on that question – there are fewer public companies and many more large private companies to worry about.

This is not just bad from a fraud perspective. Private companies are out of ordinary investors' reach. The securities laws, by definition, prevent nonaccredited investors from these lucrative opportunities. As more companies stay private, their employees who are paid in stock options find these options less valuable, since they cannot sell their shares into an open market. While the intention may have been good, legislators should have considered that, over time, companies would try to avoid these expenses. Instead of realizing this basic economic reality, well-meaning regulators and lawmakers have actually made the world a more dangerous and less lucrative place for the ordinary investor. Only the accredited investors, who can invest in private companies, stand to profit from this expensive legislation.

BIBLIOGRAPHY

Aguilar, Luis A., *The Need for Greater Secondary Market Liquidity for Small Businesses*, (2015), www.sec.gov/news/statement/need-for-greater-secondary-market-liquidity-for-small-businesses.html.

Bailey, James B. & Diana W. Thomas, *Regulating Away Ccompetition: The Effect of Regulation on Entrepreneurship and Employment*, 52 J. REGULATORY ECON. 237–254 (2017).
Bainbridge, Stephen M., *Dodd-Frank: Quack Federal Corporate Governance Round II*, 95 MINN. L. REV. 1779 (2011).
Bratton, William W. & Michael L. Wachter, *A Theory of Preferred Stock*, 161 U. PA. L. REV. 1815 (2013).
CB Insights, *Global Unicorn Club: Private Companies Valued at $1B+ (as of December 21st, 2020)* (2020).
CB Insights, *The Complete List of Unicorn Companies*, (2020), https://perma.cc/P9EP-AJY8.
EASTMAN, SCOTT, CORPORATE AND PASS-THROUGH BUSINESS INCOME AND RETURNS SINCE 1980 (2019).
Frier, Sarah & Eric Newcomer, *Things Fall Apart: Regulating the Credit Default Swap Commons*, (2015), available at https://perma.cc/N4FZ-9GBY.
FTSE Russell, *Russell 3000 Index Factsheet* (FTSE Russell ed., 2020).
Johnson, Kristin N., *Things Fall Apart: Regulating the Credit Default Swap Commons*, 82 U. COLO. L. REV. 167 (2011).
Johnson, Lyman P. Q. & Mark A. Sides, *The Sarbanes-Oxley Act and Fiduciary Duties*, 30 WM. MITCHELL L. REV. (2004).
Oranburg, Seth C., *Democratizing Startups*, 68 RUTGERS U. L. REV. 1013 (2015).
Oranburg, Seth C., *Hyperfunding: Regulating Financial Innovations*, 89 U. COLO. L. REV. 1033 (2018).
Oranburg, Seth C., *Securities Regulation and Social Media*, 52 LOYOLA U. CHICAGO L. J. 101 (2020).
PricewaterhouseCooper, *Considering an IPO?: The Costs of Going and Being Public May Surprise You* (2012).
Ribstein, Larry E., *Market vs. Regulatory Responses to Corporate Fraud: A Critique of the Sarbanes-Oxley Act of 2002*, 28 J. CORP. L. 1 (2002).
Romano, Roberta, *The Sarbanes-Oxley Act and the Making of Quack Corporate Governance*, 114 YALE L.J. 1521 (2005).
Sarbanes-Oxley Act of 2002, 107 P.L. 204.

8

Social Media Activism

The decentralization of news and information due to the use of social media has changed the financial landscape. Large corporations used to be able to control the information that shareholders receive. But Wikileaks and Twitter have democratized shareholder information by allowing them to communicate with each other. Large public corporations are not well equipped to use social media to send information to shareholders, and Regulation Fair Disclosure (Reg FD) may preclude them from doing so. But a new breed of activist shareholders who use Twitter to mobilize their co-shareholders have increasing influence over corporate activity. This social media shareholder activism is one reason why being public is not as appealing to companies as it once was.

> We currently have a large position in APPLE. We believe the company to be extremely undervalued. Spoke to Tim Cook today. More to come.
>
> – Carl Icahn via TWITTER, *August 13, 2013*

On Monday, July 27 2020, upwards of 1.6 million shares of Kodak (KODK), a near-extinct remnant of the film-photography industry, suddenly shot from $2.62 per share to $33.20 per share – a 1167.18 percent increase in just two days. Kodak has made no announcements about upcoming products, nor about changes in leadership. Their previous investor call ranged from sleepy to downbeat. What would cause such as remarkably rapid spike in price?

Social media – websites that allow users to connect and share information – was the source of the Kodak buying frenzy. A news station in Kodak's hometown of Rochester, N.Y., tweeted that Kodak was poised to receive a passive $765 million government loan – before this information was made public. Almost simultaneously, local news outlets also prematurely reported on the initiative. The repercussions were swift and momentous.

Although the leaked information was swiftly removed from news streams and Twitter, you cannot really scrub information from the internet. Kodak's shares quickly soared 8 percent within the hour. Within the week, the company's stock

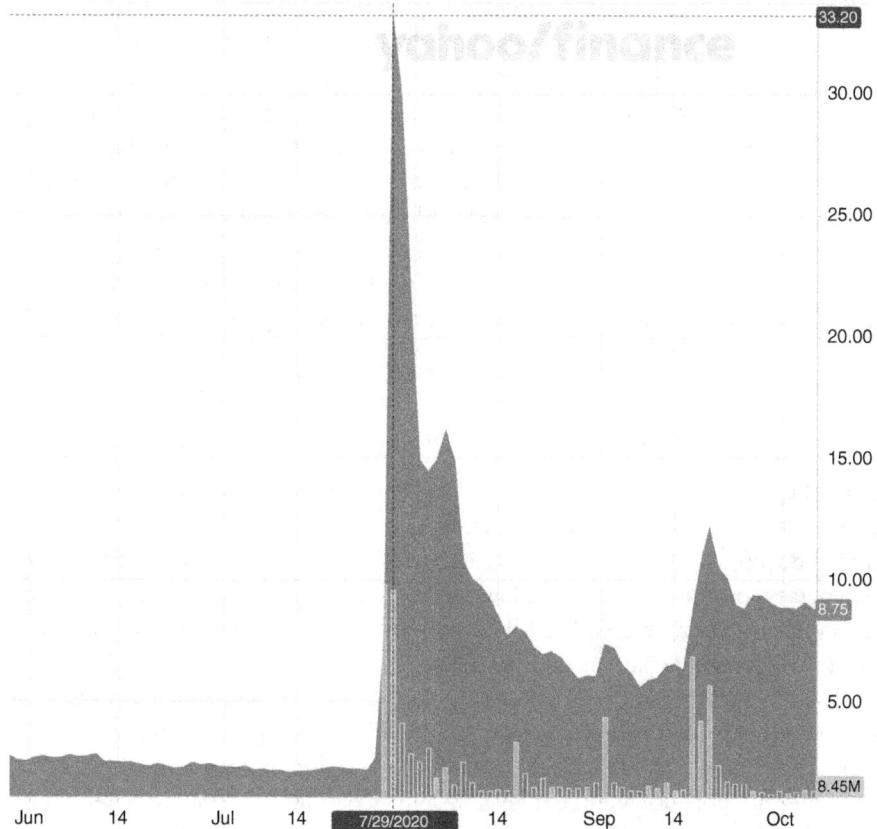

FIGURE 8.1 The Kodak price spike. Credit Yahoo! Finance.

hit a high of $60. Although the price eventually settled to around $7.50, fortunes were won and lost in a span of just six days.

While stock prices have risen and fallen due to wild speculation based on tenuous information for the entire history of stock trading, this episode reflects something new. The information was not provided by credible news sources, inside information, or word of mouth. Rather, the information was provided by random and often anonymous people via the internet.

Thanks to Web 2.0 technology, virtually anyone can send a message to the entire world. The internet has democratized information, meaning, the internet makes it much easier for people to send and receive information directly, without some intermediary like a newspaper or a television reporter. This includes financial information.

Social media thus democratized the financial landscape: using social media platforms like Twitter, Facebook, and Reddit, virtually anyone could send and receive opinions about which stocks to buy, hold, or sell.

Then, companies designed complex algorithms and other computerized techniques to analyze social media feeds, news streams, and other sources to trade stock almost instantaneously based on the available information. Now, a single tweet can set the automated stock trading systems into a flurry of activity, even when that tweet is merely a tale told by an idiot, full of sound and fury, signifying nothing.

This chapter explores how social media creates a new basic for shareholder democracies – and how it creates new risks for corporate control. Corporations can harness the power of Web 2.0 to make corporate decisions more transparent and democratic, or they can risk users creating backchannels in the gray areas of the web where cult of personality and magical thinking often defeat common sense.

DIRECT DEMOCRATIZATION OF CORPORATE GOVERNANCE

A public corporation is similar to a republic in that both employ *representative* democracy. Shareholders delegate broad decision-making powers to a board of directors, just as voting citizens delegate lawmaking powers to legislators. A *direct* democracy, on the other hand, allows citizens to directly participate in voting on policy decisions by referendum. The framers of the American constitution disfavored direct democracy, as does corporate law.

However, historic transformations in the way we communicate could make corporate direct democracy – where shareholder voters play an integral role in a broad scope of corporate decision-making – possible and even practical. This begs the question of whether such a system is desirable. With just a few SEC-sponsored tweaks to the federal securities law and some modifications to key state statutes, American public companies could be run as direct democracies. Innovations like webcasting, Twitter, Internet Protocol Security, and blockchain make it feasible for shareholders to gain immediate access to extensive managerial and operational information and securely vote in real-time on a wide array of corporate matters.

In light of the social-media organized mass movements like the Arab Spring and Occupy Wall Street – and being mindful of increasing public pressure for corporations to make social responsibility business decisions – would shareholder direct democracy be a glorious conclusion to the capitalist era, or would it be a crippling impediment to efficient economic functioning? Some may have a bias toward one approach or the other. A middle road to this modern circumstance is to let the market determine which corporate political structure is best.

INTERNET SHAREHOLDER VOTING

One way to unlock new shareholder governance regimes is simply to allow Internet voting on corporate matters. Presently, shareholders have essentially zero opportunities to formally address corporate governance issues between annual meetings. The shareholder annual meeting is an anachronism. It imposes great expenses on shareholders, effectively excluding many would-be participants. The direct beneficiaries of the current system are the institutional investors. Small shareholders who cannot afford to attend the meeting are excluded from the process, or at the very least left with limited access to information and diminished interaction with board members and management, just as small shareholders were not invited to attend the quarterly analyst calls and who were excluded from timely receiving material non-public information. Corporations may be able to modify their bylaws to allow virtual shareholder meetings and Internet voting. By opening up a new avenue for shareholder engagement, the SEC can create an opportunity for the market to decide what mixture of shareholder corporate control it values most – even if that control is democratized.

Antiquated rules mandated that shareholders submit their questions and demand that those questions be put to a shareholder vote through an arduous process. Rule 14a governs shareholders' rights to present proposals at the annual meeting. Through a series of amendments to Rule 14a, the process by which shareholders can communicate their opinions has become more democratized. Shareholder communication rules are now more liberal than they once were, but shareholder voting rules remain limited by SEC rules and securities laws. While the intricacies of 14a are beyond the scope of this chapter, it is important to note one crucial amendment to Rule 14a which allows shareholder communication in real-time through "the use of electronic shareholder forums." The problem is that no one really knows what an electronic shareholder forum is. Is it a chat room? A social media website? An open source blog? The rule does not define the term, nor does it prescribe any particular format for such a forum.

The nebulous nature of Rule 14a creates a great deal of uncertainty as to where shareholders may communicate, although subsequent cases have begun to provide a little clarity. The SEC has determined that Facebook apparently is not an "electronic shareholder forum." Social media first got CEOs into trouble on July 3, 2012, when Netflix CEO Reed Hastings posted to his personal Facebook page, "Netflix monthly viewing exceeded 1 billion hours for the first time ever in June." Netflix stock price increased 10 percent that day, and the SEC investigated whether Hastings' post violated Regulation Fair Disclosure.

REGULATION FD AND SHAREHOLDER COLLECTIVE ACTION

Social media has had a profound impact on collective action, enabling users to mobilize and swiftly communicate information with followers and other users. While its impact on social activism is well documented, its impacts on financial markets and shareholder activism are less known but equally profound. Shareholder activism, which has long been plagued by collective action problems including rational apathy and free riding,[1] has been rejuvenated by emerging social media tools like Twitter. Tweets, and other social media feeds, are a cheap and easy way for shareholders to engage with each other and build consensus and support for collective action.

As previously noted, the financial revolution will not be televised. That one-way communications channel of TV broadcasts has been predominately substituted for two-way internet communications channels. Unlike TV, which is a passive medium controlled by a few major networks, social media in an active medium where users participate in both consuming and producing information. Social media has provided users, shareholders, and investors with a platform to express their opinions and dissent with corporate dealings.

For example, Carl Icahn, the famous activist investor, grabbed Wall Street and the tech world's attention when he tweeted caustically, "All would be swell at Dell if Michael and the board bid farewell." These types of communications can have monumental impacts on corporate decisions and valuations. However, the SEC-mandated disclosure that is supposed to be included on all public securities-related communications is not among them. A major problem with using Twitter to disseminate securities information is that it might violate Regulation Fair Disclosure, or Reg FD for short, which requires public companies to disclose material information to all shareholders at the same time.

Reg FD is a relatively new rule promulgated in August 2000. At that time, only reporters and large investors were invited to the quarterly analyst conference calls, where results of the past quarter were first disclosed. Small investors who traded over the Internet wanted equal access. Reg FD granted them equal access to material nonpublic information.

Shareholders can use social media in ways management cannot. Reg FD applies unequally to Reed Hastings, CEO of Netflix, and Carl Icahn, stockholder of Apple. Activists can now access virtually all shareholders and influence public opinion through social networks, relatively unencumbered by reporting requirements under SEC rules. But management cannot simply tweet back to the critiques of activists. Despite the fact that Hastings was found not to have violated Reg FD with his Facebook post, it is not clear that management can simply respond to activist banter without risking a disclosure violation. Management has to fight proxy battles in the

[1] Rational apathy or rational ignorance occurs where the cost of educating oneself exceeds the expected value from that knowledge. For example, if it takes four hours to read corporate reports, a reasonable person who only owns $50 worth of stock in that corporation would probably not bother to make that effort, even if it leads to a better investment decision, because the cost of the effort is worth than the value of the investment. Free riding is a related concept. Where there is public information about a corporation – such as its stock price – people reasonably may rely on that information instead of educating themselves. When a stock price starts going down, people tend to sell because the price tells them that the stock is not worth its current price, even though most of these people have not analyzed the corporation's fundamental finances and prospects for themselves. Many of these investors assume that a stock prices reflects someone else's analysis of that stock's real value, but this assumption is increasing unsupportable in a social media investing world.

social network arena with one hand tied behind its keyboard while activists use the full power of social media to their advantage.

Management does have one advantage: the power of the purse. Management can pay for its own reelection campaign with corporate money. In such a "proxy contest," management might spend tens of millions of dollars of corporate money to stay in power. However, board access to the corporate coffers to fund reelection campaigns – an antidemocratic feature of corporate law – might become less significant as shareholder engagement gets cheaper and more democratized. Social media could enable low-cost yet effective shareholder campaigns against management.

For example, for four consecutive years, shareholder have organized to press ExxonMobil and other oil and gas companies to disclose the dangers of hydraulic fracking. Management vehemently opposed this corporate social responsibility initiative. It was not until the ExxonMobil shareholders got enough votes to pass a precatory proposal for fracking risk disclosure that management capitulated and stopped fracking. Nowadays, however, shareholder and even non-shareholders can pressure oil and gas companies simply by using social media. The battle over fracking has gone from the boardroom to the web where corporations that impact climate worldwide have signed on the Net Zero Carbon by 2040 Pledge. It has yet to be seen, however, whether these policies and promises are effective substitutes for shareholder votes and regime change for corporate management. Unless social media pushes corporations to take legally binding actions, not just make policy statements, actualized commitments to these action statement are as ephemeral as the tweets they puff out.

Some shareholder campaigns may be unsuccessful in moving management to change its policies, but they may yet be effective in accomplishing goals of awareness and corporate social responsibility. For example, grassroots activist shareholders – who originally organized on the Internet – descended on Safeway's annual shareholder meeting to protest genetically modified (GMO) foods. Inside the meeting, shareholders voted on a proposal to remove GMO foods from Safeway shelves that was proposed by the Sisters of Notre Dame de Namur, a Roman Catholic order, who owned 8,800 shares of Safeway stock, representing only about 0.00173 percent of the outstanding shares at that time.

Only 2 percent of shareholders supported the proposal to remove GMO ingredients from its products, and the proposal did not pass, but the demonstrations – which consisted of shareholders in biohazard suits dumping Safeway produce in garbage bins in front of the hotel where the annual meeting was held – attracted significant media attention.

Another grassroots movement, 99% Power, an offshoot from the Occupy Wall Street movement, organized protests at the shareholder meetings of major banks during their annual meetings in Spring 2012. At least 500 protesters gathered at the Wells Fargo annual shareholders meeting, of which about two dozen were arrested for chaining themselves together to block entry to the meeting at the bank's headquarters and for entering the meeting and interrupting CEO John Stumpf during his presentation. The protest, which included signs that read "Hells Fargo" and handouts of dollar bills with an image of a stagecoach (Wells Fargo's corporate logo) pulled by human beings with the caption "Debt Slavery," became so active that some shareholders were not allowed to enter the meeting. One such shareholder even used the protest's Twitter hashtag to voice her frustration that the protest prevented her from voting her shares.

Just like the physical protests in the Arab Spring that were organized through social media platforms, grassroots shareholder activism can be organized and empowered by Twitter and Facebook. In fact, the Wells Fargo protest was planned, organized, and broadcast live using social media. The web site "Stop Wells Fargo" was established to focus attention on and raise support for "major disruptions" at the Wells Fargo shareholder meeting. Visitors to that website were invited to "Follow the action on Twitter with #wf24 #wfshareholders #notfeelingwells" and on Facebook.

A New Shareholder Activism

The "Hells Fargo" protests show a dramatic shift away from "classic" shareholder activism. In the classic model, an activist would locate a company that it believed to be undervalued. It would then purchase a large percentage of a corporation's share and use its shareholder voting rights to force corporate management to make changes designed to increase the corporation's value. Classical activist means to accomplish the ends of increasing corporate value include replacing management, divesting unprofitable operations, downsizing (firing employees), or even liquidating the company in merger or asset sale. Sometimes, the threat of these actions alone would give activist leverage to force management to make more modest changes. Although classical activists' tactics were largely successful at increasing corporate stock value, these actions were seen as ruthless and against the public interest. For this reason, classical activists were often termed "corporate raiders," and their actions described as "asset stripping."

An example of a classical activist who was often considered to be a corporate raider is Phil Goldstein, founder of Bulldog Investors. In an interview with financial writer Mark Gottlieb, Mr. Goldstein described himself as a "transactional activist," but explained his standard playbook including buying enough shares to threaten the board, then demanding cost-cutting measures. If management resists, Bulldog will pursue a proxy fight, where it offers to buy shares from other investors until it has a controlling percent of shares and the ability to replace management unilaterally.

New social media might make traditional shareholder tactics unnecessary in many cases. Instead of going through the costly process of buying shares, social media activists seek to control the marketplace of ideas through likes, retweets, followers, and subscriptions. If trends continue, the future of shareholder activism may start to look more like political activism and less like Bulldog Investors. Brayden King, Professor at the Kellogg School of Management has noted that activism through social media is inherently different from "classic" activism. It is not, "we are going to tout the party line, we are going to say what the NGOs are telling us to say." Instead, King notes that it is, "we are going to personalize it. And this can catch activists by surprise. They may have gotten the ball rolling, but what actually occurs falls out of the control of any hierarchical entity." The most poignant distinction is that grassroots shareholder activism can quickly become unpredictable, because social media activists are not only motivated by corporate profits, and may in fact benefit from the corporation's economic failure.

CORPORATE GADFLIES

Grassroots shareholder activism is not necessarily directed at increasing the overall value of corporate stock, also known as unlocking shareholder value. There have been numerous studies on whether shareholders' ability to control or at least reign in corporate activity increases share prices. This inquiry is particularly pertinent to the shareholder social media activism. Many grassroots shareholder campaigns are sponsored by shareholders with minimal holdings. The old name for these pesky shareholders was "corporate gadflies." Some gadflies are peskier than others: two-thirds of all proposals submitted to Fortune 150 companies between January 1, 2008 and August 1, 2011 by individual investors came from Evelyn Davis and members of the Steiner, Chevedden, and Rossi families.

Nonprofits have formed solely to purchase minimal amounts of securities and leverage Rule 14a to make "precatory" proposals to major corporations, which are statements from shareholders expressing their wish for how management might govern the company, but these statements are merely requests and do not compel management to take action in accord with them. As You Sow, a nonprofit founded in 1992 to increase corporate accountability, launched its shareholder activism program in 1997, whereby As You Sow would purchase $2,000 in securities, hold them for one year, then make precatory proposals related to various social issues. Corporate social responsibility activist As You Sow is a perfect example of how a shareholder may purchase securities for purposes other than value creation.

Whether shareholder democracy is good or bad is an immensely personal and political question. Corporate law has not – and might never – settle on whether corporations must maximize shareholder wealth or prioritize corporate social responsibility. It is clear, however, that social media, in an age of already increasing shareholder democracy and activism, is a powerful new tool for proponents of corporate social responsibility.

INFLUENCERS

Social media not only democratized access to communications. Social media also made it possible for ordinary people to influence market behavior. In fact, social media gave rise to a new kind of endorsers who are famous for being famous. Individuals can create a brand identity based on their own identity, which they use to target audiences and sell products via social media.

Sometimes called "micro-celebrities," social media influencers are ordinary people who seek and achieve fame by creating a recognizable and marketable internet identity. This concept is not entirely new – reality TV shows ranging from The Real World to Survivor have been broadcast since the early 1990s – but what distinguishes social media micro-celebrities from those who came before is that social media allows people to make their own celebrity without any network, publisher, or political support.

The quintessential influencer is Kim Kardashian West, who is famous for being famous. She has over seventy million followers on Twitter, and many more on Instagram and other platforms. She can reach a lot of people, and she commands a high price to do so. In her 2019 complaint against Missguided (a fast-fashion brand), she alleged that she commonly receives three to five hundred thousand dollars for a single Instagram post. Recently she has posted advertisements for a new cryptocurrency, Ethereummax, on her accounts. Experts report that Ethereummax is a risky new coin with few virtues and no documentation, but the coin's advertising campaign appears to be drawing users.

In the social media era, influencers are able to generate a great deal of public interest to various opportunities, including investment opportunities, even though such influences would not have any credibility in a traditional marketplace of ideas. For example, in 2017, entrepreneur Billy McFarland and rapper Ja Rule decided to create a new music festival on a remote island in the Bahamas. Despite the fact that neither had any experience in developing such events, and despite the fact that the location was totally unsuitable to host tens of thousands of people over a several-day period, the event promotors were able to pay social media influencers to advertise the event. The resulting Fyre Festival turned out to be a total disaster, of course, and McFarland pled guilty to wire fraud to defraud investors and ticket holders, which led to his six-year jail sentence. Nevertheless, many investors and consumers lost millions of dollars in this fraud. The influencers were not held accountable.[2]

Influencers can and do effect stock prices, too. For example, when Carl Icahn, the legendary investor, tweeted that he has a large position in Apple Corporation, the

---

[2] In fact, co-authors Professor Duncan Brown and historian Nick Hayes essentially predicted this outcome in their 2008 book, INFLUENCER MARKETING: WHO REALLY INFLUENCES YOUR CUSTOMERS?, which defined an "influences" as influencer as a "third party who significantly shapes the customer's purchasing decision but may never be accountable for it."

stock price immediately rose and hit a six-month high. When Elon Musk, CEO of Tesla Corporation, tweeted that he was selling 10 percent of his shares to pay taxes, the stock price fell almost 5 percent. The SEC has investigated some of Musk's tweets because they could violate Regulation Fair Disclosure, which limits what major public companies can say to a select audience. The SEC fined Musk for his impropriety, but he continues to bend the rules to their limits.

More recently, however, Congress and federal regulators are paying more attention to social media influences' impact on public markets. In particular, an episode involving a relatively small public company, GameStock (GME), was targeted by social media influences in a potential pump-and-dump scheme that led to a Congressional hearing.

The GameStop Episode

Even people who are not already famous can impact stock prices from their desktops. Keith Gill, who posts on the social media platform Reddit under the username DeepFuckingValue, drove a frenzied mob to purchase GameStop stock in the major "meme" stock event of 2021. Gill claimed that GameStock was a good value to purchase because too many investors held short positions. If enough people purchase the stock, Gill reasoned, the price would go up. As the price goes up, it becomes more expensive to maintain a short position. Eventually, the short-sellers would have to give up their position or hedge by taking long positions too; either way, that should further increase the stock price.

GameStop (GME) was not a particularly interesting or compelling stock. For most of 2020, its stock price hovered around $5 per share. Its price rose along with the rest of the market in last 2020, but this was neither exceptional nor outstanding. Its market capitalization (the total value of all its outstanding shares of stock) ranged from about a quarter-billion dollars in early 2020 to a little over a billion dollars by the end of that year; thus, GME never accounted for more than about 0.002 percent of the New York Stock Exchange's total market value of about $50 trillion in 2020.

There were no particularly compelling announcements, either. On an investor conference call in the third quarter of 2020, GameStop announced that, like most retail companies amid the pandemic, sales and profitability were down, with a net loss of $0.53 per share. The company tried to paint a rosy picture of its so-called optimization journey, which was it plans to shutter over 1,000 stores and reduce inventory. This was hardly a cause célèbre; rather, it was seen by most investors as a generally dismal picture that was commonplace for corporations in the doldrums of the COVID-19 pandemic economy.

But the story circulating on social media painted a vastly different picture. Amateur investors organized on the Reddit forum "WallStreet Bets." There, a pseudonymous user going by the name of "delaneydi" shared his alternative thesis on why GameStop was undervalued. His, her, or its back-of-the envelope math suggested the share price should be $18. This post led to users bantering and joking that the social media investors on that Reddit forum should take over the company.

At some point, however, the joking grew serious. Sometime around November 29, 2020, the r/WallStreetBets conversation turned from the merits of GameStop to the fact that major Wall Street investors were shorting the stock. A "short" position profits when stock values go down. In brief, the short investor borrows the stock and sells the borrowed shares. If the stock price goes down, the short seller can repurchase shares at the lower market price and then return them to the investor for a profit.

Short sellers have been reviled throughout history. President Herbert Hoover blamed the stock market crash on in 1929 on short sellers. Short sellers were blamed again for the 1987 "Black Monday" crash, and again for the 2008 financial crisis, when short selling was briefly banned. A short seller even played the role of a James Bond Villain – Le Chiffre, The Cypher. The negative public impression of short sellers and regulatory uncertainty around short selling limits some managers' ability to interpret these actions and for novice investors to use such instruments.

In January 2021, a r/WallStreetBets moderator known as DeepFuckingValue prodded his community to go long on GameStop stock. Influencer and YouTube micro-celebrity Roaring Kitty goaded them to force the short sellers into a "short squeeze" just to cost them billions.

The Short Squeeze

A short squeeze can occur when a stock that has been shorted has an unexpected rise in value. When the price surprisingly goes up, short investors (who have bet that the stock price will go down, and who pay often interest for every day they maintain that position) will want to limit their losses. One way to limit these losses is to convert to a long position, that is, to buy shares immediately, instead of waiting for the price to climb even higher. Such a purchase stops interest payments, and, moreover, the formerly short investor now will instead make a profit if the stock continues to go up. But if many short investors cover in this way, the sudden demand to buy this stock sends its price even higher. A positive feedback loop buoys the stock price higher and higher, wreaking havoc upon the short investors who continue to bet that the stock price would go down, while providing a windfall to the long investors.

Short sellers usually trade on margin (meaning they pay a daily interest rate to hold the short position), which creates an additional pitfall for them. Margin is a term that simply means the money that is borrowed to purchase an investment. Investing using borrowed money is called buying on margin. When the investor borrows money from a stockbroker, the stockbroker opens a margin account, into which the margin investor must make an initial cash deposit to "cover" part of the margin. The initial cash deposit varies, but most brokers require investor to deposit an amount equal to half of the cost of the stock to be purchased. In general, such

50 percent coverage shall be maintained so long as the investor has an outstanding short position.

Margin investors are also contractually obligated to deposit additional cash into the margin account upon various events. When brokers require investors to deposit additional cash into the margin account, that is called a margin call. For example, if the investor used borrowed money to purchase a stock (taking the long position), a decrease in the market value of that stock may trigger a margin call.

Investors can also obtain short positions on margin. In fact, Federal Reserve Regulation T requires short traders to maintain 50 percent of their loan amounts in margin accounts. If the value of the equities in that account decreases, then the investor must put more cash into the margin account so it totals 50 percent of the loan value again. This is called a "Regulation T call," and it mandates that short seller put more cash into margin account as a matter of federal regulations.

In addition to Regulation T calls, lenders who lend stock to short investors may become increasingly worried that the short investors will become unable to repay that loan as the short's value decreases. Such worried lenders – who are often the investor's stockbroker, too – often demand that the short investors make additional margin calls, lest the investor's trading account be frozen.

Thus, short investors have to put more cash into margin accounts, which functions as collateral that the lenders can take if the borrower defaults on the loan, especially when the short drops precipitously in value. To get the cash necessary to true up the margin account, short investors might have to sell some of their short positions immediately, even at a loss, or as a stop-loss strategy. As short investors sell off their short positions to raise cash for margin calls, this increases the supply of short positions in the market, which puts downward price pressure on the value of short positions. As the short positions lose value, more and more short investors need to sell off larger and larger positions to make margin calls, thus creating a feedback loop that pushes the value of short positions lower and lower while the value of the long position climbs higher and higher.

In theory, long investors could force short investors into a money-spewing short squeeze if the long investors simply drove the price up enough. This is generally hard to do with the large-cap stocks that short investors tend to prefer, but stranger things have happened.

In fact, Porsche SE employed the short squeeze on investors. Volkswagen almost went bankrupt in the Financial Crisis of 2008. Short investors bet heavily that the car company would not survive. But Porsche was secretly buying up shares in the beleaguered company. On October 26, 2008, Porsche announced that it held 74 percent of Volkswagen stock. The stock price suddenly surged, and the nearly bankrupt Volkswagen briefly became one of the world's most valuable stocks, topping out at over $370 billion in total market capitalization. Short investors lost billions in what has been called the Mother of all Squeezes and the Infinity Squeeze.

The unfortunate economic fact that short investors can be put into an unrecoverable tailspin has thus been utilized by large institutional investors before, but not until recently were short-squeeze tactics used by an online rabble of amateur investors.

The GameStock Short Squeeze

In late January 27, 2021, tens of thousands of users on the free stock trading app RobinHood drove up GameStock. They were fueled by r/WallStreetBets and YouTube influencers who focusing on and asked "Have you robbed your billionaire today?" With the mantra "never sell, never surrender," this social media consortium drove the price up from an average of just under $20 per share on January 11 to an intraday high of $483 on January 28, 2021 – an incredible 2315 percent increase in less than three weeks.

Short investors lost billions. Melvin Capital, who was explicitly targeted by r/WallStreetBets users, lost 53 percent of its investment, requiring its financier Citadel LLC and Point72 Asset Management to invest another $2.75 billion just so Melvin could meet its margin calls. Meanwhile, DeepFuckingValue apparently earned over $11 million.

Damages to short investors and profits to social media influencers and others with long positions were actually cut short. RobinHood, the free trading platform on which many of the social media users purchased long-call investments, ran out of money to post collateral for its users and shut down. Within days, however, RobinHood raised at least $3.4 billion so it could meet collateral calls and continue trading.

MEME INVESTING

Some pundits quickly concluded that the GameStop Episode may be the end of short selling, but it's too early to ring the death knell for this investment technique. Short selling will always be profitable in some instances, and many economists have recognized how short selling helps markets function more efficiently. But the way in which investors take short positions may change.

Short investors should now be about concerned about backlash and attacks on social media. Not only are short sellers unpopular for profiting only when companies and economies are failing, but short sellers also make an easy target for a mob with enough money. Unless short sellers figure out how to avoid the short squeeze triggered by a social media rush into heavily shorted stocks, especially small-cap stock whose prices are more easily impacted, then short investors would be wise to keep their positions under wraps, lest their position comes into the crosshairs of a r/WallStreetBets social media influencer.

The term "meme stock" entered the vernacular in February 2021 to describe a company whose stock price experienced a spike of rapid growth not because of any underlying improvement to its fundamentals or economics but only because it was targeted by a social media campaign. This is like the pump-and-dump schemes of old, but this pump is "organized" by a loosely affiliated online group of outsiders and amateur investors, instead of the corporate insiders and Wall Street pink sheet brokers that pumped stock before. Such organization was not possible before social media "democratized" access to information and investment.

In this new era of social media investing, stock manipulation schemes have been democratized, too. Now anyone with an internet connection can try to rally a crowd to purchase stock, seemingly without regard to that stock's fundamental value, especially when doing so can be framed as an attack on the mega-rich. Meanwhile, anyone with a Twitter account can bring attention to perceived corporate wrongdoing and drive millions of people to sell that stock or even boycott the company. While investors and corporations always had to be concerned about their public image, social media investing greatly raises the risk that a variety of behavior from taking short positions to donating to certain political candidates will result in a social media backlash that can eradicate value in record time.

Ordinary investors thus found themselves between a rock and a hard place. On the one hand, regulations give wealthy investors more access and options to beat the market than ordinary investors had. On the other hand, powerful and influential personalities can move markets while common folk can at best come along for the ride – or get drowned in the wake of resulting market turbulence. With such a narrow route to financial success, investors began looking for ways make money outside of the regulated public marketplaces. They found such an opportunity in the nascent cryptocurrency market.

BIBLIOGRAPHY

Ang, Lawrence & Raymond Welling Susie Khamis, *Self-Branding, 'Micro-Celebrity' and the Rise of Social Media Influencers*, 8 CELEBRITY STUDIES 191 (2016).

Anonymous, *Complete Guide for Trading Pump and Dump Stocks* (Al Hill eds., 2018), available at https://perma.cc/DG54-DHSN.

Bowman, Emma, *Reddit WallStreetBets Founder Calls GameStop Stock Frenzy A 'Symbolic Movement'*, NPR (Jan. 31, 2021), available at https://perma.cc/C5P3-7PJW.

Boylston, Christian et al., *WallStreetBets: Positions or Ban*, ARXIV.ORG (January 28, 2021), available at https://perma.cc/A7FV-CHGG.

Carpenter, Julia, *Some GameStop Investors Got in with One Goal – to Pay Off Debt*, WSJ (January 30, 2021), available at https://perma.cc/7V2C-3KAS.

Chung, Juliet, *Melvin Capital Lost 53% in January, Hurt by GameStop and Other Bets*, WSJ (January 31, 2021), available at AQ: As above.

Demos, Telis, *Why Did Robinhood Ground GameStop? Look at Clearing*, WSJ (January 29, 2021), available at https://perma.cc/3MAM-JQJP.

Fearon, Scott & Robert Kroajczyk, *Does GameStop Signal the End of Short Selling as We Know It?*, KelloggInsight (January 29, 2021), available at https://perma.cc/6MK9-MHQL.

Fisch, Jill E., *Measuring Efficiency in Corporate Law: The Role of Shareholder Primacy*, 31 J. CORP. L. 637 (2006).

Freberg, Karen, et al., *Who Are the Social Media Influencers? A Study of Public Perceptions of Personality*, 37 PUB. RELATIONS REV. 90–92 (2011).

Gómez, Alexandra Ruiz, *Digital Fame and Fortune in the Age of Social Media: A Classification of Social Media Influencers*, 19 REVISTA INTERNACIONAL DE INVESTIGACIÓN EN COMUNICACIÓN 8 (2019).

Gottlieb, Matt (mgconsults), *Interview with Phil Goldstein and Andrew Dakos of Bulldog Investors, Part 1*, SEEKINGALPHA.COM (2018), available at https://perma.cc/D6V9-4FHL.

Grant, Charley, *On YouTube, GameStop Hearing Just Another Pumping Opportunity*, WSJ (February 19, 2021), available at https://perma.cc/4D4P-FFAE.

Hedge Funds Lose $30 Billion on VW Infinity Squeeze, MOX REPORTS (December 9, 2018), available at https://perma.cc/HKM2-XJ4Q.

Ishii, Joy & Andrew Metrick Paul Gompers, *Corporate Governance and Equity Prices*, 118 QUARTERLY J. ECON. 107 (2003).

Jenkins Jr., Jolman W., *Opinion: GameStop Was an Enjoyment of Crowds*, WSJ (January 29, 2021), available at https://perma.cc/Y4QN-7ZLZ.

Khamis, Susie et al., *Self-Branding, 'Micro-Celebrity' and the Rise of Social Media Influencers*, 8 CELEBRITY STUDIES 191–208 (2017).

Kochkodin, Brandon, *How WallStreetBets Pushed GameStop Shares to the Moon*, BLOOMBERG WEALTH (January 25, 2021), available at https://perma.cc/6GBM-AZRJ.

Loten, Angus, *Nasdaq Tech Chief Credits Cloud with Helping Manage Market Frenzies*, WSJ (January 29, 2021), available at https://perma.cc/T28D-3PHP.

Mackintosh, James, *Gambling? In the Stock Market? I'm Shocked.*, WSJ (2021), available at https://perma.cc/8TMA-KXDH.

Marsh, Sarah, *Short Sellers Make VW the World's Priciest Firm*, REUTERS (October 28, 2008), available at https://perma.cc/TDS8-C2FR.

McCabe, Caitlin, *Robinhood, Facing Ire on Many Fronts, Defends Its App to Regulators*, WSJ (January 29, 2021), available at https://perma.cc/EQU6-PY3Z.

Mendelson, Haim, *Market Behavior in a Clearing House*, 50 ECONOMETRICA 1505 (1982).

Michaels, Dave and Paul Kiernan, *Day-Trader Mania Will Challenge SEC Under Gensler, Biden's Choice for Chairman*, WSJ (January 29, 2021), available at https://perma.cc/VKE7-UWM8.

Mitts, Joshua, *Short and Distort*, 49 J. LEGAL STUD. 287–334 (June 2020).

Msika, Michael and Jake Lloyd-Smith, *Reddit Trades Crumble as GameStop, AMC and Silver Plunge*, BLOOMBERG (February 2, 2021), available at https://perma.cc/J4HC-D4GQ.

Nathan, Charles & Nicholas O'Keefe, *A Practitioner's Guide to Electronic Shareholder Forums*, LATHAM & WATKINS LLP CORPORATE GOVERNANCE COMMENTARY (January 2008), available at https://perma.cc/HWJ2-R29X

O'Mahony, Michael, *What Is a 'Meme Stock'?*, MyWallSt.com (2021), available at https://perma.cc/QA24-R23J.

Oranburg, Seth C., *A Little Birdie Said: How Twitter Is Disrupting Shareholder Activism*, 20 FORDHAM J. CORP. & FIN. L. 695 (2015).

Osipovich, Alexander & Rachael Levy Geoffrey Rogow, *Tweets and Articles Sent Kodak Shares Surging Before Official Announcement*, WSJ (July 29, 2020), available at https://perma.cc/N45F-K4B2.

Otani, Akane, *Reddit Investors Rage Against Being Shut Out of Hot Stock Trades Like GameStop and AMC*, WSJ (January 29, 2021), available at https://perma.cc/K9XW-FXNT.

Plaintiff's Emergency Complaint for Injunctive and Other Relief, *Securities and Exchange Commission v. McKeown* (Southern District of Florida) (No. 10–80748-CIV-COHN).

Ponczek, Sarah, *How a Penny Stock Explodes From Obscurity to 451% Gains Via Chat Forums*, BLOOMBERG (January 26, 2021), available at https://perma.cc/K8XN-FKH2.

Robinson, Ben Cohen Joshua, Julia-Ambra Verlaine & Gunjan Banerji, *Roaring Kitty Wanted to Break a 4-Minute Mile. He Broke Wall Street Instead.*, WSJ (January 30, 2021), available at https://perma.cc/W5K2–E625.

Rudegeair, Peter & Orla McCaffrey, *Robinhood Raises $1 Billion to Meet Surging Cash Demands*, WSJ (January 29, 2021), available at https://perma.cc/VGF3-ZNS9.

Schmidt, Krista Kjellman & WSJ Staff Jenna Telesca, *GameStop Stock, Reddit and Robinhood: What You Need to Know*, WSJ (January 29, 2021), available at https://perma.cc/5PZ4-TGAQ.

SHAKESPEARE, WILLIAM, MACBETH (1623).

u/Talonx4, *How to Find, and Ride Pumps*, Reddit.com (2017), available at https://perma.cc/HJ4B-DB2J.

Verlaine, Julia-Ambra & Gunjan Banerji, *Keith Gill Drove the GameStop Reddit Mania. He Talked to the Journal*, WSJ (January 29, 2021), available at https://perma.cc/3TX3-8WDP.

Vigna, Paul & Anna Hirtenstein, *Stocks Close Down 2% as GameStop Frenzy Continues* (January 29, 2021), available at https://perma.cc/46TY-JZBD.

Virk, Rizwan, *GameStop Trades and Meme Investing Turn Stocks into a Pump-and-Dump Scheme*, NBC NEWS (2021), available at https://perma.cc/N4VE-MGUL.

Wohlsen, Marcus, *Single Tweet Sends Apple Shares Soaring*, WIRED (August 13, 2013), available at https://perma.cc/C3Z8-FXEY.

Zweig, Jason, *The Real Force Driving the GameStop Revolution*, WSJ (January 30, 2021), available at https://perma.cc/S7SM-F6UH.

9

Cryptographic Theory and Decentralized Finance

When bitcoin was first announced in 2008, only a few anarcho-capitalists gravitated to its notions of a decentralized global currency. But the technology powering bitcoin – the blockchain – proved to be an incredibly effective means of facilitating transactions between anonymous or pseudonymous parties. In general, it is foolish to contract with someone that is not trustworthy. But blockchains enables "trustless" transactions by using a combination of cryptography, digital signatures, and incentives. As a result, people are willing to transact with strangers using cryptocurrency. Companies are now using cryptocurrency for corporate financing. Is this a return to the era of rugged individualism, or will big data and the internet pave the way for a new form of regulation?

> The Times 03/Jan/2009 Chancellor on brink of second bailout for banks.
> – Bitcoin Genesis Block, "Satoshi Nakamoto," 3 January 2009

Cryptocurrency markets are self-regulated, and increasingly popular, digital marketplaces for ordinary investors to conduct transactions – similar to the Wild West of the First Era. While self-regulating markets have some desirable aspects, the anonymity feature of cryptocurrency markets has its drawbacks which can lead to more fraud and corruption if left completely unchecked.

The "crypto" part of the word cryptocurrency refers to cryptography, which is the practice of writing and deciphering codes in order to keep messages secret. Although the concept is thousands of years old, it has evolved dramatically thanks to modern computing power.

ORIGINS OF CRYPTOGRAPHY

Cryptography dates back at least as far as ancient Greece, where it secured wartime communications between Generals. Spartans would wrap leather or parchment around a wooden cylinder, known as a scytale, and then write a message while the parchment was wrapped around it. When the message was unraveled from the scytale it would be meaningless because the letters were no longer aligned up in the proper places. The only way to decode the message was to wrap it around another scytale of the same shape and diameter, that only the intended receiver possessed, so the letters in the message could be properly aligned again. Even if the parchment was made public, its message would remain private to anyone who did not have the scytale.

But the scytale had serious limitations. It is a symmetric cipher system, meaning the encryption and the decryption is done using the same scytale. Both the sender and the receiver must have scytale that match exactly. If multiple people are sharing coding messages, each must have a copy of the same scytale. When the system gets large enough, it is hand to ensure confidentiality. For example, if a Spartan general was captured, the enemy might also capture a copy of the scytale. Not only would that enable the enemy to read encrypted messages, but would also allow the enemy to send false codes. This actually happened on May 9, 1941, when British captured a German U-110 submarine and found on board the Enigma machine that the Nazis used to encode and decode messages between German command ships.

CYPHERPUNKS

To understand the origins of modern cryptocurrency and the nature of this unique technology, one must understand the motivations of its creators: the Cypherpunks and the ever-elusive "Satoshi Nakamoto." As Chapter 6 explained, computer science research and development accelerated during World War II. The British needed computers to decrypt Nazi code. The American needed computers to build the atom bombs that would decimate Nagasaki and Hiroshima. Computer science in its infancy was thus thrust into acts of war. Some feared that computer science, although developed for the sake of saving democracy, would be used by state as a force of oppression against its own people.

The people known as the Cypherpunks developed their own computer science resistance movement and used cryptography to fight for the freedom of privacy. Cypherpunks originated as civil libertarians and privacy advocates resisted government efforts to control the emerging internet in the so-called Crypto Wars. The U.S. Government classified cryptography – computer technology that encrypts information and thereby makes information unavailable even to government agencies – as a "munition." Cryptographic devices, software, and components were listed on the United States Munitions List, banned alongside nuclear weapons. Export of cryptographic technology was effectively banned until 1992. (Export of cryptographic technology remains restricted today.)

Eric Hughes, Timothy May, and John Gilmore started the organization in 1992, meeting monthly in San Francisco. They created a mailing list where they could virtually meet and discuss their hopes for the future with their fellow cryptography enthusiasts. Hughes wrote "A Cypherpunk's Manifesto" in March of 1993. Elegantly, he said in the opening paragraph:

> Privacy is necessary for an open society in the electronic age. Privacy is not secrecy. A private matter is something one doesn't want the whole world to know, but a secret matter is something one doesn't want anybody to know. Privacy is the power to selectively reveal oneself to the world.

The manifesto speaks directly to the tension between cryptocurrency and regulation, and it boldly proclaims that cryptography will eventually prevail over efforts to regulate encryption:

> Cypherpunks deplore regulations on cryptography, for encryption is fundamentally a private act. The act of encryption, in fact, removes information from the public realm. Even laws against cryptography reach only so far as a nation's border and the arm of its violence. Cryptography will ineluctably spread over the whole globe, and with it the anonymous transactions systems that it makes possible.

Ironically, the Cypherpunk movement itself was not especially secretive or private. Most of their technology was open source. They created code that anyone can download. Writing computer code is the first step in developing software. The computer code can be read and understood by humans. Then the code is compiled into a machine-readable form called an application or simply an app.[1]

The Cypherpunks published their code so that users could see for themselves how that code functioned before compiling it themselves. This open-source strategy allowed the movement to grow quickly, but it also put additional demands on the technology they created. In a sense, the Cypherpunks also encoded their political philosophy in their cryptography efforts. The processes and products they developed contains features of classical liberalism, democracy, and anarchy within the structure of its code.

Cypherpunks needed to ensure that open-source code could be used to create private information. The solution, blockchain technology, discussed in depth later in this chapter, required an innovation in public-key cryptography. The technology used to power the first successful cryptocurrency, Bitcoin.

---

[1] Apps must be run by computers and cannot be read by human beings. (Although apps can sometimes be partially decompiled back into human-readable code, this is an imperfect and difficult process.) This means that app developers can hide nefarious programs in apps that cannot be hidden so easily in code. Recent scandals include, for example, the popular TikTok app. Security researchers discovered that TikTok was programmed to secretly access the clipboards on users' devices. If TikTok is active, even if it is just running in the background, then it can read anything written on that device. Passwords, sensitive messages, confidential emails, and financial information could thereby be secretly copied by the app and sent to TikTok's headquarters in China. The Chinese government may be able to accesses information that enters its jurisdiction, thus exposing tens of millions of American's most private and sensitive information to the world's largest communist government.

BITCOIN

Bitcoin is by far the world's most famous and successful cryptocurrency today. As of February 2021, Bitcoin alone accounted for more than two thirds of the total market cap for all cryptocurrencies. But, even though the market cap for Bitcoin is almost a trillion dollars, most people don't know how it originated or how it works.

Bitcoin was created by Satoshi Nakamoto, who stated purpose was to create a monetary regime that made it unnecessary for people to use the current centralized financial system. The technology allows parties to cut out costly middlemen, namely the banks, and replace them with a decentralized system that can operate beyond the borders of any centralized authority. Moreover, transactions were perfectly verifiable yet totally private.

Bitcoin is a network system that enables a decentralized system of trust verification between users, coupled with desirable privacy features. With a system of decentralized trust between users, there was a reduced need for a centralized financial

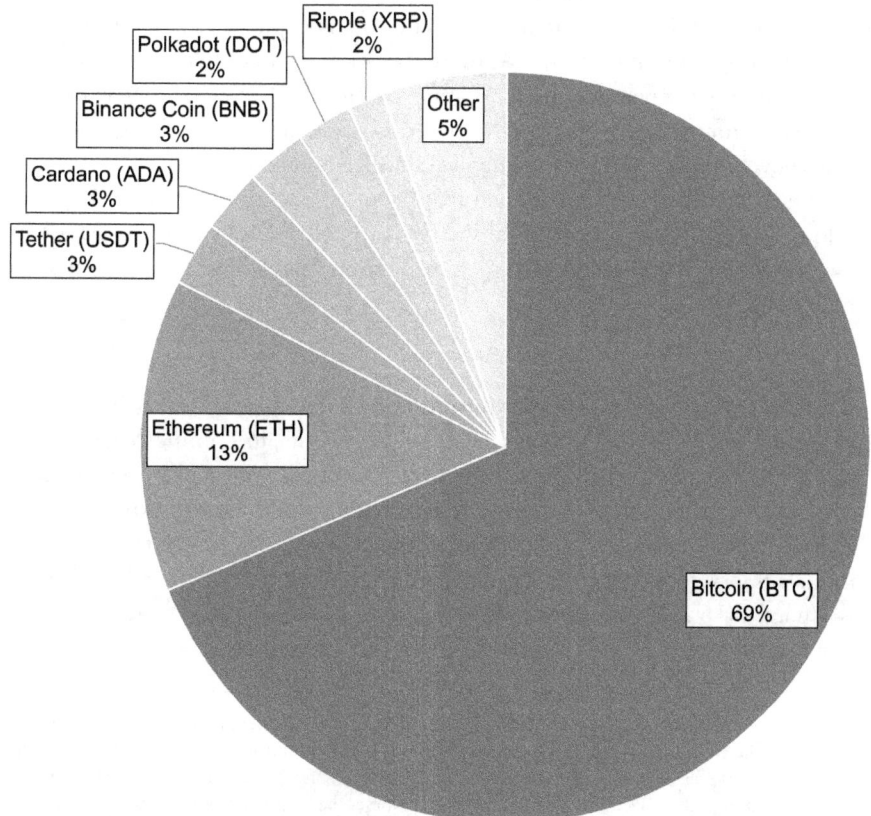

FIGURE 9.1 Market share of the top fifteen cryptocurrencies in February 2021.

authority acting as the middleman. Many have opined that Bitcoin's efficiency and its decentralized ledger have the capability to significantly reduce transaction costs in addition to eradicating corruption in the current legal, political, and transactional regimes. This may have indeed been part of its creator's intentions.

SATOSHI NAKAMOTO: WHAT'S IN A NAME?

On Halloween, 2008, someone using the name Satoshi Nakamoto sent an email to the Cypherpunks mailing list. Nakamoto wrote, "I've been working on a new electronic cash system that's fully peer-to-peer." The mysterious email directed those who read it to a website with a nine-page "white paper" document describing the plans in greater detail. That was the beginning of the dramatic roller coaster that we know today as the Bitcoin Revolution. It started as nothing more than an email to a few people who enjoyed programming, cryptography, and privacy.

Satoshi Nakamoto is a pseudonym. Understanding why Nakamoto used a pseudonym, as opposed to using a true name or posting anonymously, reveals much about why Cypherpunks and other flocked to Bitcoin. Anonymity, pseudonymity, and nonymity represent three states in which people can share information. Anonymity is untraceable privacy. Authors may write books or letters anonymously to avoid personal repercussions for stating controversial views. Such works are attributed "Anonymous." No specific name is given to the work's author. The famous novel Frankenstein was originally published anonymously, perhaps because its author Mary Shelly was concerned that people in eighteenth-century England would not take seriously a novel published by a woman.[2] Anonymity may be useful for works that speak for themselves, such as facts that lead to arrest of a criminal.

Anonymity

Anonymity is also useful for committing crimes and getting away with it. Those who know about Bitcoin have probably heard of Silk Road, the online black-market website shut down by the FBI in 2013, but which keeps popping back up with various names and forms. Silk Road was run through an anonymous network known as Tor which effectively made traceability impossible. Without fear of arrest, anonymous criminals transacted among one another without being tracked. Tor's anonymity was lauded by privacy-driven people, but its connection to Silk Road and other fraudulent activity overshadows those benefits for many others.

---

[2] If Shelly was indeed concerned that her gender would discredit her novel's political contribution, she was right. The British Critic effectively dismissed the novel because it suspected the author was female, writing "The writer of it is, we understand, a female; this is an aggravation of that which is the prevailing fault of the novel; but if our authoress can forget the gentleness of her sex, it is no reason why we should; and we shall therefore dismiss the novel without further comment." https://uminn pressblog.com/2019/01/18/frankenstein-and-anonymous-authorship-in-eighteenth-century-britain/

Moreover, anonymity is unsuitable for transactions where trust is required. A person would likely not entrust an anonymous person with their valuables. Most people would not lend their car to a total stranger or give an anonymous person cash to pay a bill on their behalf. A newspaper might not trust an anonymous source because it is not possible to verify whether the source provided true information. By putting one's name to something, one is effectively providing some basis for trust. One can consider another's reputation as a proxy for determining whether to trust that person. But an anonymous person has no reputation and therefore no innate basis for trust.

Pseudonymity

Pseudonymity differs from anonymity in that instead of providing no name a false name is given. Although the pseudonym initially has no reputation, that pseudonym can develop a reputation over time. Pseudonymous writings have long been used to inspire political action. In 1769, someone using the pseudonym "Junius" published scathing letters attacking the Prime Minister of England, who resigned in 1770 citing the Junius letters as one of the most significant reasons for his departure. During the debates over the design of the United States Constitution, many arguments were published under pseudonyms, including Publius (used by Alexander Hamilton, James Madison, and John Jay), Brutus (Robert Yates), Senex (Patrick Henry), and An Old Whig (an unknown Anti-Federalist). In more recent times, famous author J. K. Rowling used the pseudonym Robert Galbraith, who said that "being Robert Galbraith has been such a liberating experience. It has been wonderful to publish without hype or expectation, and pure pleasure to get feedback under a different name."

Pseudonyms develop a reputation and a perception over time, such that people might tend to trust or at least better understand a well-known pseudonymous author more than an anonymous one.

Nonymity

Nonymity, a term created for the purposes of this chapter, is the use of one's true identity. In a realm of nonymity, users lack all privacy. There is no hiding ideas and actions. There are no secret transactions. Everything may be tracked and monitored. Nonymity is not identical, but bears the closest resemblance to the current state of the world. Banks and other financial institutions have a hand in almost every aspect of one's life. They know people's names, where they live, their occupation, their familial status, how much they are worth, and even the digits of their social security number. That, of course, is aside from other personal information most people disclose to their doctors, lawyers, accountants and business partners – all of that is tracked too. Even to the extent that outline activities are individually anonymized, artificial intelligence can often employ mosaic theory to figure out who is who regardless.

Like Junius, Publius, and Senex, Satoshi Nakamoto assumed a pseudonymous identity in order to push for economic and social change. All of his emails were encrypted and untraceable. Just as mysterious as his arrival, so too was his exit. One day he randomly appeared with an idea; another, completely vanished – never sending another email. We can say "he," "she," or even "they" when referring to Satoshi. The search has pointed fingers at many people like Neal King, Vladimir Oksman, and Charles Bry, three men who filed for encryption patents around the time Bitcoin came to be. They could be Nakamodo. Shinichi Mochizuki, a Japanese math professor at Kyoto University, could be him. Or perhaps, as others suggest, she is an unknown woman or even a group of people.

NAKAMOTO'S EMAILS

We may never solve the mystery of Nakamoto's identity, but the emails that were apparently sent by Nakamoto are recorded and can be read by anyone. Since they are pseudonymous, not anonymous, these emails can be traced back to the same mysterious source. These writings give clues as to the political and economic philosophy behind the making of Bitcoin. The February 11, 2009 email illustrates that decentralization and perhaps even anarchy motivated the Bitcoin project.[3] Nakamoto apparently detested the centralized banking system and set out to create Bitcoin as a solution. The community of trust was born when Satoshi set the first "node" in the Bitcoin blockchain, commonly referenced as the "Genesis Block." But a transaction system cannot exist in a vacuum. By definition, a transaction requires at least two people. Moreover, Bitcoin's novel strategy requires user participation. The system needs to be large enough that no one person can control the information. Nakamoto returned to the Cypherpunk mailing list and announced his creation. Hal Finney became the second to join when he received the first transfer of Bitcoins from Nakamoto. As time went on, the community continued to grow. A larger community meant more people were checking and verifying transactions in the system. This meant communal trust, from a conceptual standpoint, was rising exponentially.

Although we may never be sure who is Satoshi Nakamoto, we credit him, her, or it for developing Bitcoin and ushering in a new era of digital finance.

---

[3] "The root problem with conventional currency is all the trust that's required to make it work. The central bank must be trusted not to debase the currency, but the history of fiat currencies is full of breaches of that trust. Banks must be trusted to hold our money and transfer it electronically, but they lend it out in waves of credit bubbles with barely a fraction in reserve. We have to trust them with our privacy, trust them not to let identity thieves drain our accounts. Their massive overhead costs make micropayments impossible."

CRYPTOCURRENCY: PRIVATE, NOT SECRET

Modern cryptography uses asymmetric cryptography. Unlike symmetric cryptography, which uses one key such as a scytale or an Enigma machine for both encryption and decryption, asymmetric cryptography uses two types of keys: a private key and a public key called a wallet address.

The Bitcoin system first generates a private key, which is a 256-bit number. A bit (short for "binary digit") is the smallest amount of data in a computer. One bit has a single value of either 0 or 1. A 256-bit number could be represented by a string of 256 binary digits, but it can also be represented in a shorter number that uses hexadecimal digits (where each bit has the value 0–9 or A-F), Base64 (where the value can be any letter or number, plus the symbols +, /, and =), or ASCII (which includes symbols, letters, and numbers). This means that a more complex representation can store more information in a shorter string. Bitcoin private keys are based on the secp256k1 ECDSA standard, which uses a modified version of Base64 called Base58 that omits the characters o, O, l, I, + and / because of the risk of visual confusion and to improve human readability.

As you can see from the chart above, all the encoding schemes produce the same information in a shorter value than binary encoding. This is called compression, as it enables information to be stored and transmitted in a shorter form. Accordingly, a 256-bit private key that is written in Base58 may be only 52 characters long, whereas that same information written in binary would be 304 characters long.[4]

After the system generates a random private key, it then runs a hash function on that private key to generate a cryptographically linked public key. A hash function is a computer program that scrambles data of any length and returns a result that is always the same length. Bitcoin uses the SHA256 and RIPEM160 hash functions to

TABLE 9.1 *Encoding schemes*

Encoding Scheme	Value
ASCII	Bitcoin
Binary	01000010 01101001 01110100 01100011 01101111 01101001 01101110
Hexadecimal	42 69 74 63 6F 69 6E
Base64	QmloY29pbg==
Base58	3WyEDWjcVB

[4] *C.f.* L2tUqZzNbBR6WKXskUTxyjRqu3YWfLRqPcn8LgLKpLtenLuc6QhD (Base58) *with* 10000000 10101001 00100001 10110101 11111000 11110111 00111110 11001010 01100011 10000001 10100101 10110010 10011101 10100000 00011110 01011000 10000111 11100010 00000110 10011011 00101001 00000110 11000101 11011001 11011000 00010101 11001111 00011011 11110110 11010110 10011010 01010000 11110101 00000001 11000100 10011010 11001110 00010000 (binary code).

Cryptographic Theory and Decentralized Finance

Bitcoin Address   **Private Key**

15snfutJNc4zJS1EaGVLLtAffHDkPdp96F

L2tUqZzNbBR6WKXskUTxyjRqu3YWfLRqPcn8LgLKpLtenLuc6QhD

FIGURE 9.2 Illustration of public and private cryptographic keys.

generate public keys through an elliptical curve digital signature algorithm that are always 160 bits long.[5] The public key is a unique identifier associated with a person. It functions like a street address or an internet-protocol address. In fact, the public key is called the Bitcoin address.

The public and private keys are mathematically linked in one direction, meaning it is easy to generate a public key given a private key, but it is nearly impossible to reverse the process and create a private key from a public key. In other words, the private key has more information than the public key. This makes it possible for one person to encrypt information using another's public key, such that the information can only be decrypted by that person's private key.

For example, imagine that an admiral wants to send a coded message to the commander of a nuclear submarine. If the commander sends his public key to the admiral, the admiral can encrypt a message using the commander's public key. Then that information can only be decrypted using the commander's private key. Since the commander does not have to send his private key to the admiral, the private key is more secure than a scytale or an Enigma machine.

If a nefarious hacker had enough time and computing power, he could attempt to discover a private key through a hacking process called brute force. In a brute force hack, the hacker simply tries different passcodes until one works. There are 2^{256} possible private keys, although the public key reveals some information about the private key such that 2^{128} private are functionally possible. Conservative estimates suggest that it would take over a half billion years to try all these combinations using modern computer power. To hack the Blockchain it would require computing power far too costly to run than the potential reward, making the blockchain a safe and secure system for verifying transactions – for now.[6]

---

[5] For example, 15snfutJNc4zJS1EaGVLLtAffHDkPdp96F.
[6] Bitcoin and Blockchain Technology are generally regarded as infallible systems that are impossible to hack. Today, the cost incurred to sufficiently power computers attempting to hack the Blockchain is, simply put, not worth the effort – the cost far outweighs the reward. This is why Bitcoin is regarded as "unhackable." However, as technology develops it become more efficient. Quantum computers pose a risk to the security of blockchain as they gain computing power efficiency. See Kotow, E., Quantum Blockchain, *Hedgetrade*, June 8, 2019.

DIGITAL CURRENCY'S DOUBLE-SPEND PROBLEM

Although cryptographic solutions for safely sharing information between novel parties was developed in the 1970s, it was not readily applicable to digital currency because of a phenomenon called the double-spend problem. Put simply, holders of digital currency can spend the same coin twice or more due to the fact that electronic communication is not instantaneous. To solve this problem, Nakamoto developed blockchain technology, which solves the double-spend problem by implementing a universal ledger with a confirmation mechanism.

For illustration, consider going to Talia's Video Arcade. You put a five-dollar bill in the token dispensing machine, and out comes five plastic Talia Tokens. These tokens have no financial value per se. You cannot take them to the corner store and exchange them for a pack of gum. But you can insert one into a Skee ball machine and get the opportunity to play that game. At the end of the night, a TVA employee retrieves all the Talia tokens from all the video game machines and puts them back into the dispensing machine. In this simple example, the Talia token can only be spent once because it returns to a central authority before being reissued. The dispensing machine acts like a mint. This is fine so long as the mint works, but it is not a robust solution, because the mint is a bottleneck. If the dispensing machine breaks down, the entire video arcade ceases to function until it is replaced. The dispensing machine is also vulnerable to attack because it is a centralized store of value. It could be literally "hacked" open with a hacksaw. Is there another way to track these tokens?

Instead of using physical tokens that are stored in a central location, we could use digital tokens. While we could still task a central mint to track the ownership of all those tokens, we have also unlocked a new solution by going digital. Digital tokens can be recorded in infinitely many places at once at virtually no additional cost. The record of who owns what tokens is called a ledger, and such a record that exists in many places at once is called a distributed ledger. For example, both the Skee Ball machine and the air hockey machine could have a copy of the distributed ledger. When you sign away your digital Talia Token by agreeing to play a game of Skee Ball, you should no longer own that token to play a game of air hockey. But the Internet does not transmit information instantaneously. Nothing can travel faster than the speed of light, so the message that you spent your token on a game of Skee Ball could take several seconds to reach an air hockey machine on the other side of the world. An enterprising American fraudster could partner with a comrade in China so they both hit "play" on their video game machines at the same time. The transaction at the air hockey table is not transmitted (or "published") to the Skee Ball table until the balls have been dispensed, and our fraudster will get to enjoy a free game. In other words, your Talia Token has been double spent.

Double spending seems like a trivial matter when it relates to video games, but what if that token represents one million dollars? Obviously, a solution to the double-spend problem is necessary if distributed ledgers are to be useful, and digital signatures are not enough. Blockchain thus adds two features, a timestamp server and proof-of-work, that solve the double-spending problem.

A timestamp server widely publishes all the transactions that occurred in a prior period of time. Each publication constitutes one block. For example, this Talia Block will show two transactions: the spending of one Talia Token to play a Skee Ball game in America, and the spending of the same Talia Token to play an air hockey game in China. Blockchain technology is programmed to invalidate double-spend transactions, so neither video game machine will accept the token, and our fraudster will be thwarted. However, our timestamp solution has created a new problem: we cannot validate a transaction until a block is published. That makes instantaneous transactions impossible. While our fraudster is thwarted, TVA's legitimate customers will be frustrated by waiting ten minutes or more to play a game of Skee Ball.

But our technologically savvy fraudster is not done yet. In a last-ditch effort to get one free play, the fraudster attempts to publish a false block that erroneously shows ownership of two tokens. Proof-of-work is a cryptographic solution to this problem.

Digital information of any length can be converted into a fixed-length hexadecimal code by a process called "hashing."[7] It is very easy to create a hash value based on any given set of input data. But it is very hard to determine the input data given only the hash value output.[8] Blockchain technology is programmed only to accept published blocks whose hash value begins with several zeros. This requires block publishers to add an arbitrary number (a "nonce") to each block until the block returns a hash value starting with the specified number of zeros. Scanning for a nonce that returns an acceptable hash value for the block takes a huge amount of computing power. It would be cheaper for our fraudster to simply buy a second Tali Token legitimately than to spend more money on computer hardware and electricity. However, this also creates a new problem: block publishers have to spend huge amounts of money on electricity to solve the blockchain hash problem, which is not only costly but also bad for the environment.

To summarize, blockchain technology uses proof-of-work to prevent double spending on a peer-to-peer network of digital signatures. Blockchain has the advantage of a decentralized system that is inefficient to hack. But it has the disadvantage of being too slow for some applications and of being extremely energy intensive. Technologists are working on solutions to these and other problems with

[7] For example, the input data "fox" results in the output hash value "776cb326abocd5-f0a974c1b9606044d8485201f2db19cf8e3749bdee5f36e200" when put through the SHA256 hash algorithm. The input data "The quick brown fox jumps over the lazy dog." Results in the hash value "ef537f25c895bfa782526529a9b63d97aa631564d5d789c2b765448c8635fb6c." Note that the hash values are exactly the same length (64 characters) even though the input data are different lengths.

[8] This feature of "one-wayness" is more technically described as "preimage resistance." Peters, G.W., Panayi, E. (2015) Understanding Modern Business Banking Ledgers through Blockchain Technologies: Future of Transaction Processing and Smart Contracts on the Internet of Money, at 4.

blockchain, and there are myriad new applications for the blockchain ledger that go above and beyond transactions in digital currency. In the meantime, it remains an infallible system of security that is virtually impossible to hack and can provide the security we need to facilitate transactions between people. The blockchain technology that undergirds Bitcoin, rather than Bitcoin itself, it more likely to transform society.

BLOCKCHAIN TECHNOLOGY

After downloading the proper software, any computer can join the existing Bitcoin network with the ability to add or withdraw funds through a "digital wallet." Each computer in the network is referred to as a "node." When a transaction occurs, it is publicized to the entire network. Details about the transaction are collected by each node and reduced to a "hash." Finally, a new "block" is created and is virtually attached to the previous block in the chain, and the public ledger is updated. Each node has its own copy of the ledger; when the public ledger is updated in one node it is updated in all of other nodes too. Since the decentralized ledger is public it becomes extremely difficult to cheat the system.

INVESTING IN CRYPTOCURRENCY

Bitcoin was not created to operate as an investment vehicle. The ups and downs of the stock market were never truly relevant to the nature of cryptocurrencies, nor were the considerations of Bitcoin as a borderless currency. At the heart of cryptocurrencies and blockchain technology is the prospect that they provide a level of anonymity from the rest of the world, and more importantly, from governments. To that end, it creates the potential for a shift from the centralized financial systems we currently use, to a decentralized publicly distributed ledger free from any centralized influence.

Despite the original intentions of the Cypherpunks to use cryptocurrencies like Bitcoin as a means to avoid centralized financial systems, others began using cryptocurrency as an alternative investment strategy. In March 2010, the price per Bitcoin was only $0.003. If you spent just $100 on Bitcoin at that time, you would have received over 33,000 Bitcoins. By 2017, your stake would have skyrocketed to more than $625 million. Some early adopters become billionaires, such as the Winklevoss twins who are otherwise famous for their involvement in the genesis of Facebook, and who invested heavily in Bitcoin and as a result became billionaires. Roger Ver, regarded as the "Bitcoin Jesus," bought in around $1 per Bitcoin to the tune of $25,000. Today, a virtual wallet with 25,000 Bitcoins stored in it would be worth over $167.5 million. Celebrities such as 50 Cent, Snoop Dog, Johnny Depp, and Ashton Kutcher, among many others, have benefited from the proliferation of Bitcoin as well.

In January of 2017, Bitcoins were valued at just over $900 each. By December 2017, the per-Bitcoin price skyrocketed to over $19,000. In February 2021, the price cracked $50,000. The drastic rise in Bitcoin's valuation was widely broadcasted, leading to an influx of new speculative investors purchasing Bitcoin at unprecedented volumes. Individuals who bought in early and sold late profited extraordinarily. The math is even more mind boggling if you set your sights on the price of Bitcoin as a whole, from the moment the genesis block was placed.

This promise of fast riches has attracted many newcomers to Bitcoin and other cryptocurrency investments, even if they are unable to understand its technological foundation. One reason why cryptocurrency is popular for investing is that doing so is easy. Just a few clicks on the Internet and you will be set up with a virtual wallet in mere minutes on sites like Gemini, Coinbase, or Robinhood. As a result of hype and ease of use, Bitcoin transformed from an underground movement to a popular and seemingly legitimate financial product almost overnight. But Bitcoin was still new and virtually unregulated. It took some time for federal agencies to figure out who should regulate this new financial product, much less how it should be regulated.

Although the idea of sending encrypted messages is ancient, its incorporation into financial transactions has a profound impact on financial markets. Initially, blockchain was created to subvert the influence of major financial institutions. However, today these same institutions have begun to incorporate their own blockchain technology in an effort to increase security. These effects will continue to proliferate as the burgeoning cryptocurrency market grows. The next chapter will discuss the government's response to this novel digital technology and the legal and constitutional challenges that have been and will likely be raised.

BIBLIOGRAPHY

About the OCC, Office of the Comptroller of the Currency. (2020), available at https://perma.cc/U7EC-NZ3W.

Alexander, Jane, *The Anonymous Writer Who Brought Down a Prime Minister*, LONDONIST (2020), available at https://perma.cc/ZC5N-6G3JN-6G3J.

Alexandre, Ana, *New Study Says 80 Percent of ICOs Conducted in 2017 Were Scams*, COIN TELEGRAPH (July 13, 2018), available at https://perma.cc/K834-35ZE.

Arner, Douglas W. et al., *FinTech, RegTech, and the Reconceptualization of Financial Regulation*, 37 NORTHWESTERN J. INTERNATIONAL L. & BUS. 371 (2016).

Aydin, Rebecca, *This 20-year-old High School Dropout Bought $1,000 Worth of Bitcoin at the Age of 12 – Now He's Worth $4.5 Million*, BUSINESS INSIDER (August 27, 2019), https://perma.cc/H6T5-SWJC.

Baraniuk, Chris, *Bitcoin's Energy Consumption 'Equals That of Switzerland'*, BBC NEWS (July 3, 2019), available at https://perma.cc/B7MD-P7RT.

Barnett, Chance, *Inside the Meteoric Rise of ICOs*, FORBES (September 23, 2017), available at https://perma.cc/2ELQ-LUJZ.

Bitcoin v0.1 released, SATOSHI NAKAMOTO INSTITUTE (January 8, 2009), available at https://perma.cc/NLC9-55E4.

Bond, Robert *Encryption – Use and Control in E-commerce*, AMICUS CURIAE (Nov. 2000).
Brandom, Russell & Sarah Jeong, *Why the Feds Took Down One of Bitcoin's Largest Exchanges*, THE VERGE (July 29, 2017).
Brito, Jerry, Houman B. Shadab, & Andrea Castillo, *Bitcoin Financial Regulation: Securities, Derivatives, Prediction Markets, and Gambling*, 16 COLUM. SCI. & TECH. L. REV. 144 (2014).
Bruss, Dagmar et al., *Quantum Cryptography: A Survey*, 39 ACM COMPUTING SURVEYS (2007).
CHAMPAGNE, PHIL, THE BOOK OF SATOSHI: THE COLLECTED WRITINGS OF BITCOIN CREATOR SATOSHI NAKAMOTO: PHIL CHAMPAGNE (2014).
Chen, James, *Commodity Futures Trading Commission (CFTC)*, INVESTOPEDIA (April 9, 2019), available at https://perma.cc/547E-TTH9.
Chohan, Usman W., *A History of Dogecoin*, School of Business and Economics University of New South Wales Working Paper (December 20, 2017).
Choudhury, Saheli Roy, *China Just Made a Huge Move Against Cryptocurrencies*, CNBC, (September 4, 2017), available at https://perma.cc/4QMQ-KGJW.
COINBASE, *Buy and Sell Cryptocurrency*, available at www.coinbase.com/.
COINMARKETCAP (2020), available at https://coinmarketcap.com/.
Conley, John P., *Blockchain and the Economics of Crypto-tokens and Initial Coin Offerings*, Working Papers, 17-00008 VANDERBILT UNIV. DEPT. OF ECONOMICS (June 6, 2017).
D'Ambrosio, Daniel, *Plattsburgh Turns Back Invasion of Bitcoin Miners*, FORBES (October 31, 2018), available at https://perma.cc/X4LQ-7BVZ.
DE FILIPPI, PRIMAVERA & AARON WRIGHT, BLOCKCHAIN AND THE LAW: THE RULE OF CODE (2019).
De Filippi, Primavera & Benjamin Loveluck, *The Invisible Politics of Bitcoin: Governance Crisis of a Decentralized Infrastructure*, 5 INTERNET POLICY REVIEW (October 17, 2016).
De, Nikhilesh, *Another Ripple Lawsuit Claims XRP Is a Security*, COINDESK (July 5, 2018), available at https://perma.cc/THD2-5NCH
Dominguez, Nick, *6 Most Logical Theories Why Satoshi Nakamoto Disappeared* (January 31, 2020), available at https://perma.cc/ZU64-TFWB.
Feng, C., N. Li, M. H. Wong, and M. Zhang, *Initial Coin Offerings, Blockchain Technology, and White Paper Disclosures*, SSRN (October 12, 2018).
Fisher, Tim, *Nodes in a Computer Network Explained*, LIFEWIRE (November 19, 2019), available at https://perma.cc/H6JY-3GQU.
Enforcement, Federal Trade Commission (2020), available at https://perma.cc/6VKR-LE2H.
Fitzpatrick, Luke, *Bitcoin Cash to Surpass BTC Market Cap, Says Roger Ver*, FORBES MAGAZINE (December 20, 2019), available at https://perma.cc/4KPA-SPBS.
Frankel, Matthew, *You'll Be Shocked by How Much $10 Invested in Bitcoin in 2010 Is Worth Today*, THE MOTLEY FOOL (September 24, 2017), available at https://perma.cc/7LE2-SUKL.
FTC Shuts Down Promoters of Deceptive Cryptocurrency Schemes, FEDERAL TRADE COMMISSION (March 16, 2018), available at https://perma.cc/RFW7-6P2S.
GEMINI, *Buy Bitcoin and Crypto Instantly!*, available at https://gemini.com/.
Gillespie, Patrick, *Venezuela Tries a Cryptocurrency to Solve Its Economic Crisis*, CNN MONEY (February 20, 2018), available at https://perma.cc/Y2TX-JTVR.
Graham, Luke, *As China Cracks Down, Japan Is Fast Becoming the Powerhouse of the Bitcoin Market*, CNBC (September 29, 2017), available at https://perma.cc/B736-DD8W.
Gruben, William C. & John H. Welch, *Banking and Currency Crisis Recovery: Brazil's Turnaround of 1999*, 2001 ECON. & FIN. POL'Y REV. 12–23 (2001).
Guo, Ye & Chen Liang, *Blockchain Application and Outlook in the Banking Industry*, 2 FINANCIAL INNOVATION (2016).

Guzman, Z., *50 Cent 'Forgot' He Had Bitcoin – Now It's Worth over $7 million*, BBC News (January 26, 2018.), available at https://perma.cc/T478-SU8A.

Hamrick, J. T. et al., *An Examination of the Cryptocurrency Pump and Dump Ecosystem*, available at SSRN 3303365 (2018).

Hu, A., C. Parlour, and Rajan, *Cryptocurrencies: Stylized Facts on a New Investible Instrument*, Electronic Journal (May 3, 2018).

Hughes, Eric, *A Cypherpunk's Manifesto*, Satoshi Nakamoto Institute (March 9, 1993), available at https://perma.cc/TD9X-9CTR.

Hunter, D. & C. Op den Kemp, A History of Intellectual Property in 50 Objects (2019).

Kharpal, A., *A Cryptocurrency Start-up Disappeared with $375,000 from an ICO and Nobody Can Find Them*, CNBC (November 22, 2017), available at https://perma.cc/6FDA-QQVB.

Kharpal, A., *Another Country Regulates ICOs for Cryptocurrency Funding – But Still Warns of 'Many Risks'*, CNBC (October 9, 2017), available at https://perma.cc/R5FA-7UMR.

Kotow, Emily, *Quantum Blockchain*, Hedgetrade (June 8, 2019), available at https://perma.cc/LHJ8-BRJC.

Lehner, Edward & John R. Ziegler, *Free Information, Not Free Labor*, CUNY Academic Works (2019).

Levy, Steven, *Crypto Rebels*, Wired Magazine (February 1, 1993).

Li, J. and Mann, W., *Initial Coin Offering and Platform Building*, SSRN Electronic Journal (January 31, 2018).

Long, Tony, *May 9, 1941: German Sub Caught with the Goods*, Wired Magazine (May 9, 2011).

Lopp, Jameson, *Bitcoin and the Rise of the Cypherpunks* (April 9, 2016), available at https://perma.cc/FS5G-LA59.

Matt, *What Is Ethereum*, Mycryptopedia (October 30, 2018), available at https://perma.cc/7P4P-L5Z3.

McGrath Goodman, Leah, *The Face Behind Bitcoin*, Newsweek (March 6, 2014 6:05 AM).

Meyer v. Nebraska, 262 U.S. 390 (1923).

Murphy, Hannah and Philip Strafford, *Zuckerberg Held Talks with Winklevoss Twins about New Currency*, Financial Times (May 23, 2019).

Nakamoto, Satoshi, *Bitcoin P2P e-cash paper*, Satoshi Nakamoto Institute (October 31, 2008 6:10 UTC), available at https://perma.cc/4ACC-9BH4.

North, M., *Bitcoin Network Surpasses 100,000 Nodes, New Data Shows*, Bitcoinist (May 6, 2019), available at https://perma.cc/Q7CN-WBHV.

Oranburg, Seth C., *Hyperfunding: Regulating Financial Innovations*, 89 University of Colorado Law Review 1033 (2018).

Our History, Federal Trade Commission (2020), available at https://perma.cc/JBS3-V6XF.

Pagliery, Jose, *FBI Shuts Down Online Drug Market Silk Road*, CNN (October 2, 2013).

Pan, D., *Vanguard Developing Blockchain Platform for $6 Trillion Forex Market*, CoinDesk (October 9, 2019), available at https://perma.cc/V3AY-CSE5.

Penenberg, Adam L., *The Bitcoin Crypto-Currency Mystery Reopened*, Fast Company, (October 11, 2011), available at https://perma.cc/M4SX-P277.

Ramírez, P., and R. Moynihan, *13 Celebrities Who Back Cryptocurrency and May Own Millions in Bitcoin*, (January 20, 2019), available at https://perma.cc/HCM9-293J.

Raskin, Max, *The Law and Legality of Smart Contracts*, 1 Georgetown Law Technology Review 305 (2017).

Rep. Soto Introduces Bipartisan Bills Preventing Virtual Currency Price Manipulation, House.gov. (2018), available at https://perma.cc/LZ9B-LZPQ.

Ripple, *The Financial Network of the Future: Easily Run a High-Performance Global Payments Business*, available at https://ripple.com/ripplenet/.
Ripple, *XRP – A Digital Asset Built for Global Payments* (2020), available at https://ripple.com/xrp/.
ROBINHOOD, *Investing for Everyone*, https://robinhood.com/us/en/.
Rogow, Geoffrey, Alexander Osipovich & Rachael Levy, *Tweets and Articles Sent Kodak Shares Surging Before Official Announcement*, WSJ (July 29, 2020), available at https://perma.cc/4LWW-5ZY6.
Rogow, Geoffrey and Michael Wursthorn, *Fortunes Won and Lost Trading in Kodak Stock: Inside a Wild Week*, THE WALL STREET JOURNAL (August 6, 2020).
Rooney, Kate, *SEC Chief Says Agency Won't Change Securities Laws to Cater to Cryptocurrencies*, CNBC Online (June 6, 2018).
Rooney, Kate, *Bipartisan Lawmakers Seek Cryptocurrency Rules to Protect Consumers and Keep US Competitive*, CNBC (December 6, 2018), available at https://perma.cc/YGM2-837J.
Rooney, Kate, *SEC Takes First Action Against a Crypto Hedge Fund*, CNBC (September 11, 2018), available at https://perma.cc/N8PH-FKJ9.
Rooney, Kate, *Federal Judge Says SEC Rules Apply to Initial Coin Offering*, CNBC (September 11, 2018), available at https://perma.cc/XY62-L9Y5.
Rosic, A., *What is Litecoin?*, BLOCKGEEKS (2020), available at https://perma.cc/TH25-LBLJ.
Russel, J., *Former Mozilla CEO Raises $35 M in Under 30 seconds for his Browser Startup Brave*, TECHCRUNCH (June 1, 2017), available at https://perma.cc/7295-SK2D.
Satoshi Nakamoto Is Female: Women in the Cryptocurrency Industry, BITCOINIST (May 22, 2018 2:00PM), available at https://perma.cc/53PT-J9S6.
SEC, *Filing Review Process*, U.S. Securities and Exchange Commission. www.sec.gov/divisions/corpfin/cffilingreview.htm.
SEC, *Spotlight on Initial Coin Offerings (ICOs)*, U.S. Securities and Exchange Commission (2018), available at https://perma.cc/8AGQ-8YFH.
SEC, *Leaders of CFTC, FinCEN, and SEC Issue Joint Statement on Activities Involving Digital Assets*, Securities Exchange Commission (October 11, 2019), available at https://perma.cc/S9NA-HFAQ.
SEC v. S.G. Ltd., 265 F.3d 42 (2001).
SEC v. W.J. Howey Co., 328 U.S. 293.
Sedgwick, K., *Benebit ICO Does a Runner with $2.7 Million of Investor Funds*, BITCOIN NEWS (January 23, 2018), available at https://perma.cc/XF4R-JQUY.
SHA create hash online, unit-conversion.info. Website that allows you to create algorithms, available at www.unit-conversion.info/texttools/sha/#data.
Sharma, R., *SEC Chair Says Bitcoin Is Not a Security*, INVESTOPEDIA (June 29, 2015), available at https://perma.cc/P4TF-7PER.
Shi, Ning, *A New Proof-of-Work Mechanism for Bitcoin*, 2 FINANCIAL INNOVATION (2016).
Shin, L., *$15 Million ICO Halted By SEC for Being Alleged Scam*, FORBES (December 4, 2017).
Son, H., *JP Morgan Rolls Out First US bank-Backed Cryptocurrency to Transform Payments Business*, CNBC (February 14, 2019), available at https://perma.cc/9T85-7RW7.
Sun, Jianjun et al., *Blockchain-Based Sharing Services: What Blockchain Technology Can Contribute to Smart Cities*, 2 FINANCIAL INNOVATION (2016).
The Token Taxonomy Act of 2019, H.R. 2144 (2018).
The U.S. Virtual Currency Market and Regulatory Competitiveness Act of 2018, H.R. 7225 (2018).

The Virtual Currency Consumer Protection Act of 2018, H.R. 7224 (2018).
Token Taxonomy Act to Address Blockchain, Innovation Flight in America, House.gov. (April 9, 2019), available at https://perma.cc/A893-XVXA.
Toomey, Patrick, *The NSA Continues to Violate Americans' Internet Privacy Rights*, American Civil Liberties Union (August 22, 2018).
US DOJ, *Former Federal Agents Charged with Bitcoin Money Laundering and Wire Fraud*, Department of Justice, Public Affairs (March 30, 2015).
U.S. SECURITIES EXCHANGE COMMISSION, *What We Do* (SEC 2013).
Vareschi, Mark, *Frankenstein and Anonymous Authorship in Eighteenth-Century Britain*, UNIVERSITY OF WISCONSIN–MADISON (January 18, 2019).
Verhage, J., *E*Trade Is Close to Launching Cryptocurrency Trading*, BLOOMBERG (April 26, 2019), available at https://perma.cc/6652-GAPQ.
Vigna, P., *SEC Chief Fires Warning Shot Against Coin Offerings*, THE WALL STREET JOURNAL (November 9, 2017).
Weisenthal, Joe, *Here's the Problem with the New Theory that Japanese Maths Professor Satoshi Nakamoto Is the Inventor Of Bitcoin*, BUSINESS INSIDER (May 20, 2013), available at https://perma.cc/HEB3-SZPN.
Williams, G., *What Is a Digital Wallet?*, US NEWS & WORLD REPORT (May 21, 2019), available at https://money.usnews.com/money/personal-finance/saving-and-budgeting/articles/what-is-a-digital-wallet.
Xu, Jennifer J., *Are Blockchains Immune to All Malicious Attacks?*, 2 FINANCIAL INNOVATION (2016).
Yan, S. and Wallace, G., *Mt.Gox CEO's U.S. Assets Frozen*, CNN BUSINESS (March 12, 2014), available at https://perma.cc/8CSB-QC8J.
Yli-Huumo, J. et al., *Where Is Current Research on Blockchain Technology?-A Systematic Review*, 11 PLOS ONE (2016).
Zakinov v. Ripple Labs, Inc., 369 F. supp. 950 (20920).
Zhao, J. Leon et al., *Overview of Business Innovations and Research Opportunities in Blockchain and Introduction to the Special Issue*, 2 FINANCIAL INNOVATION (2016).
Zhu, Huasheng & Zach Zhizhong Zhou, *Analysis and Outlook of Applications of Blockchain Technology to Equity Crowdfunding in China*, 2 FINANCIAL INNOVATION (2016).

10

Cryptocurrency Regulation

Cryptocurrency arose from open-source technology developed by anarchists. But its anti-government origins will not stop governments from trying to regulate cryptocurrency – or from creating GovCoins, cryptocurrencies owned by governments. As various cryptocurrencies go mainstream and because a larger part of national economies and international commerce, the question is by who and how – not whether – they will be regulated. In America, there are Constitutional constraints that should impact the answer to this question. The First Amendment ensures the right of free speech, and the Supreme Court has ruled that spending money constitutes speech. That same amendment provides an implied right to privacy. Since cryptocurrency involves spending money in a private way, it must have some Constitutional protections. Other Amendments and Constitutional principles bolster these rights to use cryptocurrency. But that right is not unlimited and might be regulated by some agency or another. Many agencies are vying for authority over cryptocurrency, but none seems ideally suited for the task. Perhaps some new cryptocurrency regulator should be created, lest foreign governments seize the initiative and assert themselves as the global authority over this nascent financial technology.

> You can't stop things like Bitcoin, it's like trying to stop gunpowder. It will be everywhere, and the world will have to readjust. World governments will have to readjust.
>
> – John McAfee, founder of McAfee Inc., who was later arrested for tax evasion

The last chapter introduced you to cryptocurrency and blockchain technology and discussed its impact on financial markets. This chapter focuses on the regulatory and constitutional aspects of cryptocurrency.

As we have seen financial markets evolve over the last two centuries, so have legal landscapes. In the digital age, "Crypto" and encryption technologies pose an array of constitutional questions, although few have been litigated thus far. This chapter explores the various agency, legal, and constitutional frameworks that could be applied to answer difficult questions regarding these novel technologies.

WHO REGULATES DIGITAL ASSETS?

Cryptocurrency is so new that it still has not been totally decided who should regulate cryptocurrency transactions and how they should be regulated. Moreover, the number of different kinds of cryptocurrencies have exploded in recent years. Although major cryptocurrencies in 2021 include Bitcoin, Ethereum, Ripple, Bitcoin Cash, Cardano, Stellar, and Litecoin, and these make up the majority of the cryptocurrency market, there are thousands of other cryptocurrencies. Each cryptocurrency has its own features that make it seem more or less like existing financial instruments that are already regulated by one federal agency or another.

There are several U.S. federal agencies who vie for top candidates for cryptocurrency regulator. They include the Securities and Exchange Commission (SEC), the Federal Trade Commission (FTC), and the Commodity Futures Trading Commission (CFTC). In addition, foreign government agencies (FGAs), international government agencies (IGAs), and nongovernmental organizations (NGOs) may attempt to assert some jurisdiction over certain aspects of cryptocurrency regulation.

But note that cryptocurrencies were invented and designed to avoid regulation. Comprehensive regulation of cryptocurrencies requires a new way of thinking about how financial regulation works in this third era of international and internet financial regulation. Governments cannot simply demand command and control of

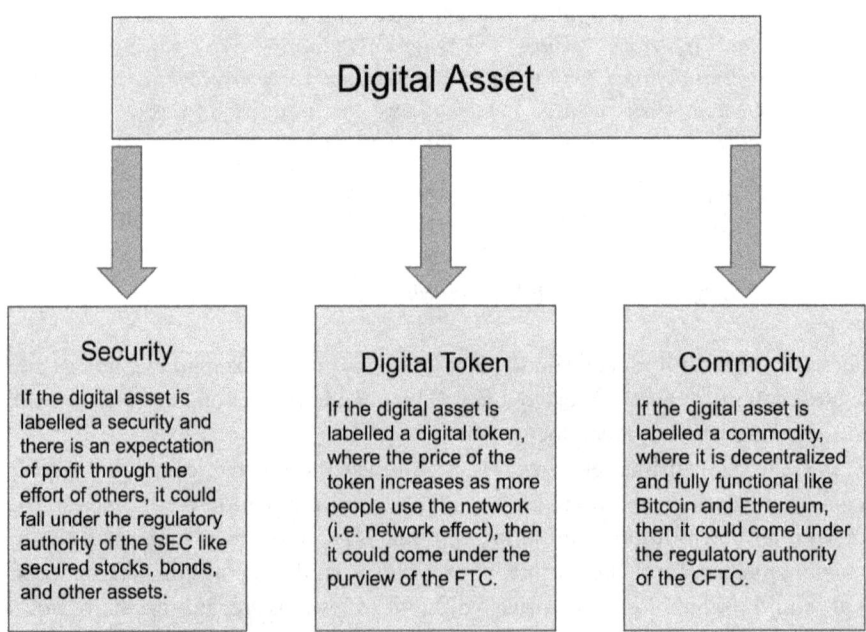

FIGURE 10.1 Regulation of Digital Assets.

cryptocurrency; rather, they must intelligently design systems that make socially beneficially cryptocurrency use preferable.

The primary challenge with regulating cryptocurrencies is that they can be used for different purposes and come in different forms. Our regulatory agencies are generally set up to have jurisdiction over certain kinds of transactions and instruments. Cryptocurrencies and more broadly digital assets do not neatly fall into any one category. Each digital asset must therefore be analyzed individually to under who may regulate it and how it should be regulated.

SEC REGULATION OF CRYPTO-SECURITIES

The SEC, as its name implies, regulates securities. What, then, is a security? The Court created a four-factor test to determine whether or not something is a security. The so-called "Howey Test" considers whether the scheme involves (1) an investment of money, (2) an expectation of profit from that investment, (3) the investment of money in a common enterprise, and (4) profits from the efforts of a promoter or third party. Cryptocurrencies come in many varieties with unique properties. Some cryptocurrencies meet the "Howey Test," definition, while many do not, making them hard to categorically regulate.

The SEC is responsible for enforcing current securities laws, proposing new securities rules, and providing general oversight of the investment industry. It monitors the nation's stock exchanges as well as publicly traded companies to ensure compliance. The Commission seems, at least initially, to be the ideal agency to regulate cryptocurrencies. Under current law, however, the SEC's jurisdiction is limited by the Howey Test.

SEC v. Howey

The Howey Test was created by the Supreme Court in the 1946 case *Securities and Exchange Commission v. W. J. Howey Co. et al.* The Howey Company owned large tracts of land in Florida where it planted orange groves. They planted some acres for themselves, but then offered half of the groves for sale to the public. Howey Co. promised to cultivate the land, harvest the crops, and distribute accrued profits to those who purchased the parcels. The Court found that this was an investment masquerading as a sale. This was similar to purchasing stock in a publicly traded company because the parcels of land acted as stock, thereby representing partial ownership in The Howey Company. The profit distributions functioned as dividends paid to investors. The Court held that the purchases of land in the *Howey* case were securities because individuals invested money with an expectation of profit from a common enterprise as a result of The Howey Company's labor to cultivate and care for the orange groves. Being classified as securities, the orange groves were thereby subject to SEC regulation.

This had the effect of an investment even though it did not follow any traditional form of investment. *Howey* teaches us that substance and not form of an instrument determines whether it is a security. Whether cryptocurrencies are securities depends on how a particular cryptocurrency functions. But it is hard to predict how a court would apply the Howey Test to a novel cryptocurrency technology. This uncertainty leads some companies to ignore SEC regulations, while it discourages others from forming in the first place. Many ICOs have been specifically designed to fail the Howey Test so they can avoid the classification as securities, thereby skirting SEC guidelines.

November 2017, SEC chairman Jay Clayton stated, "I have yet to see an ICO that doesn't have a sufficient number of hallmarks of a security." With this statement, the SEC is explicitly exerting regulatory control over ICOs and Security Tokens. Ultimately, however, many cryptocurrencies exist outside the SEC's reach because the Howey-Test is not an all-encompassing test.

Coffey *v.* Ripple Labs Inc.

The threat of securities litigation against cryptocurrency issuers may be heightened by the Superior Court of California's decision in *Coffey* v. *Ripple Labs Inc.* (2018). The plaintiff in that case alleged that Ripple created XRP "tokens" and then engaged in an ongoing "scheme" to sell XRP to the general public. The plaintiff contends that XRP tokens constitute a security because purchasers of the tokens invested their fiat currency into a common enterprise, Ripple, and expected to derive profits from their ownership of XRP.

What distinguishes the purchase of XRP from purchasing stock in any other publicly traded company is that in purchasing XRP, however, the XRP purchaser does not receive any ownership stake in Ripple. Instead, acquiring XRP merely provides the purchaser with a cryptocurrency they can use over the RippleNet as a means of exchange with other entities that also exchange XRP tokens. For this reason, XRP appears not to meet the *Howey* test for a security.

However, the SEC found that Ripple managers made "undeniably significant" effort to curate valuable opportunities on which XRP tokens could be spent on RippleNet. This curation process, according to the SEC, elevated XRP to the status of a security. Ripple's CEO Brad Garlinghouse wrote a blog post explaining why, in his opinion, the SEC is simply wrong. As of the time of this book's publication, the case is still playing out in federal court. In the meantime, however, XRP's value has been dashed. The cloud of uncertainty that hangs over XRP has driven many would-be investors to other, less contentious prospects.

INITIAL COIN OFFERINGS

The SEC has maintained that two of the most popular cryptocurrencies, Bitcoin and Ethereum, are not securities. Instead, they are viewed as commodities, which are regulated by the CFTC. Initial Coin Offerings (ICOs), on the other hand, are transactions in securities according to the SEC and fall under relevant securities laws. This distinction between commodity or security is important because most issues arise when cryptocurrencies are misclassified as securities. Understanding why an ICO of a cryptocurrency is a securities transaction even when the cryptocurrency itself is not a security provides vital insights into understanding how cryptocurrencies may and should be regulated in the future.

A distinction must be made to separate the term "cryptocurrencies" from ICOs. Standing alone, the term "cryptocurrency" is a digital asset created and designed to be a means of exchange utilizing advanced cryptographical procedures to verify and secure the transfer of value between users – Bitcoin, Litecoin, Ether, to name a few. On its own, Bitcoin and other many other cryptocurrencies are not securities. They are "replacements for sovereign currencies" similar to U.S. dollar, the yen, or the euro. In this capacity, cryptocurrencies are no different than any other currency we use every day, aside from the fact that they do not come in a physical form. As long as two contracting parties agree to use a particular cryptocurrency, they are free to exchange it for goods or services in the same fashion as we exchange U.S. treasury bills for a particular good or service with a local business. Divergence from this straightforward manner of use is where it gets murky.

One major divergence occurs where cryptocurrencies are used as investments instead of as means of exchange. Initial Coin Offerings (ICOs) can be likened to the Initial Public Offerings (IPOs) discussed in Chapter 7. Both are designed to help companies raise funds for a particular business venture. In a traditional IPO, a corporation creates and registers new issue of stock with the SEC. The corporation creates then sells that stock to an underwriter at the underwriter's price. Then the underwriter quickly resells that stock on a public stock market like the New York Stock Exchange or the NASDAQ for the issue price. When the issue price is at least 5 percent greater than the underwriter's price, the IPO is considered to be a hot issue. If the issue is hot, the stock price is likely to rise as the people who initially bought the stock at the issue price from the underwriter resell it for a higher price. Eventually, the price stabilizes at the market price. In this way, underwriters take most of the risk and get most of the reward for the change in stock price immediately after the IPO.

An ICO is similar to an IPO insofar as they both involve the creation of a new security which is sold to the public who may then resell it. But these two financial transactions are very different in that IPOs are highly regulated and almost completely standardized, whereas ICOs are almost totally unregulated and can range from IPO-like transactions to flat-out scams.

Although one might expect investors to prefer IPOs to ICOs because IPOs are more regulated and therefore safer, there are many reasons why IPOs are inappropriate and even impossible for most fundraising operations. Conducting an IPO, however, is no simple feat. Companies should expect to spend one to five million dollars on out-of-pocket costs associated with going public through an IPO.

Moreover, the regulatory requirements may occupy the company's executive leadership for several months. Given that they interfere with doing business while costing millions of dollars, IPOs have grown less popular as public-company regulations have increased.

The great difficulty in orchestrating an IPO is consistent with the theme that too much regulation stifles innovation and decreases efficiency. Congress has set forth heavy burdens in their mandatory disclosure requirements for companies who wish to become publicly traded. Although Congress' intent was to protect unsophisticated investors from the dangers of the free market, the requirements for an IPO have become unduly costly in our information age. This is evidenced by the fact many organizations choose to hold private offerings through one of the Securities Act exemptions, rather than listing publicly. Those private-offering exceptions are discussed in Chapter 7.

But not all companies and transactions fit into one of the private-offering exemption regulatory safe harbors. Some such companies and transactions sought ICOs as a means to fundraise where traditional legal avenues were closed to them. The cryptocurrency world crafted the new ICO mechanism to solve the costly IPO dilemma. The SEC is just beginning to understand and explain how to regulate these ICOs.

Blockchain startups have embraced ICOs as a vehicle to raise early capital for a wide varied set of roles on different platforms. Part of the challenge with regulating IPOs is that they come in so many different forms. In a typical ICO, to the extent that one can truly call an IPO typical, an entrepreneur presells virtual tokens which will later serve as the medium of exchange on a peer-to-peer platform. Some tokens are similar to currencies while others act more like securities in a publicly traded company, and even more have properties that are entirely new. The sheer volume and speed of ICOs allow people to raise millions of dollars in as short as thirty seconds.

It is tempting to find false parallels between IPOs and ICOs. For example, in an IPO, the issuer and the underwriter must produce a voluminous prospectus, which includes all the marketing, accounting, business, legal, and other information that an investor needs to make an investment decision. The contents of the prospectus are governed by decades of federal statutes, SEC regulations, stock exchange rules, generally accepted accounting principles, and established expectations and traditions. The SEC may subject the prospectus to a full cover-to-cover review. SEC staff may provide comments that must be addressed by the company in order to enhance compliance with applicable requirements. If an issue engages in fraudulent conduct during an IPO, the SEC can investigate and press civil and criminal charges.

ICOs might go off without any regulatory review at all. Although most ICOs are backed up by so-called white papers, a term that apparently originated in England around 1920 to describe policy documents, such as Winston Churchill's 1922 plan titled "Palestine. Correspondence with the Palestine Araba Delegation and the

Zionist Organisation," which maintained England's commitment to the Balfour Declaration and its promise of a Jewish homeland in Israel. In cryptocurrency white papers, coin issuers concisely explain their novel technology. But these white papers are not even subject to peer review, much less government review. ICOs may be conducted by anonymous or pseudonymous parties, limiting, or eliminating, the ability to bring these issuers to court to answer for fraud or other crimes. Or they can be entirely legitimate and profitable. The issue with all these different ICOs is the same problem we see with cryptocurrencies as a whole: there is no one size fits all test to determine whether or not they fall under SEC regulatory reach.

Even ICOs can be broken down into smaller classes. There are at least two types of tokens issued in ICOs. First there are Utility Tokens which allow buyers to access and pay for usage of the blockchain software. Second, there are Security Tokens. Security Tokens are more akin to shares listed in an IPO. They are distributed to purchasers and grant voting power just like shares in a publicly traded company permit the shareholder to vote. In some cases, ICOs even offer a share of the company's profits. ICOs are rapidly growing as the red tape-free method to raising capital quickly with the potential to dwarf Venture Capital fundraising in the coming years. Unfortunately, even though ICOs have been labeled as securities, it is difficult for the SEC to properly regulate them because many operate outside of the United States.

Investors in ICOs generally do not have much information about the venture – all that is needed is a "white paper" providing basic information about the project. Contrast this with the extensive mandatory disclosures required for IPOs. As a result, white papers vary in style and in what they disclose. With zero legislative structure for guidance, hackers and other nefarious fraudsters have taken advantage of ICOs as exit scams.

ICO Fraud

A wide range of examples already exist regarding ICO fraud. The ICO advisory firm Statis Group recently published a study claiming more than 80 percent of ICOs conducted in 2017 were scams. In November of 2017, Confido, a cryptocurrency startup, raised $375,000 through one such ICO before vanishing with investors' money. Another company, Benebit, pulled a similar scam and made off with at least $2.7 million. The SEC stepped in and froze the assets of PlexCoin in December of 2017 after they raised over $15 million and promised investors profits of 1,354 percent within a single month. In 2015, two federal agents were indicted and charged with wire fraud, money laundering and theft of virtual currency during their joint investigation into the Silk Road.

There have been some instances of judicial action. A federal judge in Brooklyn refused to throw out a case in 2018 where the defendant argued two cryptocurrencies were beyond the reach of federal securities laws. Although Judge Raymond Dearie stopped short of defining RECoin and Diamond, the two cryptocurrencies at issue, as securities, he did say that a jury should be able to assess them using existing laws, namely, the Howey Test.

The distinction between currency or security is important because most issues arise when cryptocurrencies are misclassified as securities. IPOs are too costly and too time consuming. Only large corporations can afford to host an IPO. The disparity in one's ability to raise funds has led to the swing away from the nonymous environment of the current market. Instead, people choose to operate in an unregulated space because it is cheaper. Some scammers may incidentally prefer that it is a pseudonymous alternative, if not entirely anonymous. Although some endeavors are credible, there is still a high risk involved.

REGULATION OF CRYPTOCURRENCIES

Cryptocurrencies are novel and varied, making them hard to define. This definitional problem leads to overlapping authorities by various regulatory bodies. The United Stated Congress, the Federal Bureau of Investigation (FBI), the Commodity Futures Trading Commission (CFTC), the Internal Revenue Service (IRS), the Federal Trade Commission (FTC), the Office of the Comptroller of Currency (OCC), individual states, cities, and even foreign governmental agencies (FGAs) have asserted their jurisdiction over cryptocurrencies and imposed regulations according to this purported authority. In addition, cryptocurrencies are privately regulated by miners and other market participants. To make matters even more confusing, there is always the prospect of some new agency being created to regulate cryptocurrencies. Moreover, cryptocurrencies are decentralized. They are designed by crypto-anarchists to resist regulation by anything other than consensus amid users.

Congressional Regulation of Cryptocurrencies

There has been little statutory intervention against cryptocurrencies as whole. This is true, at least in some part, because confusion still exists around blockchain technology and cryptocurrencies. U.S. Rep. Darren Soto, (D-FL), and U.S. Rep. Ted Budd, (R-NC), cosponsored two bipartisan bills in 2018 that sought to alleviate some of that confusion. The bills titled "The Virtual Currency Consumer Protection Act of 2018" (VCCPA) and "The U.S. Virtual Currency Market and Regulatory Competitiveness Act of 2018" (VCMRCA) were aimed to allow for innovation in the developing market while protecting U.S. consumers. They also were designed to facilitate the development of a description and classification system that would grant current agencies the ability to regulate cryptocurrencies. The two separate pieces of legislation work in tandem to accomplish the goal of creating a safe market. The legislation states that virtual currency means any digital representation of value that does not have legal tender status and that functions as a medium of exchange, a unit of account, or a store of value.

Two important provisions exist in the VCCPA, which are intended to aid in promoting the policymakers' goal of providing safe innovation in this arena. The first provision states that the CFTC, along with the SEC, will submit a report that will help position the United States to implement policies to become a leader in the virtual currency market while protecting consumers. This report will include a brief description discussing manipulation of the prices of virtual currencies, an analysis of how the CFTC and other agencies currently address virtual currencies and provide recommendations on future legislation to increase the effectiveness of regulation in this realm. The bill aims to identify possible issues in the virtual currency sphere, analyze what is currently being done to address those issues, and then create new solutions for those issues. It is mainly geared toward research so that the United States can better understand cryptocurrencies in general. To properly regulate cryptocurrencies, we must first fully understand them.

FBI Regulation of Cryptocurrencies

The FBI is charged with conducting domestic intelligence and is the primary security service of the United States. As the lead agency in day-to-day national security functions, the FBI must prevent cryptocurrencies from being used for nefarious ends, such as domestic terrorism, the drug trade, and organized crime.

The first intervention by the U.S. government over cryptocurrencies occurred in 2013 when the FBI shut down the Silk Road – the dark web black market. Then in 2014, Mt. Gox's CEO, Mark Karpeles, had his U.S. assets frozen after over 1.75 million Bitcoins vanished from the Mt. Gox website.

But the FBI does not have a cybercrime strategy that comprehensively addresses cryptocurrency. In fact, the Department of Justice Office of Inspector General (OIG) issued a report to the FBI in December 2020 calling for the FBI to develop a plan to systematically disrupt illegal activities on the web, including those facilitated by the anonymous and pseudonymous nature of cryptocurrencies and blockchain transactions. Thus, one might expect the FBI to more aggressively seek to regulate cryptocurrencies in the future.

CFTC Regulation of Cryptocurrencies

The CFTC is another independent federal agency that could potentially regulate the cryptocurrency market. The CFTC was created to regulate the commodity futures and options markets. It is tasked with "the promotion of competitive and efficient futures markets and the protection of investors against manipulation, abusive trade practices, and fraud." They, along with the SEC and the Financial Crimes Enforcement Network (FinCEN), recently issued a joint statement regarding cryptocurrencies. In it, the agencies set forth a reminder that activities involving "digital assets" are still subject to the anti-money laundering obligations financial institutions must abide by under the Bank Secrecy Act. The release also noted that the CFTC has jurisdiction over commodity futures and a wide array of derivatives, such as interest rate swaps.

The CFTC's jurisdiction over cryptocurrencies is not clear, but recent legislation seeks to clarify its dominion over cryptocurrency regulation. H.R. 923, the U.S. Virtual Currency Market and Regulatory Competitiveness Act (VCMRCA) of 2019, is a bill that would direct the CFTC to report on virtual currency markets and U.S. competitiveness. It is directly focused on making the U.S. a leader in the global virtual currency market. This bill tasks the CFTC, in consultation with other agencies, to provide a report to congressional committees in order to better understand what cryptocurrencies are and how to regulate them. The report will include: (1) a comparative study of U.S. regulation on the virtual currency industry and of the regulation of the virtual currency industry by foreign countries, (2) an analysis of the possible benefits of virtual currencies and the underlying blockchain technology in the U.S. commodities market, then (3) conclude with recommendations on legislative changes to promote competitiveness in the industry. The bill is designed to encourage growth of virtual currencies, clarify virtual currencies as commodities for existing and future currencies, and to create a new regulatory structure for virtual currency markets.

IRS Regulation of Cryptocurrencies

U.S. Rep. Soto and U.S. Rep. Budd joined U.S. Rep. Warren Davidson, U.S. Rep. Josh Gottheimer, U.S. Rep. Scott Perry and U.S. Rep. Tulsi Gabbard in introducing "The Token Taxonomy Act" in 2019, around the same time as the VCMRCA. The bill explicitly defines "digital token" as a digital unit that is not a representation of a financial interest in a company, and then proposes amending the Securities Exchange Act to exclude "digital tokens." U.S. Rep. Davidson stated, "as blockchain technology continues to emerge, it is clear that there must be a framework in place that not only provides a much clearer path forward for open blockchain projects, but also will establish the United States as a leading force in this space."

FTC Regulation of Cryptocurrencies

The Federal Trade Commission (FTC) was created to protect consumers and promote competition. It enforces antitrust laws and federal consumer protection laws to prevent fraud or unfair business practices. Perhaps the FTC is best suited to become the agency that exerts control over the cryptocurrency world. In 2018, the FTC filed a complaint against four individuals who were alleged to be promoting deceptive "money-making schemes involving cryptocurrencies." The FTC was able to target those individuals because, as a single agency, the FTC is afforded a larger range of oversight so they are able to adequately protect and promote competition. Yet, despite having this broader reach, it does not extend far enough tocover all cryptocurrencies.

OCC Regulation of Cryptocurrencies

The Office of the Comptroller of the Currency (OCC) was created to "ensure that national banks and federal savings associations operate in a safe and sound manner, provide fair access to financial services, treat customers fairly, and comply with applicable laws and regulations." The OCC may be better suited for regulating cryptocurrencies used in the United States by current banks and financial institutions. In February 2019, JPMorgan created the "JPM Coin," a digital token they intend to use for settling transactions instantly between clients within their network, similar to the use of XRP. The JPM Coin only operates on a private network within JPMorgan, and only between JPMorgan business units, in contrast to Bitcoin which operates on a public network that any person can join. The OCC might be the agency that could regulate this arena most effectively when cryptocurrencies are localized to private institutional networks such as JPMorgan's. This, of course, will not solve the entire problem because there are few cryptocurrencies that exist in such a controlled and localized format, necessitating a broader focus.

Local Regulation of Cryptocurrencies

In other cases, intervention came in the form of blanket regulatory action. One such instance occurred in 2018 when the City Council of Plattsburgh, New York issued an eighteen-month moratorium on new cryptocurrency mining operations.

Cryptocurrency mining is the process of rewarding people for validating cryptocurrency transactions. Without detailing how mining works varies based on how each cryptocurrency itself works, the overall concept is that people with a huge amount of computer power use those computers to confirm that transactions posted to a blockchain must have been authentically created. In the case of Bitcoin, the first miner to validate the current block of transactions is rewarded with a new Bitcoin (or a fraction of a Bitcoin) attributed to them in the next block. A vast amount of electrical power is required to operate such computers.

The quiet town of Plattsburgh was first targeted by bitcoin mining companies because it offered cheap rates per kilowatt consumed thanks to its proximity to the St. Lawrence River and the neighboring hydro-powerplant. When cryptocurrency mining companies came to town the citizens of Plattsburgh saw a spike in their energy prices by as much as 50 percent. Mining rigs consume enormous amounts of energy. The City Council imposed the moratorium to lift the energy burden the Bitcoin mining rigs placed on their independent citizens.

Non-U.S. Regulation of Cryptocurrencies

The VCCPA and the VCMRCA are not straightforward regulations that actually regulate the industry, they are designed to enhance our nation's understanding. While the United States has not enacted legislation to actively regulate cryptocurrencies, other countries have gotten the ball rolling. Abu Dhabi's Financial Services Regulatory Authority (FSRA) stated that, "if an ICO has the characteristics of a security, such as giving a person ownership of shares in the company, then the FSRA will regulate it" just as it would if they were a company issuing stock. A company wishing to execute an ICO is required to approach the FSRA to see if it will fall under their purview and publish a prospectus just like a firm entering into an IPO would be required to do.

China, on the other hand, has put an outright ban on ICOs from being used to raise funds. The China Securities Regulatory Commission, China Banking Regulatory Commission, People's Bank of China and China Insurance Regulatory Commission released a joint statement where they said ICOs will be regarded as illegal fund-raising activity. In stark contrast, Japan has embraced cryptocurrencies. In September 2017, Japan's Financial Services Agency officially recognized eleven companies as registered cryptocurrency exchange operators. In registering, the companies are required to build a "strong" computer system to support their cryptocurrency and check the identity of users to prevent money laundering. Japan even officially recognized Bitcoin as legal tender.

In February 2018, Venezuela's government launched the world's first sovereign cryptocurrency dubbed "The Petro" (₽). The Venezuelan government claimed that ₽ is linked to the value of its fiat currency (the bolivar) and backed by the country's reserves of crude oil and precious metals. But ₽ provides no ownership stake in these natural resources, nor did the government explain how such a cryptocurrency could be "linked" to fiat money while acting as an independent reserve currency. The Brookings Institution analyzed ₽ and found it pretends to create a reserve currency from thin air. Famous economists and even Bloomberg news concluded that ₽ was a sham and a fraud. It seems that even sovereign nations can use the hype of cryptocurrency to deceive investors. This casts serious doubts on whether we can rely of foreign nations to make cryptocurrencies safe and efficient through their regulations.

Private Regulation of Cryptocurrencies

Blockchains are controlled by miners and users. Both groups utilize the blockchain and manage the distributed public ledger for all to see. They do so through a variety of economic incentives, relying on sophisticated software, hardware, and other intermediaries, like Internet service providers, to keep the entire system going.

The companies and organizations that service these technologies usually sit in at least one jurisdiction and therefore are subject to its laws whether that be state or federal. It could be easier to regulate these companies rather than regulate cryptocurrencies as a whole. Internet service provider Comcast, for example, has their headquarters in Philadelphia, thereby subjecting themselves to Pennsylvania and federal law. If the government regulates cryptocurrencies and the blockchain, it might be most reasonable to regulate it on a federal level to avoid additional confusion because of varying laws between all the states. It was only recently that such regulation has been proposed in the legislature.

A New Cryptocurrency Regulator?

There does not seem to be a clear-cut answer to the question: Who is best suited to regulate cryptocurrencies? Each organization described above can claim a relationship to cryptocurrencies in some way, yet none have the broad reach needed to cover the entire cryptocurrency arena. The best solution may be to combine the capabilities offered by each independent department into a hybrid agency. Congress could create a new agency: The Virtual Asset Commission (VAC).

The VAC could have a board of administrators that oversee everything related to cryptocurrencies. The SEC, OCC, FTC, FDIC, and CFTC would each nominate one individual for appointment to the board of administrators, to be approved by the President, and function as a joint task force. Each nominee would be selected as representative for their prior agency's interests within the VAC. That is, each administrator would have an area of expertise that aligned with the goals of the agency they were nominated from. The VAC members would have their own areas of expertise allowing them, as a group, the ability to cover a comprehensive range of issues under one roof. The FBI may even have a part to play considering they already have experience shutting down criminal activity like Silk Road. The FBI could be the criminal arm, enforcing laws while preventing fraud.

The hypothetical Virtual Asset Commission presents an interesting option for Congress to consider. On the other hand, a different approach might be by regulating classes of individuals, or large corporations. Instead of trying to control the entire Bitcoin ecosystem, the government could extend regulatory authority on individual criminals directly, just as the FBI did with Silk Road, or when they shut down Mt. Gox. However, with over one-hundred thousand nodes within the Bitcoin network alone, it is reasonable to assume monitoring them all would be extraordinarily difficult. With millions of users worldwide, regulating cryptocurrencies on such an individual level seems inefficient. Of course, this is in addition to the fact that such a style of oversight too closely resembles the type of surveillance performed by the National Security Agency (NSA).

Direct and individual enforcement is probably not the ideal method for regulation. Presumably, it would be very costly and labor intensive. Instead, what if we exerted control over cryptocurrencies through corporate mandates, perhaps through an amendment to an already existing Act? Cryptocurrencies do not have the same physical attributes as paper money. They depend on computer code to create the architecture of their existence. One angle that could be exploited is the code itself. The government might enact legislation targeting software developers at large financial and technology institutions who work directly with cryptocurrencies or with blockchain technology. For example, "new laws could mandate that software developers introduce specific features – such as a government backdoor – directly into a blockchain's underlying protocol." The government would be permitted to shut down blockchain-based applications or even autonomous smart contracts when they are not in compliance with relevant laws.

Only one thing is for certain: there is much work that needs to be done if we, as a society, are ever to fully understand or regulate the cryptocurrency universe. The United States already has a number of agencies who have the potential to exercise oversight for cryptocurrencies and blockchain technology. As the virtual cryptocurrency landscape continues to grow and evolve, it becomes increasingly important for the government to take decisive action and provide supervision over this unregulated space. Whether that be through an already existing department, by means of a conglomerate-like hybrid formed by several agencies, or through direct legislation against people and corporations, it is time for legislators to start tackling the question of who should regulate cryptocurrencies.

CRYPTOCURRENCY MARKETS

As discussed above, there is an absence of legislative oversight over the cryptocurrency realm. Without regulations in place, there has been a growing trend of consumer confusion regarding cryptocurrencies. The average, and frequently uninformed, citizen can buy and sell cryptocurrencies just as they would buy or sell stock in a publicly traded company. Robinhood already boasts their capabilities as a cryptocurrency exchange aside from their core business of fee-free trading for investors in publicly traded companies. Traditional stock investment platforms like E*Trade and Vanguard are not far behind – both are building out their existing platforms as they reach for a piece of the crypto-pie market share. The barriers to entry are low for sophisticated and unsophisticated investors alike, which means everybody could be vulnerable to loss.[1]

---

[1] For instance, investors can sign up for Robinhood and instantly have access to a handful of cryptocurrencies like Bitcoin, Litecoin, Ethereum, and more. The "disclosure" they provide is lackluster at best. Essentially, Robinhood warns that cryptocurrencies are volatile and are not covered by either FDIC or SIPC insurance. Even the most basic limitation to entry is diminished – price. Some may avoid buying bitcoin because of the sheer cost. At over $50,000 per share, only the wealthy can "invest."

The astonishing growth in the cryptocurrency market in the past decade has inevitably led many to investing in essentially a virtual stake of nothing. Many have invested substantial sums of cash in cryptocurrencies despite the fact they do not meet the traditional definition of "a security." This is important because it could determine the proper regulatory authority responsible to regulate cryptocurrencies.

Specifically, if not determined to be a security, the SEC cannot protect investors under securities laws. For the SEC to enforce securities regulations on cryptocurrencies, they must be securities. Numerous lawsuits have been filed as a result of this consumer confusion, and lead us to ask and evaluate the question first at issue here: What is a security?

The Howey Test can be applied to all publicly traded companies today. If you were to purchase 100 shares of Microsoft Corp. (MSFT), you would be (1) paying an investment of money – stock is not free. You would be doing so with (2) an expectation of profit from that investment. It would be foolish to invest in anything if you anticipated it would depreciate in value. The (3) investment of money in a common enterprise element has been explored more extensively and has been summarized as the presence of an "investment contract." In this case, the third element is satisfied. Finally, you (4) expect profits from the efforts of a promoter or third party. Your investment appreciates in value through the efforts of Microsoft employees by means of product development, via sales of those products, and through the corporation's management within the company, including the oversight provided by the board of directors.

The Howey Test remains the landmark assessment used today when we ask the question, "What is a security?" Yet, despite this seemingly straightforward analysis, confusion persists. Lawmakers have found it challenging to evaluate cryptocurrencies as a class in accord with the Howey Test. This is because "[p]ublic watchdogs and legislatures lack the capacity to keep up with emerging FinTech like blockchain and cryptocurrency." The problem is exacerbated by the fact that Bitcoin is not alone in the crypto-space.

Today, there are thousands of "Altcoins" in virtual circulation, each touting themselves as the superior alternative to Bitcoin. Some were created to operate similar to cash, that is, as a medium of exchange. Others were created with their own unique sets of characteristics setting them apart from other cryptocurrencies. The proliferation of Altcoins is relevant because, with so many existing variations, it makes it difficult to determine if one Altcoin is, or is not, a security under the Howey Test. This means it is impossible for a one-size-fits-all test; each must be considered independently because each exhibits distinguishing traits. Some of the most notable altcoins include Litecoin, Ethereum, Dogecoin, and XRP, albeit over 5,000 other

> Robinhood's solution: allow purchases of fractional shares. If you do not have enough for a single Bitcoin, but maybe have $500 instead, you could put that amount down and receive a fraction of Bitcoin. Although seemingly insignificant, this illustrates the low bar to entry in the cryptocurrency investing realm.

altcoins exist at the time of this writing. An extensive list can be found through CoinMarketCap.

CONSTITUTIONAL QUESTIONS

Now that we have discussed the various legal frameworks and agents who may have the power to regulate cryptocurrency, we can explore the constitutional issues posed by this novel technology. Does one have the right to anonymous financial dealings? And if so, under what doctrinal theory? What are the Constitutional limits imposed on agencies who would seek to regulate such anonymous transactions?

Cryptography and the Freedom Not to Speak (Publicly)

Some argue that a right to pseudonymous financial transactions finds support in the First Amendment.[2] Most Americans know that the Constitution assures citizens the right to free speech. But this implies an equal right not to speak. Legal scholar Milton Konvitz argued that "freedom not to speak, not to profess beliefs, may be more important than the freedom to speak, since the profession of beliefs that one does not maintain may do more violence to the conscience than the failures to express beliefs that one does not maintain."

The freedom not to speak has been routinely upheld, from the right to refuse to say the pledge of allegiance and salute the American flag[3] to the right to refuse to profess a state motto on a license plate.[4] The salient question is how these rights extend to the digital realm, especially with regards to the competing interests of balancing economy interests, public policy, and efficiency in financial markets.

The Supreme Court has emphatically pronounced that spending money is a form of speech. In simple terms, people "vote with dollars" by making consumer decisions that accord with their beliefs. People literally put their money where their mouth is when they purchase free-range chicken and organic broccoli. In *Buckley* v. *Valero*, 424 U.S. 1 (1976), the Court found that making donations to a political candidate counts as political speech. The Court extended the doctrine that spending money is speech through several later cases, including the contentious decision of *Citizens United* v. *Federal Election Commission*, which struck down bans or limits on campaign contributions by corporations.

---

[2] "Congress shall make no law respecting an establishment of religion, or prohibiting the free exercise thereof; or abridging the freedom of speech, or of the press; or the right of the people peaceably to assemble, and to petition the government for a redress of grievances."
[3] *West Virginia State Board of Education* v. *Barnett*, 319 U.S. 624 (1943).
[4] *Woodley* v. *Maynard*, 430 U.S. 705 (1977) (note Justice's Robert's dissent that New Hampshire's mandate that the State motto be present on a license plate without violating a person's constitutional rights because the law only required it be present in order to own the vehicle, not that the person *express* their belief in the motto.)

The Court expressly held that the right not to speak extends to not to be compelled to spend money on social and political activities that go against core beliefs. In *Abood v. Detroit Board of Education*, 431 U.S. 209 (1977), the State of Michigan had a law permitting unions to extract dues from members, and these dues were used to fund political activities. The Court held that the members had the right of "negative association" and could not lawfully be compelled to pay for political activities.

While there are deeper tensions in the jurisprudence of freedom not to speak that are beyond the scope of this book, the key takeaway for present purposes is that there is some right not to publicly speak, and that includes the right to spend or not to spend money on certain kinds of activities. This relates directly to cryptography because cryptography is a technology that keeps speech private. By encrypting a political message, two people can privately communicate without that information becoming public. As illustrated later in this chapter, people rightfully fear that their private communications will be intercepted by the state or publicized by other actors. Without cryptography, people rightfully fear that their private communications will be intercepted by the state or publicized by other actors. This fear may chill people's general willingness to express dissident views.

This logic extends to finance. One may want to support a political message or to purchase a good or service that supports an ideological agenda, but one may not want that support to become public. Cryptocurrency arose precisely to give people the ability to spend money without easily being identified. While anonymous (or, more accurately, pseudonymous) tools can be used for nefarious ends, such tools can also be used to fund unpopular political positions. There is, therefore, an argument that there is some constitutional right to use cryptocurrencies for anonymous transactions under the First Amendment.

However, contrary to popular opinion, there are limitations to the freedom of speech. For example, it is commonly understood that one cannot shout "fire" in a crowded theatre. Less understood is the freedom not to speak, especially when the right is outweighed by other concerns. At present, it is not clear whether the right not to speak would extend to the right to have pseudonymous financial transactions. Courts may look to other doctrinal basis to support the assertion that one has a right to remain anonymous in a financial setting.

Cryptography Regulation and the Freedom of Association

The First Amendment also protects people's right to assemble. In the seminal decision, *Nat'l Ass'n for Advancement of Colored People v. State of Ala. ex rel. Patterson*, decided in 1958, the Supreme Court held that requiring the National Association for Advancement of Colored People (NAACP) could not be compelled by the Alabama government to publicly disclose its membership documents because it would jeopardize its member's safety and ultimately lead to a decline in membership.

Things get more complicated, however, when national security interests are at stake. The government's modern ability to spy on its citizens in the name of national security can be traced back to the Foreign Intelligence Surveillance Act of 1978. Despite its name, FISA actually allows the National Security Association (NSA) and the Federal Bureau of Investigation (FBI) to tap into domestic phone lines. After terrorists attacked the World Trade Center on September 11, 2001, Congress passed the USA Patriot Act. Title II of the Patriot Act is entitled "Enhanced Surveillance Procedures," and it greatly expands governmental ability to tap phone lines and listen into private communications. The extent to which the federal government leveraged FISA and the PATRIOT Act to spy on American citizens was famously exposed in 2013 by Edward Snowden, who revealed that Verizon Wireless provided detailed domestic call records to the NSA on a daily basis. Snowden subsequently penned an essay from his self-imposed exile in Russia titled "Without Encryption, We Will Lose All Privacy. This Is Our Next Battleground."

Encryption via cryptography makes it more difficult for governmental agents to tap into private communications because, even if they can intercept those communications, they cannot understand them. This is obviously a problem when, for example, terrorist groups can use commonly available encrypted-communication software like WhatsApp to secretly plan mass atrocities. One key function of government (and some would say its only function) is to ensure domestic tranquility by monopolizing the use of force and preventing acts of violence. This critical ability may be stymied by cryptography. While there may be some reasonable legislative approach that balances the policy goals of domestic security with personal freedom, such legislation has not yet been advanced.

On the other hand, citizens clearly have rights to conduct their non-terrorist affairs in private. A person is permitted by the Constitution to join the Communist Party USA and to peacefully advance the goals of that political organizations. This right to freely associate requires some privacy, as public association with these groups could result harms ranging from reduced career opportunities to assassination attempts.

Yet a person is not free to associate when the purpose of that association is to conspire to commit a crime. Cryptography is necessary to keep membership lists and communications private, but it can also obscure nefarious and criminal behavior. This tension continues to play out in courts and legislatures today.

Cryptocurrency is directly implicated in the freedom of association because payment of membership dues or donations to organizations can make association public. If associations are to remain private so that membership in them is not unduly chilled, payment of dues and other financial support must also remain private. Cryptocurrencies are designed to ensure maximum privacy in payment systems. This privacy is desirably and in fact mandated by the Constitution where the association is for protected ends such as peaceful political protest and legislative change. Cryptocurrency's financial privacy is dangerous when used to funnel cash to terrorist organizations. But such financial mobility could have saved countless refugees from dire poverty. Unfortunately, it is difficult to tell the difference before the encryption is cracked.

Search and Seizure of Cryptocurrency

Government seizure of electronic assets will likely invoke the Fourth Amendment.[5] In general, the Fourth Amendment provides the right to security in one's papers and effects. The Fourth Amendment has thus been interpreted by the Supreme Court to create "a right to privacy, no less important than any other right carefully and particularly reserved to the people." Because the Fourth Amendment provides this right to privacy of one's possessions, it prohibits unreasonable searches and seizures, and governmental agencies must obtain a search warrant prior to intruding on one's person or property (although there are a great many carveouts that allow police to perform stock-and-frisk searches, search motor vehicles, etc.). In general, in order for a violation of this right to occur, the individual must have (1) an actual (subjective) expectation of privacy and (2) the expectation was one that society is prepared to recognize as reasonable.

Recently, the Fourth Amendment has been applied to data. Scholars have argued that the Fourth Amendment does not create a reasonable expectation of privacy in cyberspace. Although strong cryptography makes it nearly impossible for an unintended party to read and understand the encrypted message, cryptography does not make it difficult for the government to access that communication. The messages are private, not secret.

Consider Bitcoin as an example. When two parties transact in Bitcoin, the Blockchain ledger records that transaction and propagates that ledger entry to every system on the Bitcoin networks. The information itself is unreadable to anyone who does not have the private key, which is a sort of password that will descramble the encoded transaction into readable text. But the information is widely accessible. In fact, by design, that information is available to everyone on the network. The government can easily access that information, and therefore there is no reasonable expectation for the information itself to be protected against unreasonable search and seizure. The government can therefore retrieve and attempt to decrypt this information without violating the Fourth Amendment.

The Supreme Court has not yet decided whether encrypted information that is on the internet is protected by the Fourth Amendment, but other courts recently ruled

---

[5] "No person shall be held to answer for a capital, or otherwise infamous crime, unless on a presentment or indictment of a grand jury, except in cases arising in the land or naval forces, or in the militia, when in actual service in time of war or public danger; nor shall any person be subject for the same offense to be twice put in jeopardy of life or limb; nor shall be compelled in any criminal case to be a witness against himself, nor be deprived of life, liberty, or property, without due process of law; nor shall private property be taken for public use, without just compensation."

that records of virtual currency transactions do not enjoy Fourth Amendment protections. In 2017, the Internal Revenue Service (IRS) served a subpoena on Coinbase Inc., a virtual currency exchange, to provide customer information and transaction logs for approximately 13,000 taxpayers who were potentially using Bitcoin transaction to avoid paying taxes. In July 2020, The Fifth Circuit ruled that Bitcoin data in the hands of a third party is not protected by the Fourth Amendment.[6] This accords with *Zietzke v. United States*, a Fourth Circuit decision from 2019 which held that the government may subpoena records from the virtual currency exchange Bitstamp because an individual does not have a reasonable expectation of privacy in financial records that were already exposed to a third party, even when those records were in an encrypted form.

While the Fourth Amendment may not prevent the government from attempting to decrypt and use encrypted information including records of cryptographic transactions, that does not mean this information cannot be protected. Rather, state and federal legislatures are able to protect this information by passing new laws. Whether or not they should do so is a matter of policy.

Cryptography and the Freedom from Self-Incrimination

The Fifth Amendment[7] in its Self-Incrimination Clause enables the citizen to create a zone of privacy which government may not force him to surrender to his detriment. *Griswold v. Connecticut*, 381 U.S. 479, 484 (1965). Whether or not this protection extends to encrypted information in general or to cryptocurrencies in particular is an unsettled issue that has little precedent in law. However, there are analogies that help illustrate the constitutional issues with government investigation of cryptocurrency transactions.

In the 1966 case of *Miranda v. Arizona*, the Supreme Court determined that police must inform people of their Fifth Amendment rights when they are taken into police custody. This so-called Miranda warning stipulates four basic rights: (1) you have their right to remain silent; (2) anything you say can and will be used against you in a court of law; (3) you have the right to an attorney; and (4) if you cannot afford an attorney, one will be appointed for you. These are sometimes summarized as the right against self-incrimination.

These rights are challenged by changes in technology. For example, the question of whether police may force you to unlock your iPhone using your passcode,

---

[6] *United States v. Gratkowski*.

[7] "No person shall be held to answer for a capital, or otherwise infamous crime, unless on a presentment or indictment of a grand jury, except in cases arising in the land or naval forces, or in the militia, when in actual service in time of war or public danger; nor shall any person be subject for the same offense to be twice put in jeopardy of life or limb; nor shall be compelled in any criminal case to be a witness against himself, nor be deprived of life, liberty, or property, without due process of law; nor shall private property be taken for public use, without just compensation."

fingerprint biometrics, or Face ID has not yet been settled. At least one district court ruled that forcing a person to unlock their phone violates the Fifth Amendment rights against self-incrimination, but these lower court decisions are not binding on all courts. Therefore, it is not clear whether the state can force the owner of encrypted information to decrypt that information using their private key, which functions like a sort of passcode.

Things get more complicated, however, when a third party has that passcode or private key. In 2015, Syed Rizwan Farook and Tashkent Malik attempted to bomb the San Bernardino County Department of Public Health and then shot a group of employees at a Christmas party there. Fourteen people were killed and twenty-two were seriously injured. The couple fled. Police pursued them and killed them in a shootout. The officers recovered Farook's iPhone 5C, but they were unable to unlock it due to its encryption and security features. The FBI sought a court order compelling Apple to unlock the phone on the grounds that it is likely to lead to information about other terrorist activities. Apple refused, and the legal battle persisted until the FBI eventually cracked the passcode themselves, thus rendering the legal battle on whether Apple must crack the encryption moot.

A similar event happened again when FBI asked Apple to unlock and decrypt iPhones belonging to Mohammed Saeed Alshamrani, the terrorist gunman who killed three people at a naval base in Pensacola, Florida. Alshamrani was shot dead at the scene, so he couldn't be asked to unlock his iPhone. Apple once again refused to cooperate, and once again the FBI managed to crack the code themselves. Although the FBI found information on that phone linking Alshamrani to Al Queda, it did not resolve whether a third party must provide federal assistance in decrypting such information.

Cryptography cases might come out differently. Unlike Apple, who does not keep individual passcodes or biometric identifiers on file, Bitcoin exchanges like Coinbase and Bitstamp do maintain their users' private keys. The private key to a unit of cryptocurrency acts like its passcode, enabling the users to transact with the cryptocurrency. The exchange needs to know the private key in order to engage in transactions on behalf of its users. It would therefore seem more likely that a court would force Coinbase to reveal users' private keys than forcing Apple to crack an encrypted iPhone.

The cryptocurrency community seems concerned with this lack of Fifth Amendment protection. Most websites advise storing private keys in "cold wallets," which are maintained on personal computers that are not connected to the internet, or even written down in physical books that are kept in a private safe. Private keys stored in these ways are more likely to be immune to police search and seizure due to Fourth and Fifth Amendment protections. Cryptography information stored on third-party exchanges, however, are more likely to be subject to government subpoena.

Cryptography as a Natural Right

The Ninth Amendment[8] has been construed to broaden the privacy protections under the first eight amendments to the Constitution. Some legal scholars argue that the Ninth Amendment checks federal power and guarantees individual liberty by granting to the people all the unenumerated natural rights that they possessed prior to the formation of the United States government.

If this argument[9] is correct, then a historical look at the civil liberties that people enjoyed prior to 1787 (when the U.S. Constitution was ratified) might illuminate whether the Ninth Amendment gives some private rights to engage in encoded transactions. Unfortunately, such a historical study does not appear to have been conducted yet. Moreover, not all legal scholars, judges, or lawmakers believe that the Constitution and the Bill of Rights can be best understood through the lens of its original meaning. There have not yet been any cases where the Supreme Court has decided whether the Ninth Amendment grants a right to privacy above and beyond what the preceding eight amendment provide. Therefore, the question of what the interaction between the Ninth Amendment and cryptocurrency is will remain unanswered for a time.

Cryptocurrency and Freedom from Economic Slavery

The Fourteenth Amendment is not found in the original Bill of Rights. The Fourteenth Amendment came nearly 100 years later after the country formed itself into a nation. In its Section 1, the states are required to provide people with equal protection under the law.[10] This was a direct response to forces that threatened to tear the union asunder, in Civil War.

The result of several more years of Reconstruction-era wrangling was the Fourteenth Amendment, which effectively made the Bill of Rights applicable to the States. Its Due Process Clause prohibited state and local governments from depriving persons of life, liberty, and property without fair procedures. Its Equal Protection Clause requires states to provide equal protection under law to all people, including noncitizens. The Fourteenth Amendment thus became the legal basis for many antidiscrimination lawsuits. It is germane to our study our corporate finance

---

[8] "The enumeration in the Constitution, of certain rights, shall not be construed to deny or disparage others retained by the people."

[9] Randy B. Barnett, "The Ninth Amendment: It Means What It Says." He argues that this amendment should be understood literally: "The enumeration in the Constitution, of certain rights, shall not be construed to deny or disparage others retained by the people."

[10] "All persons born or naturalized in the United States, and subject to the jurisdiction thereof, are citizens of the United States and of the state wherein they reside. No state shall make or enforce any law which shall abridge the privileges or immunities of citizens of the United States; nor shall any state deprive any person of life, liberty, or property, without due process of law; nor deny to any person within its jurisdiction the equal protection of the laws."

because courts have found that the Fourteenth Amendment includes a right to privacy.

A series of cases beginning in the 1970s laid the foundation for a Constitutional right to privacy in general. Whether a woman has the right to induce an abortion was the central issue in *Roe v. Wade*, 410 U.S. 113 (1973), which held that the Fourteenth Amendment "protects against state action the right to privacy, including a woman's qualified right to terminate her pregnancy." Finding that such a right existed, the Court reasoned that if the Fourteenth Amendment gives a woman the right to have an abortion, it must also give her the right to keep the fact of that abortion private, as she might be intimidated into not having that abortion by fear of its fact becoming public. Subsequently, *Planned Parenthood of Se. Pennsylvania v. Casey*, 505 U.S. 833 (1992) clarified that privacy is a fundamental right, even while it recategorized the right to have an abortion as a matter of personal autonomy and not a matter of privacy. And *Washington v. Gluckberg*, 521 U.S. 702 (1997) further established that the Fourteenth Amendment specifically provides a right of privacy of the home and the family life, while refusing to extend that right to assisted suicide.

This book is not about induced abortion or assisted suicide, so it will not discuss the merits of those decisions. However, the *Roe* decision and its progeny clearly indicated that the Fourteenth Amendment includes a right to privacy. That right to privacy applies to economic and well as family matters. It could be extended to the right to privacy in personal transactions. Although a Fourteenth Amendment right to economic privacy has not yet been tested in our nation's highest court, it could be applied to cryptocurrency ownership and transactions. Accordingly, the right to use cryptocurrency may be protected by the Fourteenth Amendment.

In fact, the right to privacy may be found in various Constitutional sources. Cryptography, the use of codes to keep messages private, and cryptocurrency, which keeps transactions private, thus may well be deemed fundamental rights that are part and parcel of the American pursuit of life, liberty, and happiness.

Indeed, the US government has long recognized that economic freedom is essential to the fulfilment of people's inalienable rights. This has occasionally led Congress to enact laws that enhance people's ability to earn a living through entrepreneurship. Entrepreneurship is the ability to "make something" of oneself, and this has often been symbolic of the American dream. Although the merits of cryptocurrency to fulfill this dream are still being debated, other laws enabling "crowdfunding" were recently enacted to give a wider range of people access to the ability to make something of themselves through entrepreneurship. This new phenomenon of crowdfunding will be addressed in the next chapter.

BIBLIOGRAPHY

Complaint, *SEC v. Ripple Labs, Inc.* (January 22, 2020) (No. 20–10832), available at https://perma.cc/AY35-9LXF.

Department of Justice Office of the Inspector General, *Audit of the Federal Bureau of Investigation's Strategy and Efforts to Disrupt Illegal Dark Web Activities* (2020).

Garlinghouse, Brad, *The SEC's Attack on Crypto in the United States*, RIPPLE.COM (2020), available at https://perma.cc/6TKK-8HLN.

Kerr, Orin S., *Applying the Fourth Amendment to the Internet: A General Approach*, 62 STANFORD L. REV. 1005 (2010).

Martin, Vince, *Even If Ripple Beats the Charges, XRP Is No Longer Worth the Risk*, INVESTOR PLACE (2021), available at https://perma.cc/R5M6-TQAU.

Snowden, Edward, *Without Encryption, We Will Lose All Privacy. This Is Our New Battleground*, THE GUARDIAN (October 15, 2019), available at https://perma.cc/Q6WN-V9QZ.

11

Crowdfunding

Congress designed and passed The Jumpstart Our Business Startups (JOBS) Act of 2012 to help a broad range of entrepreneurs leverage the internet to gain access to capital. Corporate finance was to be democratized by emerging growth companies, digital investing, crowdfunding, and mini-IPOs. But these simple principles got bogged down in rulemaking processes that resulted in over 1,000 pages of rules and red tape, leaving investors and entrepreneurs frustrated by their narrow prospects.

> The JOBS Act will allow Main Street small businesses and high-growth enterprises to raise capital from investors more efficiently, allowing small and young firms across the country to grow and hire faster.
> – President Barack Obama White House Press Release, April 5, 2012

Crowdfunding – raising money from a large number of people via the internet – went online just as the Dot-Com Bubble was beginning to hyperinflate. In fact, crowdfunding may have arisen because the internet challenged traditional ways for artists to benefit from their craft. Although there has always been copyright infringement and theft of intellectual property, the internet made it far easier to illegally distribute creative content like books and songs. What started as a response to this intellectual property problem eventually turned into an entirely new means of corporate finance.

CROWDFUNDING'S ORIGINS IN THE DOT-COM ERA

Napster was founded in 1999, amid the Dot-Com Bubble, to facilitate sharing of digital audio files on the internet. Although Napster ended up in legal trouble for facilitating copyright infringement, the threat to the traditional music industry became clear by the turn of the millennium. After Napster shut down, decentralized projects including LimeWire, Freenet, Gnutella, Soulseek, and others popped up like mushrooms after a storm.

Donative Crowdfunding

Artists are by nature creative, and some got creative about how to deal with copyright infringement. Some turned to a new way to finance music. Instead of creating music and then selling access to songs, artists began raising funds to create music, which would then be shared for cheap or free. To raise awareness, bands turned to the internet. In 1997, the rock band Marillion deployed a crowdfunding campaign to raise money for a U.S. tour. The band raised $60,000 in donations from fans who simply wanted to see the British act come to America.

Rewards-Based Crowdfunding

Donative crowdfunding remains popular today, while other entrepreneurs realized that many fans want to receive something exclusive in exchange for their contribution. This led to a number of crowdfunding websites with different business models. One of the first was ArtistShare, which was cofounded by the artist and activist Willie Nelson. ArtistShare pioneered the notion that fans would not only finance costs for album production and tours, but they also would receive unique rewards such as an autographed copy of the record, a prop from a movie set, their names in the credits, or some other reward that is not otherwise available for sale. This reward crowdfunding business model remains popular today, where it is also employed by IndieGoGo and GoFundMe.

Pre-purchase Crowdfunding

In 2009, however, a startup named Kickstarter would take crowdfunding in a new direction. Kickstarter did not rely on charitable impulse, as donative crowdfunding did. It did not rely some people's desire to get a unique or personalized reward either, as rewards crowdfunding did. Instead, Kickstarter focused on pre-purchase crowdfunding, which appealed directly to many people's consumer desires.

In pre-purchase crowdfunding, startups would offer consumers a lower pre-purchase price for an item they intend to bring to market. If the product is successfully designed, Kickstarter patrons receive the product first and for a discount. If the product fails, however, many patrons may be surprised when they get nothing. Since the pre-purchase crowdfunding model is more transactional than donative crowdfunding (where no one expects anything in return) or rewards-based crowdfunding (where one receives a talisman or keepsake that is symbolic of a relationship with the creator), startups who fail to deliver on pre-purchase crowdfunding products end up in a heap of trouble.

Perhaps the biggest fiasco in crowdfunding was the 2014 campaign for the Coolest Cooler. Although its promoters received over $13 million to build a portable battery-powered beverage cooler, they were unable to get the product to market. The startup eventually called it quits, offering its 60,000 backers only a $20 payment in return for their $200 "investment."

The pre-purchasers were furious. It seems that they did not understand the risk that they could end up with nothing. They did not treat Coolest Cooler as a startup that faced a substantial risk of failure. Rather, "investors" treated this project as a consumer would treat a mature company. They expected a guaranteed return. This was an error.

Crowdlending

More recently, crowdlending arrived on the scene. The entire industry of peer-to-peer lending originated with LendingClub, which was founded in 2005. Under the crowdlending or debt crowdfunding model, an entrepreneur, small business, or individual posts a business or project on a web site via Lending-Club or another crowdlending platform and asks to borrow a certain amount. The platform estimates the risk that the borrower will not be able to repay the debt and assigns an interest rate accordingly. Then, it matches this borrowing with dozens, hundreds, or even thousands of lenders who believe that interest rate represents an attractive investment.

Here's how it worked. People who want to borrow money create a loan listing on LendingClub's website. The listings usually provide both financial and personal details, sometimes including a photo of the prospective borrower. LendingClub evaluates the borrower's ability to repay the loan based on factors including the borrower's credit score, credit history, loan amount, debt-to-income ratio, and other factors, and it scores the borrower with a grade from A to G and a subgrade of 1 to 5, such that A1 is the highest score and G5 is the lowest.

Investors then visit the LendingClub website to find borrowers they want to loan to. Depending on lender's risk preferences, then can select an A1 borrower, who will pay the lowest interest rate but has the highest chance of repaying the loan, a G5 borrower, who pays the higher rate but also is the most likely to default on the loan, or anyone in between. Each lender commits only a small fraction of the total loan, with a minimum investment of just $25, so it may require hundreds of even thousands of lenders to cobble together a loan for the borrower.

Although LendingClub was initially set up as a social networking service that simply played matchmaker between borrowers and lenders, it quickly pivoted its business plan. In 2008, LendingClub registered with the SEC so it could make loans itself. Once enough lenders have made commitments, LendingClub acts as an intermediary, lending money to borrower members and through its partner WebBank. LendingClub then issues a promissory note (a promise to pay) its lending members, which it pays to their member account regularly. LendingClub profits by charging its borrower members an origination fee and by charging its lender members a service fee. In this way, the borrowers and the lenders never interact except via their usernames on the LendingClub platform.

This financial model puts the platform front and center. The platform adds a great deal of value not only by connecting borrowers with a network of lenders, but also by analyzing basic deal attributes like a reasonable interest rate and payment schedule. Ordinary lenders with no significant financial experience would otherwise find it very hard to price the risk of nonrepayment.

Equity Crowdfunding

LendingClub's success as a social media lending platform opened the door to a new type of online investing which would eventually become known as equity crowdfunding. This requires a brief distinction between lending debt and buying equity.

When a lender makes a debt investment, the borrower commits to make a stream of regular payments over time, until the loan is repaid, plus any applicable interest. Most personal loans are at a fixed rate, which does not vary based on the borrower's ability to use the loaned money profitably. The lender takes the risk that the borrower will become unable to pay, and the interest is meant to offset this risk. But interest rates are limited by state statutes. For example, Pennsylvania residents may be charged a maximum of 24 percent per annum, according to state consumer finance laws.

This means that loans have some limitations. Some projects or borrowers are simply too risky for a 24 percent loan. Some businesses might not be able to make monthly payments. A brand-new startup company that is not yet generating any profits would be making these payments out of the loaned funds, which defeats the purpose of getting a loan to use for research and development. And some investors may want a higher-risk and a higher-return investment to meet the needs of their portfolio.

Equity investments address these limitations. When an investor purchases stock in a company, there is usually no expectation that the investor-stockholder will be paid back on a regular basis. Rather, the investor-stockholder expects the stock value to increase because of the efforts management makes to improve the business. There is virtually no limit on how much the company can improve. Early-stage companies might sell initial shares of stock for one dollar and then go on to have a share value of five hundred dollars or more within a few years. Equity investing is potentially very lucrative.

But until 2015, regulations made it infeasible to offer and purchase equity investments via a social media platform like LendingClub did with loans. Soliciting equity investors such as stockholders is highly regulated under numerous securities regulations. Solicitations for the sale of stock must either be registered under the Securities Act of 1933 or subject to an exemption thereto. From 1933 to 2012, there was no significant exemption through which startups could sell stock to the general public. This began to change, however, when Congress passed the Jumpstart Our Business Startups (JOBS) Act of 2012, and when the SEC promulgated in final rules allowing equity crowdfunding in May 2015.

THE JOBS ACT

Although the financial crises of the Third Era generally led to legislation that made it harder and more expensive to issue stock to the general public, the JOBS Act of 2012 represented a counterpoint to this regulatory trend. Lawmakers across the aisle realized that financial markets were becoming increasingly inaccessible for ordinary investors and main street entrepreneurs. To address this, Representative Patrick McKenry (R-NC) and Representative Carolyn Maloney (D-NY) introduced the JOBS Act. This bipartisan bill would eventually become the law that at least theoretically allowed the general public to invest in startups. In President Obama's words, "These proposals will help entrepreneurs raise the capital they need to put Americans back to work and create an economy that's built to last."

The JOBS Act permitted the general public to invest in the market for entrepreneurial finance through several means, including equity "crowdfunding," "mini-public offerings," and an "IPO on-ramp." Crowdfunding can be generally understood as the practice of funding a project or venture by raising many small amounts of money from a large number of people, typically via the Internet. Equity crowdfunding – which involves selling a relatively small amount of stock to a large number of people via web sites called funding portals – is a more specific application where the reward to the investors in the fundraising is the opportunity to share in the profits of the venture.

It is worth briefly reiterating that the JOBS Act did not only enable equity crowdfunding. Title I gave "emerging growth companies," public startups with annual gross revenues less than $1 billion per year, a slight break on certain mandatory disclosure requirements. Title II allowed startups to raise money via internet "funding portals" from accredited investors. This resulted in Regulation D Rule 506(c), which led to Platforms including AngelList, Manhattan Street Capital, Crowdstreet, and Ourcrowd. Title III, also known as Regulation Crowdfunding or Reg CF, is the focus on this chapter. Title IV allows companies to raise $25–50 million via a "mini-IPO" that essentially has fewer disclosure requirements that a traditional IPO and a limited offering amount. Title V increased the number of stockholders that a private company may have before it needs to publicly register with the SEC, while Title VI increased the threshold for total assets. Title VII ordered the SEC to improve its web presence and to reach out to small businesses, woman owned businesses, veteran owned businesses, and minority owned businesses to inform them about the JOBS Act. But none of the other provisions held as much promise as Regulation Crowdfunding.

EQUITY CROWDFUNDING IN 2021

Equity crowdfunding promised to make financial markets fairer and more equal. But regulators were desperately afraid that equity crowdfunding campaigns would defraud the most vulnerable members of our financial society. To avoid this risk, regulator wrapped equity crowdfunding in miles of red tape. Although the equity crowdfunding portion, Title III, of the JOBS Act is only nine short pages (with two-inch margins), the SEC's final rules for Regulation Crowdfunding spans 685 pages.

Equity Crowdfunding was illegal in the US until the JOBS Act created a new exemption to the Securities Act of 1933. Specifically, the JOBS Act amends Section 4(a)(6) of the Securities Act of 1933 (the Securities Act) to allow a private corporation to offer and sell up to $1 million worth of equity securities (stock) in a twelve-month period to the general public without registering the securities with the SEC.

The SEC increased this limit to $5 in on November 2, 2020, effective January 1, 2021. This very recent change (as of the printing of this book) makes it difficult to say whether the higher thresholder will make crowdfunding useful. In my 2015 article, *"Bridgefunding: Crowdfunding and the Market for Entrepreneurial Finance,"* I argued that raising the limit in this manner would make equity crowdfunding much more successful. I am eager to see whether crowdfunding become more useful with this higher limit. On that same day, the SEC also clarified what "demo day" means, which give startups comfort that they can attend certain events without violating securities laws. I expect these changes to increase the use of Regulation CF.

According's to the SEC's final rules on equity crowdfunding, individuals who have between $100,000 and $1 million in annual income or net worth may invest 10 percent of it each year in startups through equity crowdfunding. Individuals who have or annually earn less than $100,000 may invest the greater of $2,000 or 5 percent of their annual income each year in this way.

The JOBS Act requires the development of a new kind of website called "funding portal," which is a financial intermediary that can sell startup stock online to nonaccredited investors. A private company raising capital under the crowdfunding exemption from the Securities Act must sell the stock through either a registered broker-dealer or a funding portal. Any broker-dealer or funding portal that engages in crowdfunding must register with the SEC and the Financial Industry Regulatory Authority (FINRA). The funding portal may not solicit transactions for securities displayed on its website or portal, compensate anyone for soliciting investors, pay compensation based on the sale of securities on its website or portal, hold customer funds or securities, or offer investment advice or recommendations.

Recall that President Obama proclaimed that the JOBS Act would further the policy goal of democratizing startups, which means providing more capital to diverse entrepreneurs – including women and minorities in novel geographies outside of Silicon Valley – for new business projects beyond high technology. But this promise has not been realized. Although women obtain a higher share of venture capital through equity crowdfunding then they receive from angels and VCs, women still receive less than their pro rata share. Moreover, the total amount raised via Reg CF is so miniscule that it cannot make more than a nominal impact. Companies raised more than $1.7 trillion – $1,700,000,000,000 – via Reg D in 2018 alone. Meanwhile, from its inception in May 2015 to 2020, the entirety of Reg CF capital raised to date is only $337 million. Equity crowdfunding is therefore less than 0.0000198 percent as financially significant as Reg D – however, this may change, thanks for the 2021 updates to Reg CF.

Why did such a promising idea as equity crowdfunding turn out to be less than a blip on the global financial radar, at least so far? On the company side, the government hamstrung Reg CF with some many protocols and precautions that it cost more than it was worth to most startups. The high cost of equity crowdfunding was compounded by the originally low fundraising limit of $1 million per year. With the newly changed higher fundraising limit, the effective cost of capital is lower, since most of the financing costs are fixed, so we may see more use of Reg CF with offerings of $5 million.

On the investor side, the lack of liquidity is a dealbreaker for many. Ordinary investors cannot easily afford to hold onto stock indefinitely. Without a resale market, it is harder to imagine buying these stocks in the first place. Investor groups typically worked through illiquidity and other economic issues (such as rational apathy and agency costs) by creating Special Purpose Vehicles (SPVs), but for reasons that were never explained SPVs are illegal under the JOBS Act. More recently, however, the SEC received comments that SPVs should be allowed under Reg CF. In 2016, legislators were exploring how to correct for the SEC's regulatory excesses with the Fix Crowdfunding Act. Unfortunately, that bill seems to have been pigeonholed. But anyone who wants to reboot the Fix Crowdfunding process should consider the issues involved in equity crowdfunding.

LIMITED FUNDRAISING

As designed by the drafters of the JOBS Act, the $1 million cap is intended to protect the general public from investment fraud or from simply making outright poor investment decisions. Instead, it makes crowdfunding expensive, complicated, inefficient, and risky for unsophisticated investors. Some reports suggest that complying with JOBS Act costs startups up to $150,000 (e.g., to obtain independent audits, disclosure documents, filing fees, and legal fees) before selling equity via crowdfunding. Raising money from angel investors is not only up to six times cheaper than crowdfunding, but angel investment costs are mostly incurred after financing is assured, whereas startups have to sink costs up front in order to try crowdfunding. Under current regulations, therefore, it seems that only startups that are unable to get funding from other sources will seek crowdfunding.

Fortunately, that cap was recently raised. On November 2, 2020, the SEC voted to increase the limit to $5 million. While it is still too early to empirically determine the magnitude of this effect of the marketplace, it is very likely that this change will make Reg CF equity crowdfunding into a viable option for entrepreneurs across America.

LACK OF RESALE OPTIONS

One foundational problem with startup securities in general, and equity crowdfunding securities in particular, is a lack of resale options that creates a financial problem called "illiquidity discount asymmetry." Illiquidity discount asymmetry means that an investment is harder for some people to unload than it is for others. A simple example can illustrate this problem. Imagine there are two investors who both have one share of Microsoft stock (MSFT). One investor has a physical stock certificate, which he keeps in a lockbox under his bed, in his isolated cabin in the woods, with no internet access. The other has a digital record of stock ownership through his Merrill Lynch brokerage account, which he accesses on the smartphone in her pocket via high-speed 5G wireless connectivity. If the tech stock market suddenly crashes, who will be able to respond quicker? Our tech savvy investors will likely be able to know and respond much quicker than our investing hermit. The connected investor may be better able to take advantage of daily market movements and protect against sudden sells offs.

The ability to sell may, ex ante, impact one's desire to buy. Our savvy investor knows that he can easily track MSFT and sell it if its value goes too low, while our hermit investor is in the dark. Knowing that he might not be able to respond to market moves, such that his stock might be worth nothing when he finally gets into town, might discourage him from making this investment in the first place. While some investments are designed to be long-term buy-and-hold strategies, not all investments can be ignored. A rational investor who does not have time to monitor a volatile investment will value that investment to be worth less than would an investor who has the time and expertise to monitor it and sell it, if needed.

A less abstract way of putting this is through another example. Imagine two brothers, Joe and Frank. Joe works sixty hours per week as a highly paid dental surgeon. Frank is a former bricklayer who is now unemployed. Both receive the opportunity to purchase a rundown house that needs repairs. Who is this investment better suited to? If Joe purchases the property, he will have to add home renovations to his already overwhelming work schedule, which would either come at a great cost to his personal life or simply be an obligation he ignores from time to time. If Frank purchases the property, he now has a valuable way to spend his free time and perhaps can also ply his trade in furtherance of his investment prospects. All else being equal, Frank should value this investment opportunity more than Joe does, because Frank has the time and ability to monitor and oversee it and ensure it succeeds, whereas Joe does not.

What if, however, the ability of one investor to see and respond to market moves was not the result of a personal lifestyle choice but rather the consequence of economic law or government mandate? In startup investing, not all investors are equal. Ordinary investors have many disadvantages. First, they only purchase small amounts of stock, so they cannot effectively command or discipline management.

Second, they do not have the time or geographic possibility of visiting the investment's headquarters to meet with management and confirm that things are on track. Third, they do not own enough stock to make it worth their time to spend hundreds of hours tracking the startup and its competitors.

Fourth, the government limits ordinary investors' access to resale markets, while mega-wealthy investment corporations have almost unlimited access to make markets. As a result, startup stock is worth substantially less when held by employees and poorer investors, yet that exact same stock is worth much more in the hands of upper management and the wealthiest investors. This raises obvious fairness concerns. It also frustrates the JOBS Act by chilling venture investment by poorer investors.

The unfortunate truth of our securities regulations is that they require poorer investors to hold private stock for longer than the wealthiest investors. Laws further restrict poorer investors' access to resale markets. This causes private stock to have a bigger illiquidity discount and thus be less valuable in the hands of poorer investors than in the hands of wealthier ones, who can access the resale market quicker and easier. Ironically, this is the unintended consequence of securities regulations that were designed to protect poorer investors, yet those regulations have the actual effect of creating an illiquidity discount asymmetry favoring wealthier investors over poorer ones.

Securities regulations create the illiquidity discount asymmetry by allowing large banks to host private stock markets for their Qualified Institutional Buyers (QIBs), who must have more than $100 million in net investments. Smaller stockholders, and employees with stock options, are systematically disadvantaged by Rule 144A, which creates the QIB restriction on private-stock resale. The lack of an equal-access safe-harbor exemption harms poorer stockholders and employees disproportionately more than it harms wealthier stockholders and management. And the lack of a general solicitation provision keeps transactions off exchanges, so trading mainly occurs in over-the-counter transactions in private stock markets called "dark pools."

In short, Rule 144A's safe harbor provides liquidity only for QIBs, who are large institutions that own over $100 million in net investments. It does not provide liquidity to many other startup investors. Angels, who invest about twenty-five billion dollars annually in startups, are be classified as accredited investors (AIs). Each AI must have at least one million dollars in net assets (not including primary residence) or $200,000 in annual income ($300,000 joint if married) to purchase private-company equities in the large Regulation D market. Wealthy angels and small venture capital funds may also be classified as qualified purchasers (QPs), but even QPs with ninety-nine million dollars in net investments cannot purchase equities on a 144A market.

This disparity in access to a resale market means that even AIs and QPs have an "illiquidity discount" on their shares, while QIBs enjoy the full value of their shares. Meanwhile, ordinary investors have an even larger illiquidity discount, effectively giving the poorest investors the worst deal as a matter of law. Startup employee might have the worst of the lot, as they often forgo cash compensation in exchange for securities that might turn out to be worthless and, in any event, cannot be sold for years at a time. The 144A regime makes private-company stock most valuable to the wealthiest class of investor and least valuable to the poorest class of investor. This problem makes crowdfunding unattractive. No one wants to cast lots when one is preordained to get the short straw.

NO SPECIAL PURPOSE VEHICLES

For reasons that are not clearly stated, the SEC forbid the use of Special Purpose Vehicles (SPVs) in equity crowdfunding. SPVs are business entities that are formed for the sole purpose of organizing investors. Members fund the SPV by contributing money, then the SPV uses that money to purchase stock in a target business. The SPV is the stockholder, which simplifies the target business's capital structure, stockholder ledger, and voting mechanisms. The SPV can be professionally managed, so the investing members take a more passive role.

SPVs have been misused in the past; perhaps this makes regulators cautious about allowing them in the future. For example, Enron Corporation used an SPV to transfer some of its riskiest assets into an SPV, which took that risk off its main balance sheet. This was just one part of Enron's massive accounting fraud, but it gave SPVs a bad name.

Perhaps because of this negative attitude toward SPVs, the SEC prohibits their use in investment crowdfunding. Although there is bipartisan, bicameral support in Congress to allow SPVs in equity crowdfunding, and despite the fact SPVs are common in investing generally, the SEC has not yet allowed it. Until that happens, we might expect equity crowdfunding to remain inconsequential. This is a shame, however, given that it would not be so hard to fix crowdfunding, and doing so could produce benefits for a wide range of investors and entrepreneurs.

HOW CROWDFUNDING COULD WORK

Regulators have suggested that allowing ordinary people to invest via the internet generates untold new risks for folks who are unable to protect themselves. But there are economic reasons to believe that investing in startups over the internet might actually be safer than investing in startups in more traditional ways, such as attending demo days and negotiating a preferred stock purchase agreement. To understand why, first we must establish why startup investing is dangerous in general. Then we can see how the internet helps solve these problems.

Startup investors have three economic problems, which professional- and public-company investors can generally mitigate, but ordinary investors might not be able to avoid. First, there is an information asymmetry problem: entrepreneurs know more than investors about what entrepreneurs will do. Professional investors join the board and oversee the entrepreneurs, so they gain information about how hard and how well the entrepreneur is working, but ordinary investors do not get board seats. Second, there is great uncertainty as to whether the venture will succeed. Professional investors invest in stages, over time, but ordinary investors may not have the cash or the time to performed staged investments. Third, there are agency costs, specifically, residual loss: entrepreneurs have incentives to shirk and self-deal, especially when the investor does not understand the entrepreneurs' technology. Professionals generally invest in familiar technical areas, but ordinary investors might not have technical expertise.

Ordinary investors probably cannot mitigate this trio of problems in the traditional ways. Given a legal limit of $10,000 per investor per year, it is doubtful that they will have the time, inclination, or ability to join two or three corporate boards, manage a multistaged private-investment portfolio, and get technical expertise in the latest app-coding languages. In addition, crowdfunding theoretically has the additional problem of competition with professional investment. The most promising startups receive multiple offers from the most prominent venture-capital investors, who contribute not only money but also professional services, workspace, mentorship, advice, management, and, of course, access to yet more money. Offline, nodes of well-connected venture capitalists (VCs) with MBAs from Stanford share information about leads over lattes in Palo Alto. They meet founders daily, and their financial resources are virtually unlimited. Their associates process data from expensive, manicured databases into custom analytics reports, fine-tuned to each principal's predilections.

Ordinary investors who want to invest in startups, on the other hand, go, for example, Crowdfunder.com, click "Search," and are presented with a long list of companies and projects that are soliciting investors. Can the ordinary investors who are by definition amateurs compete with investment professionals in finding, acquiring, servicing, and monitoring the best investment opportunities?

Crowdfunding investors, however, can collaborate in *new* ways that could mitigate this trio of problems. There are three ways that crowdfunding investors might solve the trio of problems: (1) harnessing the wisdom of the crowd, (2) crowdsourcing of information, and (3) leveraging online reputation. These crowdfunding investment strategies may come into play both during the campaign and after the company receives the money, and they give reason for hope that crowdfunding might work out after all.

Wisdom of the Crowd

Groups of people can act as wise crowds or foolish mobs. In general, a large group of diverse individuals who are able to communicate effectively will come up with better predictions and more intelligent decisions than would a skilled person acting alone. But this obviously comes with many conditions and caveats. The wisdom of the crowd is only expressed where crowds can grow sufficiently large, evaluate information that can be perfectly known, or are organized around a thought leader.

When these conditions are not met, however, crowds degrade into herds and mobs. Like the proverbial lemming who runs off a cliff because the group is running in this direction, members of crowds can also make fatal errors. When one member of a group witnesses the behavior of another, the first member may assume the second member is acting on information that is private to that second member. The first member, who may also have some private information, may infer the second member's private information from the action that is observed. The first actor may then take a similar action based both on private information and inferred information.

A familiar example makes this theory clear. When a person decides to watch a video on a website like YouTube, that person can see how many others have watched that video, which suggests something about the quality of that video. That person may decide to watch the most-watched video because the group information suggests that video is the highest quality.

This may seem quite innocuous, but as the crowd gets larger, the information from crowd behavior begins to overwhelm the prospective viewer's private information. The extreme form of this group-think behavior is called an "information cascade," where even rational individuals will choose to abandon their private information (or not make efforts to gather private information in the first place) and instead to follow the crowd. In this case, the wisdom of the crowd can be sublimated into herd behavior.

Crowd science theory deems a crowd "successful" when it aggregates "asymptotic information." In other words, from a systems-sciences perspective, a "wise" crowd is one that efficiently produces and distributes unique information about the true state of the world.

Avoid Crowd Failures

Crowds fail due to "herding" or "information cascades." Herding is when individuals merely mimic others' actions, ignoring their own private information, as opposed to "learning aggregation," when the crowd converges on the right result by leveraging both public and private information.

Are crowdfunding investors likely to be wise crowds or dumb mobs? That depends on the other factors discussed in this section. If equity crowdfunding is worthwhile enough that large groups of ordinary investors consider investment crowdfunding opportunities, then the information produced by that large group is more likely to solve information problems. If equity crowdfunding is deemed a fringe activity, crowds may never grow large enough to produce superior results. In this way, crowdfunding is a self-fulfilling prophecy. Success will generate a positive feedback loop leading to more success, while failure will generate a negative feedback loop. This is a typical chicken-egg problem that many new markets face.

To alleviate this problem, regulations could allow or even encourage crowdfunding networks to grow large. An alternative solution is to require crowdfunding companies to have an influential agent. A single influencer can have an outsized impact on the entire crowd. This can be for good or bad, so it is better not to be left to chance or drive. Rather, influencers on crowdfunding platforms should require some sort of accreditation. These modifications to the law will help ordinary investors benefit from the wisdom of the crowd.

Crowdsourcing

As mentioned earlier, the JOBS Act not only permitted equity crowdfunding. It also permitted companies to generally solicit investment from accredited investors like angels and VCs. Prior to the JOBS Act, private companies could not put an ad for the sale of stock in the newspaper or post about an investment opportunity on social media. Now there is a new Regulation D Rule 506(c) that allows private companies to publicly advertise investment opportunity, so long as the stock is only sold to wealthy accredit investors.

This new rule has resulted in an interesting new type of web portal. The largest 506(c) web portal is Angel List. On this portal, you can "follow" famous venture capital investors or join an investment syndicate, which is a group of investors who share the workload of sourcing and negotiating deals.

Following lead investors and joining investment syndicates has emerged as a key aspect of online investing because this solves some of the problems with investor group dynamics. Crowdfunding might need to take a page from Angel List's book, if it is to succeed.

Rational Pathos

Small shareholders have a problem that economists call "rational apathy." To put this problem simply, if you only have $100 invested in a company, it's not worth more than $100 of your time to monitor that investment. Monitoring the investment does not guarantee that you will not lose your money, while simply ignoring the investment and spending your time working on a lucrative project or even simply doing something that gives you $100 of enjoyment is a better bet. In fact, it would be irrational for you to spend countless hours obsessing over your $100 investment. That time would be better served, as an economic matter, but engaging in some other activity that has a higher return on the investment of your time.

Reg CF has, unfortunately, built rational apathy problems into the equity crowdfunding system, and this problem is worse for the less wealthy participants in the system. The average American full-time worker earned about $25 per hour, totaling about $50,000 per year, in 2019. Pursuant to Reg CF, such a person can only invest up to $2,500 per year in crowdfunding. Since crowdfunding is risky (it carries an especially high degree of idiosyncratic risk), a wise investor will diversify and invest in approximately twenty companies. That adds up to a $125 per company investment for the wise average investor. Such an investor should not spend countless hours sourcing, diligencing, negotiating, and monitoring crowdfunding investments. In fact, he or she would be ill-advised to spend more than five hours thinking about any one company, as spending this time would have negative expected returns.

Rational apathy will likely lead to additional problems for crowdfunding. Limitations on the dissemination of information, primarily when the cost of acquiring the information is greater than the benefit received, and the lack of incentives to produce and share information, may hinder the potential benefits of crowdsourcing behavior. Professional analysts are generally better trained in analyzing equities than an average person who may participate in crowdfunding. Accordingly, the information from crowdfunding investors shareholders is likely to be weak, infrequent, and unreliable.

But there is a flip side to rational apathy, which I call rational pathos, or caring, where an investor has natural incentives to monitor investments at an appropriate level. If we allowed crowds to form naturally as investor groups, members would specialize in certain tasks and share information for the mutual pathos. In other words, the total amount of pathos produced by a crowd can be more than the sum of the individual's rational apathy. Under these conditions, the group makes smarter decisions than rational individual investors would make.

The SEC should revise Reg CF to encourage the kind of behavior we see in Reg D Rule 506(c) markets like Angel List. Instead of forbidding investors to share information, the SEC should encourage investors to take the lead and organize investment syndicates that divvy up the work. Instead of each single investor spending up to five hours reviewing financial information for twenty companies, totaling a whopping 100 hours of work to make a measly $2,500 investment, a syndicate of twenty investors could each review one company and then share the results with others. Now, each average investor in the syndicate can spend five hours of work on a $2,500 investment. This represents a twenty-times increase in efficiency, and it could result in better information that sets off the positive feedback loop discussed in the section above on Wisdom of the Crowd.

And that was just as small example of allowing existing synergies to make investment groups more efficient. We could even kick the crowdfunding system into hyperdrive by allowing Special Purpose Vehicles (SPVs). As discussed above, SPVs are legal entities (usually limited liability companies) that are formed for the sole purpose of organizing an investment group. The SPV LLC typically has one manager, who makes decisions on behalf of the group, and an unlimited number of members, who put in money but then often have an otherwise hands-off role. The manager might be compensated for her time through a common venture-capital formula called the Two and Twenty (or "2 and 20"). This means that the manager gets 2 percent of the assets under the SPV's management plus 20 percent of the SPV's profits. If twenty ordinary investors each invest $25,000 to become members in a crowdfunding SPV, the SPV could pay a manager $1000 plus 20 percent of profits. The manager would thus be incentivized to keep proper tabs on the investment companies, and these desirable incentives increase as the SPV adds more members. Moreover, the manager should be a person who has special financial skills. A professor manager who is trained in analyzing equity securities could do a better job than an average person who does not have this training or experience.

Currently, it is difficult to form syndicates under Reg CF because the law does not permit investors to form special purpose vehicles (SPVs) or special purpose entities (SPEs). These obstacles will have to be addressed if equity crowdfunding is to make a meaningful impact.

Reputational Effects

Even if the SEC were to permit lead investors to create SPVs and manage an investment group in crowdfunding, the severe limits on how much each person can invest could limit incentives to manage these groups well. However, receiving the Two and Twenty is not the only reason to manage a small fund carefully. Managers also care about their reputation. If they manage well, they might be rewarded with the opportunities to manage more and larger funds later. Reputational effects are a significant driver of human behavior. Designing investment platforms that allow users to build reputational status may encourage superior results. Moreover, the SEC should continue to increase crowdfunding limits as the technology provides to be effective at eliminating fraud.

Gamification

Gamification – the use of game design elements in non-game contexts – is another way to motivate online investors to organize and share information. Gamification methods create a positive user experiences that improve user retention and utilization – but it also can over-stimulate users and encourage gambling behavior.

Gamification is already becoming popular in higher education. For example, Goose Chase is a new company that offer mobile-powered scavengers hunts for K-12 students. Students use their smartphone to watch videos, answer riddles, and find prizes. Along the way they learn skills like reading comprehension, time management, and map reading.

RobinHood, the free stock trading platform discussed in Chapter 8, applies gamification to make stock trading more fun and approachable for millennials and Gen Z users. For example, it sends daily push notifications reminding users to participate, and showers users with a virtual rain of confetti when they trade. Articles about stock information include emojis and simple language, and notifications push users to lists of "top mover" stocks. But, as discussed in Chapter 8, RobinHood users do not necessarily tread stocks as investments. Rather, they might alternate between playing games like Candy Crush, betting on apps like SportsBets, and "investing" on RobinHood, all while sitting in a waiting room or taking the bus to work. The casual nature of RobinHood makes it much friendly for people to invest, but it may result in people taking investment less seriously and treating it as a game and not a profession.

Gamification can facilitate online reputation by "scoring" the reputation of users; in fact, there are business-method patents pending to this effect. Gamification of reputation has been applied in varied contexts such as encouraging software developers to include comments in their code and creating leaderboards to encourage classroom learning. This could be applied to social media investing, where an ordinary users can become an influencer by virtue of scoring highly in peer reputation.

Gamification has even been used to attract and retain reliable crowdsourcing tasks such as relevance assessment, which could be directly applied to crowdsourcing for online investors. Relevance assessment is the process of attributing a relevance level to a set of information, so that users can access the most relevant information first, instead of wading through hours of irrelevant information looking for the proverbial needle in the haystack. There is so much information about investment opportunities that ordinary investors may elect to review none of it, since without a way to sort what is relevant from what is irrelevant it would take an unreasonable amount of time to learn anything meaningful from the data.

Gamification for relevance assessment already exists on social media forums like Reddit. Users can save, comment, and even give an award to useful posts, while hiding, reporting, or downvoting irrelevant ones. Future users see more of the posts deemed relevant by the prior ones, and fewer of the irrelevant ones. This could be applied to crowd review of financial information, or large-scale discussions about investment opportunities. It could also lead to users earning a relevance score based on how relevant other users find their posts to be, thus identifying and elevating influencer.[1]

While the SEC does not mandate relevance or reputation scoring systems, it also does not prevent it. So long as there is sufficient competition in the market for crowdfunding portals, some enterprising portals may employ gamification to encourage crowdfunding investors to contribute high-quality efforts to investment crowdsourcing, which may indeed help crowdfunding in general overcome information asymmetry and agency costs in crowdfunding.

These techniques, however, must be used carefully. RobinHood is currently under scrutiny for making investors too much fun. According to allegations, the confetti and leader boards causes some users to trade too often and maybe even become "addicted" to trading. Whether these allegations are true is yet to be

---

[1] Elevating influencers could also create an echo chamber, where misinformation cascades are common, if the social media platform is improperly designed, or if it has the wrong economic incentives.

determined, but platforms should be careful regardless because the optics of employing gamification techniques may seem unfavorable to some investors' and regulators' eyes.

WHY SHOULD WE CARE ABOUT CROWDFUNDING?

Fixing crowdfunding seems like a lot of work. Why should we bother? Because crowdfunding has the potential to make corporate finance safer and more equitable for ordinary investors. If we do not find a way to fix crowdfunding, frustrated ordinary investors will continue to probe deeper into the nether regions of cyberspace, looking for opportunities far beyond the reach of regulators or financial police. Meanwhile, entrepreneurship in America is at a critical point. Small businesses that were already suffering have recently been ravaged by COVID-19. The demise of small business means the death of the American dream for many of our most vulnerable citizens. Crowdfunding could help save American small business and restore the American dream to a wider range of entrepreneurs.

Protecting Investors

At first blush, it may seem that the best way to protect ordinary people from losing their money in bad investments is to prevent them from investing in the first place. After all, one cannot make a bad investment if one cannot invest at all. However, this thinking is flawed on many levels.

First, this ignores the reality that most people must make investments if they are to survive life events including illness and retirement. Unlike most first-world nations, America does not have a public pension system. Indeed, most of America's employers no longer provide pensions – also known as defined-benefit plans because they guarantee a specific pay out or lump sum benefit – but rather American employers provide defined-contributions plans like a 401(k), where the employer contributes some percentage of an employee's salary to a retirement account and the employee determines how and where he wants to invest the funds. Whether that retirement account is sufficient to carry that employee through retirement, therefore, is subject to market forces. In other words, even our defined-benefit plan system is still subject to investment risk.

Second, relatively safe investments, like keeping money in an FDIC insured bank or buying government bonds, generate relatively low returns these days. The Federal Reserve committed to keeping interest rates low for the foreseeable future. With so much cheap cash available to borrowers, it is very difficult for lenders (working savers) to charge profitable rates.

Ultra-safe investments can actually lose money over time because of inflation. In 2019, the annual inflation rate was about 1.8 percent. Meanwhile, as of September 2020, government-backed treasury bonds return about 1.25 percent per year. That means that someone who invests in treasury bonds will effectively lose about 0.5 percent of their spending power annually. This is hardly a way to prepare for retirement! Until interest rates rise again, pensioners need access to higher-reward investment opportunities.

Third, and most relevant to the lessons from this book, it is no longer reasonable to assume that Americans can be prohibited from investing in too-risky assets. The internet has eroded geopolitical barriers. Nowadays, investors in Omaha, Nebraska can invest in startups in the United Kingdom via web sites like Seedrs.com just as easily as they might purchase publicly traded stocks on eTrade. Moreover, investors now have access to much more exotic and risky investments, including initial coin offerings and decentralized autonomous organizations. While regulators might mean to protect people, in reality they are driving them to explore these exotic financial markets, because there seems to be no lucrative and reasonably safe space to invest domestically.

The securities regulators need to wake up to the Third Era of corporate finance. In this era, ordinary people see venture capitalists and a handful of Silicon Valley startup founders getting incredibly rich, while big banks keep getting bigger. Meanwhile, opportunities for ordinary investors to make decent returns through traditional instruments like savings accounts and treasury bonds have disappeared. Even stock market investing seems like a losing proposition where high-frequency traders with super-fast computers are able to make short-swing profits at the expense of long-term buy-and-hold investors.

The solution cannot be more red tape and tighter controls. As this book has shown, controls did not prevent recent crisis and crashes. Moreover, we cannot keep people from investing in Bitcoin, Ethereum, and other harder-to-understand cryptocurrency assets. We cannot stop people from participating in initial coin offerings. We cannot keep everyone safe from exploring possibilities to strike it rich in a world that presents no safe alternatives to generate meaningful wealth.

Rather, we should shift our thinking. By recognizing the reality that ordinary investors in America feel that they have no government-backed investment options that can generate substantial wealth, while recognizing that it is easy for domestic investors to invest abroad or in cyberspace, we can start to shift toward generating competitive regulations – regulations that make investing in America attractive again.

Forming Capital for Entrepreneurs

Entrepreneurship provides a path to prosperity for many people.[2] In particular, women and minorities prefer entrepreneurship as their path to achieve the

---

[2] Entrepreneurship is the ability to "make something" of oneself. As coined in 1931 by John T. Adams, entrepreneurship symbolized the democratization of opportunity that is the American Dream.

American Dream. In their striving, their startups and small businesses benefit our entire society.[3] Entrepreneurial innovation has a positive impact on social welfare. For these reasons, the federal government has implemented numerous policies designed to support small businesses and promote startup innovation. In fact, President Obama expressly stated improving access to capital for startup entrepreneurs and small business is a primary goal of the JOBS Act.

However, these policies appear to be inadequate. Recent studies have shown that startups and small businesses are less successful than large, incumbent firms. Despite what the shows Shark Tank and Silicon Valley depict, outside of certain high-tech fields, American entrepreneurship is declining. It is well documented that startups have an access-to capital-problem. The JOBS Act was designed to fix this problem, but, as the result of overregulation, the JOBS Act has so far failed to produce a meaningful amount of capital for entrepreneurship.

SEC regulators including Commission Luis A. Aguilar have recognized that small businesses need greater access to capital and liquidity. But the securities regulator's inability to craft a system that works demonstrates a seemingly irreconcilable tension between the agency's goals. The SEC states it has three goals: protecting investors, maintaining orderly capital markets, and facilitating efficient capital formation. In the case of equity crowdfunding, the SEC, who promulgated a 685-page Reg CF, have focused too much on investor protection at the expense of capital formation. This is due in large part because the SEC failed to consider how the internet changes investment.

SUMMARY

This chapter has shown how the internet ushered in a brand-new information era. Instantaneous multilateral worldwide communication networks are not just plausible, they already exist. Admittedly, these information networks suffer from problems of their own – for example, consider the rise of fake news shared on Facebook – but they also solve traditional problems in new ways.

The future of investment on the internet may be bifurcated. While some platforms will seek SEC approval and offer strong anti-fraud protections, others will avoid registration and liability and offer a *laissez faire* (hands-off) marketplace on the principles of *caveat emptor* (buyer beware). We are already seeing this bifurcation today, with some registered investment portals like AngelList and

---

Rebecca Gill, *The Evolution of Organizational Archetypes: From the American to the Entrepreneurial Dream*, 80 COMM. MONOGRAPHS 331, 337 (2013).

[3] Entrepreneurship positively impacts social welfare in two ways: by major innovations that shock the equilibrium through creation of a new product or process, which is also referred to as Schumpeterian entrepreneurship or creative destruction, and by minor innovations that bring the market price close to equilibrium, which may be called Kirzner entrepreneurship. *See* Samuel Bostaph, *Schumpeter vs. Kirzner on Entrepreneurs*, MISES INST. (May 16, 2019), https://mises.org/wire/schumpeter-vs-kirzner-entrepreneurs [https://perma.cc/D2GY-YRFP]; *see also infra* Part III.

Manhattan Street Capital focusing on Reg. A and Reg. D offerings, while operating as unregulatable decentralized autonomous organizations that have marketplaces for cryptocurrency, non-fungible tokens, digital property, and other assets that are not subject to securities regulations. While both constitute crowdfunding, the platforms' incentives to protect investors by informing them of risks, policing against fraud, and engendering productive research and conversation vary widely.

BIBLIOGRAPHY

Aldrick, Philip, *With Startups Declining, the American Dream Is Beginning to Fade*, THE TIMES (July 2, 2018), available at https://perma.cc/T4PH-VFSS.

Barasinska, Nataliya & Dorothea Schäfer, *Is Crowdfunding Different? Evidence on the Relation between Gender and Funding Success from a German Peer-to-Peer Lending Platform*, 15 GERMAN ECONOMIC REVIEW 436 (2014).

Baxter, Lawrence G., *Adaptive Financial Regulation and RegTech: A Concept Article on Realistic Protection for Victims of Bank Failures*, 66 DUKE LAW JOURNAL (2016).

Bostaph, Samuel, *Schumpeter vs. Kirzner on Entrepreneurs*, THE MISES INSTITUTION., available at https://perma.cc/D2GY-YRFP.

Case, Steve, *Can Startups Save the American Dream?*, THE CASE FOUNDATION (January 14, 2015), available at https://perma.cc/Z9XJ-AUJ2.

Casperson, Nicole, *Robinhood under Pressure for Bringing 'Gamification' to Investing*, INVESTMENTNEWS (December 18, 2020).

Clough, Paul, Mark Sanderson, Jiayu Tang, and Amy Warner, *Examining the Limits of Crowdsourcing for Relevance Assessment*, available at www.marksanderson.org/publications/my_papers/IEEE-IC-2012.pdf.

Conerly, Bill, *Innovation Benefits Society, Not Just the Rich*, FORBES (October 21, 2018).

Cumming, Douglas J. et al., *Equity Crowdfunding and Governance: Toward an Integrative Model and Research Agenda*, ACADEMY OF MANAGEMENT PERSPECTIVES (2019).

Geiger, Mark & Seth C. Oranburg, *Female Entrepreneurs and Equity Crowdfunding in the US: Receiving Less When Asking for More*, 10 JOURNAL OF BUSINESS VENTURING INSIGHTS (2018).

Gerber, Elizabeth M. et al., *Crowdfunding: Why People Are Motivated to Post and Fund Projects on Crowdfunding Platforms*, Northwestern University Evanston, IL (2012).

Gill, Rebecca, *The Evolution of Organizational Archetypes: From the American to the Entrepreneurial Dream*, 80 COMM. MONOGRAPHS 331 (2013).

Klein, Tobias J. et al., *Adverse Selection and Moral Hazard in Anonymous Markets*, § 13–050.

Massa, Annie and Edward Robinson, *Robinhood's Role in the "Gamification" of Investing*, BLOOMBERG WEALTH (December 19, 2020).

McKenny, Aaron F. et al., *How Should Crowdfunding Research Evolve? A Survey of the Entrepreneurship Theory and Practice Editorial Board*, 41 ENTREPRENEURSHIP THEORY AND PRACTICE 291 (2017).

Nordhaus, William D., *Schumpeterian Profits in the American Economy: Theory and Measurement*, NAT'L BUREAU OF ECON. RESEARCH, Working Paper No. 10433 (2004).

Oranburg, Seth C., *Bridgefunding: Crowdfunding and the Market for Entrepreneurial Finance*, 25 CORNELL JOURNAL OF LAW AND PUBLIC POLICY 397 (2015).

Oranburg, Seth C., *A Place of Their Own: Crowds in the New Market for Equity Crowdfunding*, 100 MINNESOTA LAW REVIEW HEADNOTES 147 (2016).

Oranburg, Seth C., *Democratizing Startups*, 68 RUTGERS UNIVERSITY LAW REVIEW (2017).

Ordanini, Andrea et al., *Crowd-Funding: Transforming Customers into Investors through Innovative Service Platforms*, 22 JOURNAL OF SERVICE MANAGEMENT (2011).

Press Release, Comm'r Luis A. Aguilar, U.S. Sec. & Exch. Comm'n, *The Need for Greater Secondary Market Liquidity for Small Businesses* (March 4, 2015).

Press Release, Office of the Press Sec'y, President Obama to Sign Jumpstart Our Business Startups (JOBS) Act (April 5, 2012).

Quittner, Jeremy, *The American Dream Is Dying: How Entrepreneurs Can Change That*, INC. MAGAZINE (January 14, 2015), available at https://perma.cc/E6UV-Z2PC.

Robb, Alicia M., *Entrepreneurial Performance by Women and Minorities: The Case of New Firms*, 7 J. DEVELOPMENTAL ENTREPRENEURSHIP 383 (2002).

Schwartz, Andrew A., *The Digital Shareholder*, 100 MINNESOTA LAW REVIEW (2015).

Solomon, Lewis D. & Garry S. Grossman, *Tax and Non-Tax Policies to Promote Capital Formation: Stimulating High Technology in the 1980's*, 1 AM. J. TAX POL'Y 63 (1982).

U.S. Senate Committee on Small Business & Entrepreneurship, *Access to Capital*, available at https://perma.cc/JJP7-A5DU.

Conclusion

This book journeyed through time to show how many of the seemingly new and incomprehensible financial technologies in the modern world have analogues in the past. The goal of this journey was to make those seemingly abstruse and inexplicable current events more readily understandable. Hopefully, this gives readers the context needed to make better financial decisions. But the greater goal is to show that current events demonstrate that the era of traditional financial regulation is over. This is a call to action for scholars, lawyers, judges, and policymakers to rethink law and regulation in light of a digitally connected world.

The story of American financial history unfolds across three eras. The First Era (1791–1932) is characterized by financial markets that were loosely regulated by the states and subject to few national regulations. The Second Era (1932–2002) is defined by the rapid expansion of the national regulatory apparatus in political responses to the financial crises, beginning with the Great Depression. The Third Era (2002–present) was also born from financial crises, the Dot-Com Bubble and the Great Recession, but is characterized by a private, technological response to perceived over-regulation and over-reach by a government that has decayed from free-market capitalism to cronyism. We are now living in the Third Era, when technology offers alternatives to federally regulated financial markets – and when millions of people are choosing to migrate from regulated markets onto the vast unregulated financial internet.

The First Era began when America's founding fathers enacted the Constitution of the United States, which became effective in 1789. This supreme law created a small national government and reserved many financial powers for the states who were recently colonies. This new style of government, called federalism, allowed different states to experiment with various financial regulations. States, in turn, created various laws that allowed people to charter corporations.

Corporations are entities that are treated by law as separate from their owners. Corporations are necessary for industrial society because they allow people to contribute money (capital) and effort (labor) toward a joint enterprise. Investors in corporations today enjoy limited liability, meaning investors cannot lose more than their investment. This encourages investment and productivity, but it also has a social cost. If a corporation cannot pay its debts or otherwise meet its obligations to credits, then creditors lose their claim. In technical terms, corporations externalize risks onto society.

States sought (and still seek) to balance the social benefit of corporations – enhanced productivity, faster innovation, lower costs of goods and services, etc. – with the social cost of externalized risk. In the early days of the First Era, state legislatures needed to authorize the creation of every new corporation. This resulted in the creation of few corporations, many of which were created by rich and powerful people. For example, Alexander Hamilton, who was the state representative for New York before the Constitution and a primary force for the Constitution's ratification, founded the Bank of New York. Corporations, money, and politics were thus closely intertwined from America's origin.

During Hamilton's tenure as the first Secretary of the Treasury of the United States, New York developed toward being the financial center of the fledgling nation. A group of stockbrokers and merchants formed the New York Stock Exchange in 1792. In that same year, the Federalist party formally organized itself as the first political party in America. Known as the party of merchants and bankers (contrasting with the Jeffersonian anti-Federalists who tended to be landowners and farmers), the Federalists dominated the early national government and enacted policies favoring banking corporations and stock markets. Congress, which was majority Federalist at the time, created the First Bank of the United States in 1971.

The Federalists did not maintain power for long. President Thomas Jefferson, a notable anti-Federalist, defeated incumbent President John Adams in 1800. Jefferson, a wealthy landowner, opposed the national bank in particular and investment in general, which he decried as speculation. He ostensibly preferred productive labor, such as farming for crops, even those this labor was to come from the hundreds of slaves he owned over his lifetime. President James Madison, another slaveowner, succeeded Jefferson in 1808. Both men shared views about abrogating the national bank. Madison succeeded in this ambition in 1811, when the Senate voted not to renew the bank's charter.

Madison's timing turned out to be terrible, as the nation needed funds for the upcoming War of 1812. Without a national bank to borrow from, the national government borrowed from private banks. This led to a boom in private banks, which is ironic, considering that the policy was established by two men who wished to shift power from the bankers to the landowners. This is just one of many examples of unintended consequences in the history of finance. Madison apparently recognized this folly, however, and oversaw the charter of the Second Bank of the United States in 1816.

In 1929, however, President Andrew Jackson, cofounder of the Democratic party, defeated President John Quincey Adams (a son of John Adams who shared many of his father's Federalist beliefs, including that slavery is morally wrong). Jackson followed in Jefferson's and Madison's footsteps: Jackson owned slaves and despised bankers. He campaigned to destroy the Second Bank of the United Stated, and he succeeded in 1832, when Jackson vetoed a bill to renew the bank's charter.

The connection between pro-slavery and anti-national-bank is no coincidence. Leading politicians of the time believed that a national bank could undermine slavery. Nathaniel Macon (Democrat-North Carolina) remarked, "If Congress can make banks, roads and canals under the Constitution, they can free any slave in the United States." John Tyler (Democrat-Virginia) concurred, "if Congress can incorporate a bank, it might emancipate a slave."

Jackson's campaign succeeded in destroying the national bank, but it did not help the economy of his pro-slavery constituents. Rather, it led to the Panic of 1837, a financial crisis. Ironically, this crisis harmed the agrarian Southern states more than the industrial Northern states. Cotton plantations, which were powered by slave labor, had a particularly had time selling their goods, since merchants could not borrow money to buy them.

States responded to the Democrat's opposition to national banking by passing new state laws allowing state banks to be easily created. This led to an explosion in new state banks, many of which issued their own currency. About half the banks failed in the next crisis, the Panic of 1857. Now armed with evidence that free banking did not prevent crises, states rescinded free banking laws. This pendulum swing in policy reflects the general tenor of financial regulation that persists to this day: whenever there is a financial crisis, governments seek to change policy to prevent it from happening again. But politicians do not always learn from the past. The result of failing to learn lessons from history is a flip-flop in policy from crisis to crisis, but not an end to financial crises at large.

The national division between slave states and free states proved unsustainable. In the early 1860s, Southern states formally seceded from the Union to form the Confederacy, and this "house divided" went to war on July 21, 1861. To fund the Union war effort, the U.S. Congress passed the Legal Tender Act of 1862, which permitted the federal government to issue the familiar "greenback" dollar bills we still have today. Controlling the money supply helped the Union pay for and eventually win the Civil War.

The end of the Civil War marks the beginning of the period known as the Reconstruction Era. To knit the war-torn United States back together, Congress helped fund the Transcontinental Railroad. Private investors built a rail network that connected East and West, North and South. Railroads, however, are expensive to build. To raise funds for these ambitious projects, financiers developed a new form of investment contract called preferred stock.

Unlike common stock, which reflects ownership rights in a corporation and conveys rights to profits and limited voting rights, preferred stock includes "preferences," such as greater governance rights, rights to be paid a dividend, rights to inspect books and records, and rights to sit on the board of directors. This hybrid of common stock and debt was initially criticized for favoring the wealthy who could afford to purchase such preferences over the common people who could not. But preferred stock appealed to moneyed interests, who funded rail projects across America with this investment vehicle. Over time, more preferences evolved, such as liquidation rights and rights of first refusal, and there is now a complex venture capital industry that deals mainly in this once-innovative form of stock.

Alongside the railroads, Western Union built telegraph poles. Through a network of electric wires strung on these poles, people could communicate almost instantly used a telegraph. The first telegraphs could only make and receive a buzzing noise, and people used Morse code, a series of short and long sounds, to communicate messages. Then, David Edward Hughes developed a telegraph that could translate these electrical signals into letters and numbers, which it printed on reel of tape. One of the predominate use cases for this new communication device was to transmit financial information. The New York Stock Exchange began sending out information about current stock prices, and people everywhere began "watching the ticker."

The stock ticker created a heightened interest in financial markets, but ordinary people still were not able to easily participate. The New York Stock Exchange, for example, only permitted eleven hundred stockbrokers to trade on the exchange. At its First Era peak, a "seat" on the New York Stock Exchange cost the equivalent of over ten million dollars today. Stockbrokers had to recoup these costs by charging commissions. Since it was no more difficult to trade ten thousand shares than one hundred shares, commissions decreased on a per share basis as order size increased. Orders of less than one hundred shares were considered odd lots and subject to additional fees. This cost structure, which discouraged small transactions and encouraged large ones, made it difficult for low-wealth investors to afford stockbrokers and thus to participate in stock markets.

It was likely frustrating for many to watch the ticker and hear about others becoming wealthy through stock ownership with no real means of investing. Some such people who could not invest with established stockbrokers found other means to parlay their money in bucket shops, which was akin to gambling.

By the 1900s, bucket shops had popped up across America. Although cleverly designed to look like high-end stockbrokerage firms, bucket shops were merely gambling dens. Unlike stockbrokers, who are paid for making trades or when clients make money, bucket shop traders only profit when their clients lose. What's more deleterious and unethical, the bucket shop traders manipulated the market to earn profits for themselves. Although bucket shops were eventually shut down as the First Era of unbridled financial markets ended, their popularity shows that the distinction between investing, speculating, and gambling can easily blur. This also hints at the unintended consequences that may arise where people are kept from investing.

Investing can be a safe and socially productive activity. Investors who purchase stock in a corporation get legal rights, and the directors of the corporation owe duties to those investors as a matter of law. Invested money helps corporations do business. Gambling, on the other hand, lacks legal protections and offers few social benefits. Instead of funding innovation, money goes to whoever is luckier or less scrupulous. In the First Era, people were not able to invest simply because it was too expense, and so they gambled. Soon, however, in the Second Era, governments prohibited people from investing as a matter of law. Now, in our Third Era, these prohibitions are under tension. People who lack access to investment opportunities are once again gambling, although now they are doing this on the internet, where government prohibitions are hard to apply.

America's First Era and its investment craze ended abruptly in late October 1929, when the New York Stock Exchange suddenly crashed. Premier stocks in famous corporations lost 11 percent of their value in a single day. Lower quality stocks fared worse. Then the market kept crashing. Over the course of three brutal years (1929–1932), the premier stocks lost almost 90 percent of their value. (The market did not fully recover until 1959.) In this face of yet another financial crisis, the government once again flip-flopped on its financial policy. First, President Franklin Delano Roosevelt, a Democrat, beat incumbent President Herbert Hoover, a Republican, by a landslide election in 1932. Then, Roosevelt, who campaigned in 1932 as a fiscal conservative who promised traditional economic policies including balancing the federal budget, changed his politics radically. During his twelve years in office Roosevelt oversaw the largest expansion of the federal government in American history. He even threated to subvert the Supreme Court of the United States if they dared opine that his far-reaching policies were unconstitutional. His tactics worked, insofar as Roosevelt changed America from a federalist system, with a relatively weak central government compared with the power of the states, to an administrative system, with a large central bureaucracy.

In this time known as the New Deal – which this book identifies as the beginning of the Second Era in American financial history – Roosevelt oversaw the creation of the Securities and Exchange Commission (SEC), a federal agency with sweeping power over financial markets. He charged the SEC with the triumvirate purpose of protecting investors; maintaining fair, orderly, and efficient markets; and facilitating capital formation. These purposes are often at odds with one another. For example, the SEC prevents fraud by requiring corporations to disclose information about their business to stockholders, which protects investors; but this disclosure regime is costly, making capital markets less efficient and inhibiting capital formation.

In the Eastern United States, New York became the financial center for publicly traded corporations, which preferred to list on the prestigious New York Stock Exchange. Listed corporations must comply with SEC disclosure requirements and stock exchange requirements. These expensive requirements result in only relatively large corporations being able to profitably list on a stock exchange and trade publicly. Commissions for small orders remained high, and this made it difficult for small investors to be sufficiently diversified by investing in many different corporations.

To overcome this challenge, Massachusetts Inventors Trust created a new financial technology: the mutual fund. A mutual fund is a professionally selected bundle of stocks. By purchasing a share of a mutual fund, investors get a smaller share of all the stocks in the bundle. In this way, investors can get broad exposure to the stock market without purchasing hundreds of individual shares.

In 1939, Nazi Germany invaded Poland. Thus began World War II. World War II demonstrated some of the worst qualities of humankind. Yet the war also motivated nations to develop new technologies that might give them an edge on the battlefield. Some of these technologies have financial uses that provided benefits after the costs of war are paid. World War II prompted the U.S. government to partner with universities and invest massively in developing computer technologies. Early computers solved a very simple problem: how to calculate ballistic firing trajectories.

Alongside the well-known Manhattan Project, the research and development project that produced the nuclear bombs that were detonated over Hiroshima and Nagasaki, the government also sponsored research and development on computers. The ENIAC (Electronic Numerical Integrator and Computer) project resulted in the world's first general-purpose computer. When it was first switched on in 1946, it could solve ballistics problems in thirty seconds that would have taken a human twenty hours to solve. But despite ENIAC's power, it was extremely clunky and unreliable. The machine weighed thirty tons, and it was dysfunctional for about half of its ten-year service life.

ENIAC's huge size and problematic reliability stemmed from its use of vacuum tubes to perform computations. Vacuum tubes look like complicated light bulbs, and, like conventional light bulbs, they require heat to operate. This heat causes them to burn out easily. Taking the next step in computing technology required developing an alternative to vacuum tubes. In 1947, Bell Labs developed a field-effect transistor (FET), a device that could replace some of the functions of a vacuum tube without relying on heat to perform calculations. In 1949, Siemens AG developed a way to arrange several transistors on a single chip called an integrated circuit (IC) chip. In 1959, Fairchild Semiconductor presented the first IC chip that was made of silicon.

From 1961 to 1965, NASA's Apollo Program used silicon ICs to perform the various calculations needed to send men into space and return them safely to earth. The space race encouraged further advances in computer power, and industry responded by researching new chip technology that was easier to miniaturize and mass produce. In 1968, RCA revealed the complementary metal-oxide-semiconductor (CMOS), which featured both a more efficient fabrication process and less heat waste. This product marks a breakthrough, the beginning of the so-called MOSFET (metal-oxide-semiconductor field-effect transistor) revolution, because from this time forward companies could continue making MOSFET ICs smaller and faster.

Gordon Moore, who worked at Fairchild Semiconductor, predicted that, thanks to MOSFET technology, ICs should double in power every two years. His prediction, now called "Moore's law," has so far proved reliable. Thanks to MOSFET technology, the availability and power of computers increased exponentially from the 1970s. The financial industries quickly adopted this new technology. Computer engineers found that computers which can solve physics problems can solve financial problems, too. By the mid-1970s, computer technology matured enough to enable a critical evolution in financial technology: the index fund.

Index funds are essentially mutual funds that are managed by computers. Programmers give computers a set of criteria, called an algorithm, to buy and sell stocks, then computers execute trades according to their program. This presents several advantages. Computers are not influenced by emotion. Computers do not get anxious, tired, or fatigued. Computers can trade stocks at thousands of times per second. Computers do not shirk or self-deal. But while computers do not commit fraud, programmers might. Computers can be programmed to scam markets using various techniques. When the SEC outlaws one index fund scam, another seems to pop up to take its place. That said, for every scam, there are millions of fair, value-creating trades.

But the story of the index fund is not all rosy. While computers rarely make mistakes, programmers do. Errant programming leads to strange market movements that can destroy billions of dollars of value per second. There have been several such "flash crashes" in history. Perhaps the first occurred on Black Monday, October 19, 1987, when all major world markets experienced a sharp decline. U.S. markets fell 20 to 40 percent that day. Some of the blame was foisted upon index funds, who were all programmed to sell shares in such an event, causing a sudden market drop to quickly spiral down to new depths. Regulators established circuit breakers, temporary measures to curb panic-selling. Under these regulators, markets automatically stop trading with indexes fall by certain daily limits. These regulators appear to stop panic selling – and such protections are notably absent in cryptocurrency markets today.

Despite some drawbacks to index funds, many experts highly recommend that unsophisticated investors should mainly purchase index funds from reputable financial companies. There are few human investment advisors today who can generate more value than computer-powered index funds can.

While algorithmic trading began influencing Wall Street in the 1970s thanks to new computer technology, the computer industry itself began developing rapidly on the other side of the country. In Silicon Valley, a region of California spanning from San Francisco to San Jose, an entrepreneurial spirit and appetite for taking big risks led investors down a separate path. Instead of using computers to make a few fractions of a cent per trade over millions of trades, why not invest in the next big thing? Instead of investing in established public companies, perhaps there was a way to earn higher returns by investing in new ventures or startups.

The American Research & Development Corporation established itself as the first venture capital firm. ARDC focused on investing in startups, nascent businesses with little track record and big promises. When ARDC formed in 1946, hundreds of thousands of soldiers were returning home from war. Many of these soldiers decided to make something of themselves through entrepreneurship, and ARDC was intent on financing them. For a while, it was the only game in town. This gave it a huge advantage. But investors are not likely to leave money on the table for long. An entire financial industry would eventually move into Silicon Valley.

The early venture capital playbook was hard for other investors to follow, as it required personal knowledge and connections. Investing in this way also involved legal risks. The Securities Act of 1933 allowed sophisticated investors to purchase stock in unregistered corporations so long as they did not involve a public offering. This legal standard was so vague that the SEC attempted to clarify it in 1935 by establishing a four-factor test. That test also did not provide enough clarity to comfort investors. Then, in 1982, the SEC promulgated Regulation D, which finally provided a clear rule regarding who could invest in startups. In short, "accredited" investors (defined as having more than one million dollars in net assets, more than two hundred thousand dollars in single income, or more than three hundred thousand dollars in joint-marital income) could invest in private, unregistered corporations so long as there was no "general solicitation" (advertising the sale of stock to the public). This legal safe harbor gave the venture capital industry the legal certainty it needed to grow. Annual contributions to venture capital funds rose from just over one hundred million dollars in the 1970s to over four billion dollars by the end of the 1980s.

The United States experienced a brief period of deregulation in the 1980s. President Ronald Reagan, a Republican, succeeded President Jimmy Carter, a Democrat, in 1981 and introduced "Reaganomics," economic policies that reduced tax rates, reduced government spending, privatized industries, and deregulated banking. Forty years later, people are still debating the efficacy of his policies. On the one side, Nobel Prize-winning economists Milton Friedman and Robert Mundell asset that Reaganomics improved the economy into the 1990s. On the other side, Nobel Prize-winning economist Robert Solow asserts that Reaganomics was such a failure, at least in the public's perception, that his successor, President George H. W. Bush, also a Republican, reversed his campaign promise of "no new taxes." Bush's successor, President Bill Clinton, a Democrat, took office in 1983. But despite the change in party, Clinton did not radically change economic policy during his tenure. In fact, Clinton oversaw the repeal of the Glass-Steagall Act, which further deregulated banking.

From the 1980s to the turn of the millennium, venture capital firms out West invested in private startup corporations through staged investment until the startups were large enough to go public and list on a stock exchange. When a company goes from private to public and lists on a stock exchange, that is called an initial public offering or IPO. Although traditional companies listed on the prestigious New York Stock Exchange, tech startups were attracted to another innovator: the NASDAQ. The National Association of Securities Dealers formed the NASDAQ in 1971 as an alternative to the New York Stock Exchange. Although it lacked prestige, it made up for this with innovative financial technology. Unlike traditional stock exchanges, which have a trading floor on which stockbrokers call out buy and sell orders, the NASDAQ used a fully electronic trading system. It was ready made for the emerging index funds because computer trading algorithms essentially plugged into the NASDAQ, allowing for fully automated trading. The NASDAQ allowed companies to list using a wider variety of names. It permitted trades of just a penny, paving the way for penny stocks to enter public markets. Perhaps most importantly, it was cheaper to list on the NASDAQ than the New York Stock Exchange.

NASDAQ's advantages led not only to NASDAQ becoming a popular choice for startup IPOs. It also encouraged more IPOs to occur. The advent of the Regulation D safe harbor for private financing and the NASDAQ listing option for when it was time to go public correlated with a five fold increase in IPO activity: from 1973 to 1982 (pre-Regulation D), there were an average of 66 IPOs per year; and from 1983 to 2000, there were an average of 343 IPOs per year. The IPO market peaked in 1996, where there were almost 700 IPOs. The NASDAQ's total value also spiked over this period, reaching a peak in March 2000.

Then the stock market crashed again. The late 1990s investment craze was later termed the Dot-Com Bubble because there seemed to be a mania for investing in any company that purported to do business online. Traditional rules for valuing stocks went out the window and were replaced by convictions that profits were not important; rather, growth was the predominant factor for Dot-Com investors. Some fast-growing companies even went public without having any meaningful revenues. It is not clear what drove this magical thinking, but the mindset shifted from focusing on fundamentals to growing large as fast as possible. The idea seemed to be based on the notion of first-mover advantage, that the first company to get huge would dominate its sector of the internet, at which point it could stop burning cash and start making incredible profits. This did happen to a few companies like Amazon, but most flamed out quickly.

As with seemingly every financial crisis, the Dot-Com Bubble was followed by another regulatory attempt to take the risk out of markets. President George W. Bush, a Republican who campaigned as a fiscal conservative slogans, signed the bipartisan Sarbanes-Oxley Act of 2002 (SOX) into law, which was designed to protect investors from fraud by requiring more financial reporting by public corporations and setting tougher penalties on violators. At the signing, Bush declared, "today I sign the most far-reaching reforms of American business practices since the time of Franklin Delano Roosevelt." It seemed like 1932, when popular sentiment drove Roosevelt to abandon his traditional economic policies and grow the administrative state.

SOX echoes the zeitgeist of the Securities Act and its presumption that required disclosures are the most effective bulwark against fraud. SOX amped up disclosure requirements, which were already onerous, on public companies. All of this was expensive, and, in retrospect, seems unlikely to solve the problem that created the Dot-Com Bubble. In the bubble mindset, no one seemed to care that they were buying stock in companies that lost millions of dollars per year. It was not that this fact was undisclosed; rather, it was disclosed and ignored. The solution of more disclosures, therefore, did not seem to fit the problem.

Moreover, SOX's great expense upon public companies strongly discouraged companies from going public. In the years immediately following SOX's enactment (2003–2007), IPOs fell by almost two-thirds. The unintended consequence of this investor-protection regulation was, ironically, even less disclosure and therefore, according to SOX's own philosophy, less protection. As the cost-benefit analysis of going public turned negative, companies stayed private. Private companies do not need to make hardly any disclosures under the securities laws.

This did not mean, of course, that investors stopped investing. Rather, they switched from investing in public corporations, where they had at least some disclosure requirements and federal oversight, into private corporations and ever more exotic financial instruments. Prior to SOX, corporations almost always went public in an IPO before becoming worth one billion dollars. The rare company that exceeds one billion dollars in value while still private is called a unicorn. The only startup company that seems to have accomplished this in the 1990s and prior is Google, which is now public. But after SOX, unicorns proliferated. There were over 900 unicorns in 2021, collectively worth over three trillion dollars. There are other factors, of course, including additional regulations such as the Dodd-Frank Act of 2010 that made it yet more expensive to go public (and thus further encouraged staying private). But the fact remains trillions of dollars more wealth is concentrated in private companies who have no public disclosures requirements after Congress passed laws requiring public companies to make more disclosures. The net effect of these disclosures mandates, therefore, seems to be less disclosure, which is precisely the opposite of what Congress intended.

Moreover, SOX did not prevent an even worse financial crisis. Less than six years after SOX passed, the Great Recession of 2007–2008 roiled America and indeed the world. Financial crises rarely have simple causes, and myriad forces cased the Great Recession. But perhaps the most egregious culprit behind this crisis was a new financial instrument called a collateralized debt obligation.

In the early 2000s, investment banks on Wall Street, who perhaps were looking for a new line of business after the IPO market dried up, decided to get creative and invest in some new, and questionable, financial products. The investment banks purchased bundles of home mortgages from retail banks, who make loans to home buyers. The investment banks then performed some complicated math to divide these pools into "tranches" based on risk. Each tranche got a risk rating from AAA (best) to F (worst). Tranches with the same rating were combined, and then divided again, resulting in a new financial product called a collateralized debt obligation (CDO). Some repeated this process several times, creating CDO^2, CDO^3, CDO^4, etc.

Ratings agencies gave these CDOs low risk ratings, based on the theory that you could rarify away risk with math. The ratings agencies also got huge fees for blessing these products, which makes their ratings at least somewhat suspect. The investment banks then sold the CDOs for much higher prices than they could have sold its components. It was like turning lead into gold.

But even lead must be mined. It is much easier to sell a photograph of lead, especially if you can sell it as real gold. Investment banks realized it would be easier to create entirely synthetic products. They created the synthetic CDO. These derivates represent future values of CDOs. Like a hologram, synthetic CDOs have no substance of their own. Synthetic CDOs are merely a projection of an idea. Investment banks issued over sixty billion dollars of synthetic securities in 2006 alone.

It turned out that investment banks cannot turn F rated "lead" into AAA rated "gold." By mid-2007, it became evident that our financial system was riddled with unanticipated risk. These complex and synthetic financial products, dreamed up by PhD physicists and mathematicians, had very little relationship to reality.

Back in reality, homeowners who couldn't afford their mortgages began defaulting on their loans. These defaults drove home prices down, which meant more people were underwater on their loans (they owed more than the house was worth). Recognizing that paying the mortgage would financially ruin them, homeowners began abandoning properties. That pushed home prices down further. This led to more defaults. Within months, purportedly risk-free assets were looking risky. The risk rating agencies finally acknowledged their error and downgraded thousands of CDOs. Now the CDOs were not worth what banks paid for them.

The federal government called these CDOs "toxic assets" and, to avoid an economic meltdown, congress passed the Troubled Asset Relief Program (TARP) in 2008. TARP enabled the U.S. Treasury to purchase these toxic assets, thus saving Wall Street from total ruin. This turned out to be a good bet for the Treasury, who eventually sold its holdings for a profit. Moreover, the global economy did not collapse, but rather slowed into what is now called the Great Recession.

While the economy did not technically enter a depression because of this financial crisis, it did push society into the Third Era of financial technology. A movement known as the Cypherpunks used computer science to create alternative technologies that resisted government control. The term "cypher" refers to a secret code. This movement worked on making secret codes using cryptography, secure communication techniques that enabled anonymous messages and transaction.

The loosely affiliated group was organized by Eric Hughes, who wrote *A Cypherpunk's Manifesto* (1993), which predicted that "cryptography will ineluctably spread over the whole globe, and with it the anonymous transactions systems that it makes possible." The group generally believed in decentralized structures, and they encoded their political philosophy in their digital cryptography projects. But it would take about fifteen years – and a financial crisis – to push their technology out of the shadows and into the mainstream.

The 2007–2008 financial crisis apparently prompted the Cypherpunks to redouble their efforts. On Halloween, 2008, someone using the pseudonym Satoshi Nakamoto emailed the group a link to a nine-page paper describing what is now called Bitcoin. On January 3, 2009, Nakamoto started the Bitcoin program. The program then created the Genesis Block, which contained the first fifty Bitcoins and this cryptic message: "The Times 03/Jan/2009 Chancellor on brink of second bailout for banks." Many interpret this message in the context of the Bitcoin project to express the Cypherpunks' distrust of central banking and desire to create a decentralized currency that governments could not control.

The Bitcoin protocol simply allows people to exchange digital currency. Newer protocols have even more advanced features. The Ethereum network, for example, allows users to write smart contracts that operate on its blockchain.

Smart contracts are essentially small computer programs. They automatically execute a command when certain conditions are met. For smart contracts to be really smart, however, they need information about the outside world. The next generation of blockchain technology uses "oracles" to feed data from external systems into the blockchain. Blockchain technology can now react to the happenings of the world.

While the Cypherpunks used cryptography to preserve their anonymity, thus creating Bitcoin and blockchain technology, others use technology to become famous. Social media technology has created a new means of influencing financial markets. "Influencers" are people who have cultivated a reputation as an expert and leverages that to charge for endorsements and product placements, and "microcelebrity" means a person who is famous within a niche group of users on social media. Thanks to social media, there are now "insta-famous" influencers, who are famous for being famous.

Influencers can and do affect stock prices, too. For example, when Carl Icahn, the legendary investor, tweeted that he has a large position in Apple Corporation, the stock price immediately rose and hit a six-month high. When Elon Musk, CEO of Tesla Corporation, tweeted that he was selling 10 percent of his shares to pay taxes, the stock price fell almost 5 percent. The SEC has investigated some of Musk's tweets because they could violate Regulation Fair Disclosure, which limits what major public companies can say to a select audience. The SEC fined Musk for his impropriety, but he continues to bend the rules to their limits.

Even people who are not already famous can impact stock prices from their desktops. Keith Gill, who posts on the social media platform Reddit under the username DeepFuckingValue, drove a frenzied mob to purchase GameStop stock in the major "meme" stock event of 2021. Gill and others on the Reddit forum r/

WallStreetBets stoked passions about sticking it to the hedge fund managers who took short positions (bets that the stock price will go down) in Game Stock by buying the stock and driving the price up. The plan worked. In January 2021, users of the RobinHood stock trading app piled into GameStop stock, whose price increased 1500 percent in two weeks. Gill turned his fifty-three thousand dollar investment into forty-eight million dollars.

Gill's success set off a meme stock craze. Meme stocks are stocks that are popular because they are popular, like how insta-famous influencers are famous for being famous. Even if there is no underlying value-based reason to buy a meme stock, investors (or gamblers, as the name r/WallStreetBets implies) are expecting the stock price to go up because others expect the price to go up. Meme investing reflects a herding mentality known in crowd science as an information cascade, where people make decisions based solely on other people's decisions. This is dangerous because social media creates an echo chamber environment, where people tend to hear from others who already agree with them. Outside the echo chamber, the herd's behavior might seem bizarre or irrational.

Regardless of whether today's popular social media channels cause negative behaviors, corporations cannot afford to ignore social media. Accordingly, social media has changed how corporations behave. Corporations used to focus on key shareholders, who might threaten to vote for new management, to sell out their shares, or to purchase enough shares to take over the company. That focus has shifted somewhat to social media influencers who may not own shares at all. "Greentrolling" is mocking, embarrassing, harassing, and otherwise drawing negative attention to corporations perceived not to be environmentally friendly. Social media users engage in greentrolling campaigns against companies like Exxonmobil to embarrass them into changing corporate practices. This creates new risks for management, who have an obligation to make profits for shareholders, but also need to maintain a positive brand identity.

Although Twitter, Facebook, Instagram, and other platforms are designed to generate "likes" and "followers," not accurate information or critical thought, other platforms are designed differently. AngelList, for example, uses social media tools to organize investment groups. Prospective investors first need to apply to prove they are accredited to invest. Then, investors must follow a listed lead investor who was subject to additional scrutiny. The lead investors present biographies that explain in detail their credentials and strategy. The investors then must apply to follow a lead investor, which usually results in personal communication between the would-be follower and the lead. Only after the two decide to work together can the investor began looking at prospective deals. At every step of the way the platform warns, "Investing in startups is risky – most go out of business." Startups who are seeking funds can post on the AngelList platform, then investors critically appraise the company and discuss its value proposition. The lead investor typically negotiates the deal on behalf of the group.

AngelList is an example of equity crowdfunding, a new concept in digital investing that was enabled by the Jumpstart Our Business Startups Act of 2012. Crowdfunding websites, called portals or platforms, have strong incentives to create a safe and secure experience for investors; otherwise, they can lose their license. Moreover, investors will leave the platform if it does not ensure some measure of fraud prevention. These portals function like little islands in the internet where personal trust and a human connection is still valued. Ratings are based on past performance, not on likes, and everyone goes by their real name.

So far, the experiment in equity crowdfunding is going well. There have been virtually zero stories of fraud in equity crowdfunding. This is particularly commendable when compared to what's happening in highly regulated markets: Bernie Madoff perpetrated the largest Ponzi scheme under the nose of regulations; an anonymous guy with an expletive for a screen name moved public stock markets with the theme of stick it to the fat cats; and celebrity influencers are promoting exotic cryptocurrency investments to a hundred million followers on social media. In comparison to the highly regulated world of public financial markets, where frauds, scams, and gambling appear rampant, the relatively unregulated world of crowdfunding appears tame.

This relative lack of fraud in equity crowdfunding conduction on registered portals, as compared with both the highly regulated public markets and the unregulated and perhaps unregulatable cryptocurrency markets, merits further analysis. It could be found that there are alternatives to traditional investor-protection agencies and regulations that are more effective at preventing fraud. In the future, scholars might consider whether Web 2.0 and Web3 technology can be employed to simultaneously reduce regulatory burden, enhance capital formation, stimulate efficient markets, and reduce fraud.

The SEC appears to recognize that crowdfunding is relatively safe and effective. On November 2, 2020, the SEC announced it would raise the Reg CF exception from one million to five million dollars that could be raised per company per year by equity crowdfunding. It simultaneously raised the limit for Regulation A mini-IPOs and the amount that entrepreneurs can raise from friends and family. Meanwhile, it simplified and harmonized much of its complex set of rules. It is too early to evaluate how effective these amendments have been at achieving the goal of facilitating capital formation, or whether they have unintended negative consequences in the form of fraud risks to investors. But preliminarily, there are still no reports of significant fraud in related financial markets. This should encourage entrepreneurs and investors to participate more activity in crowdfunding, which will hopefully prove safer and, in the long run, more productive for society than cryptocurrency and other trending alternative investments.

As this book goes to press, alternative investments are emerging daily. Since I began writing this book, Cypherpunks developed an entirely new asset class, the non-fungible token (NFT). Facebook changed its name to Meta, and dozens of startups are now racing to build the "metaverse," which is an immersive digital

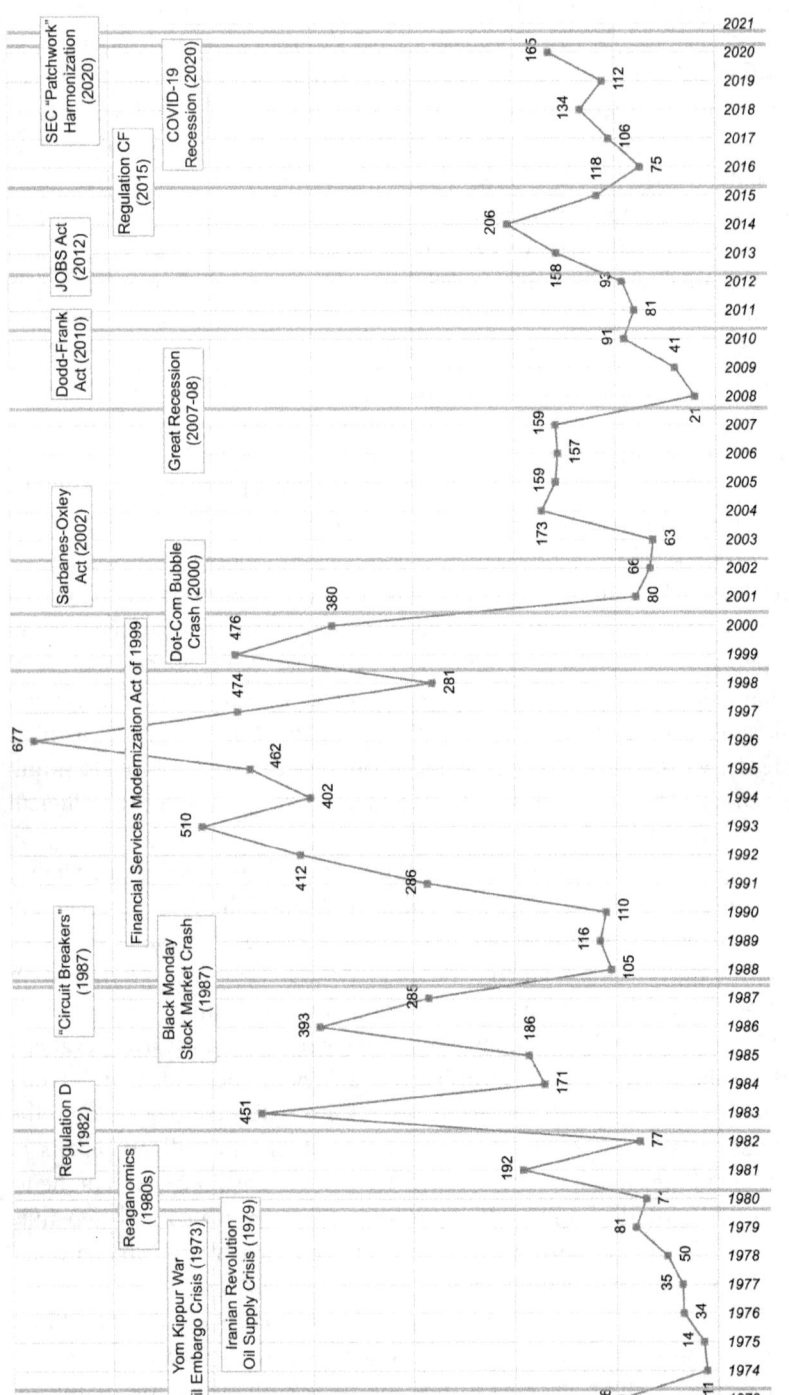

FIGURE 12.1 Financial crises, regulations, and the IPO market from 1973 to 2020.

space. Sandbox and Decentraland are new user-generated worlds that feature property rights, their own currency, voting mechanisms, marketplaces, live concerts, and, of course, advertisements. Investors are racing to buy up this new digital property, resulting in some absurd valuations.

Some people are going to get extremely rich extremely quickly in this Third Era of investing. Others will be tempted to mimic their strategies. Some will lose more than they can afford to lose. This is a dangerous game that not everyone should play. While the global market for goods and services in the metaverse may well be worth a trillion dollars someday, no one can yet say which metaverse, if any, will succeed in what appears to be a winner-take-all game.

The emergence of the metaverse and the rapid investment into it is yet another data point showing that we cannot simply continue to try and regulate financial markets as if it were still the Second Era. In this Third Era, people can easily choose to leave the protection of regulated markets from the safety and comfort of their homes simply by going on the internet. We cannot simply force people to be prudent by prohibiting them from investing in startups, for example, because they will find new ways to invest that may be even riskier.

It is critical to find new ways to balance protection and opportunity in financial markets because the future is likely to be even more tumultuous than the past. The rate of change seems to be accelerating. Perhaps alternative markets are already mainstream. In the 1990s, a fringe group of hackers called Cypherpunks sought to avoid government control by developing cyphers and cryptocurrency. In 2021, millions of people and corporations are looking to escape from the administrative bureaucracy that regulates the American economy by moving their financial activities onto an encrypted and anonymous internet. Before dismissing all these people as simply irrational or foolish, it is worth considering whether this trend reflects a rational and long-standing frustration with business as usual.

Over the past twenty years, the government has substantially grown its influence over financial markets to protect citizens from financial crises. But financial crises keep happening. The response to each crisis has traditionally been more regulation. But regulation encourages people to migrate to unregulated markets. Despite ratcheting up disclosure and compliance regimes, the financial world does not seem to be a safer place.

Albert Einstein (apparently) said, "insanity is doing the same thing over and over and expecting different results." Perhaps it is time to consider alternative approaches, especially considering that the regulatory state has huge and disparate social costs. After two decades of increasing regulation, American wealth inequality is at an all-time high. According to the World Bank, America's Gini coefficient, which statistically measures wealth inequality, rose from 0.38 in 1990 to 0.414 in 2018. Statistica reports it increased to 0.49 in 2020. This growing gap between rich and poor fuels social tensions and raises doubts about the efficacy of the entire financial system.

While correlation does not prove causation, it is notable that, as the federal government increasingly regulated the financial sector in this Third Era, the rich got richer while the poor got poorer. Across the political spectrum, many people perceive that free-market capitalism has irredeemably collapsed into bureaucratic cronyism, where the most powerful one percent award favors to each other, while the other ninety-nine percent face a rigged system and play a game they cannot win.

In this light, the fact that millions of people are abandoning the financial protections of the regulatory state and flocking into uncharted territory makes sense. People appear to be attracted to emerging financial technologies because this new digital environment promises to return financial power to the people. Just as people once came to America seeking the land of opportunity, they are now leaving because of a sentiment that America is not fulfilling its promises to them.

There is a serious risk that this financial flight toward cryptocurrencies, NFTs, digital property, and other novel assets will result in a crash. If history has shown us anything about markets, it is that bubbles are inventible, as is their bursting. If or when these new markets crash, there will likely be a cry for government to step in with more regulations. But that may or may not be the best response. More regulations might drive people even further toward harder-to-regulate assets, where risk and fraud may be even more pervasive, making yet another crash more likely. The result of such a process would be ever-increasing regulations, with increasing inefficiencies and inequalities, but not necessarily a safer financial world.

Instead of creating some new federal agency in response to whatever the next crisis will be, perhaps we can begin to think about alternatives to the administrative state that can protect investors without driving them away. In our Third Era, where ordinary people can easily choose to invest in unregulatable assets, too much regulation can dangerous, just as too little regulation can be. We should think creatively about alternative ways to design optimal regulations so that the future of financial technology leads a safer economy with equal financial opportunities for all.

Index

Abacus, 67
Abood v. *Detroit Board of Education* case, 145
Accredited investors (AIs), 10, 78–80, 94, 157, 161, 165
Activist investors, 100
Adams, John T., 16, 170
Adams, Samuel, 16
Adelphia Communication Corporation scandal (2002), 92
Advanced Research Projects Agency Network (ARPANET), 91
Agency costs, 36, 62, 64, 163
　in index funds, 62–63
　and misaligned interests, 56–59
Aguilar, Luis A., 171
Alshamrani, Mohammed Saeed, 149
Altcoins, 143
American Research & Development Corporation (ARDC), 69–70, 75
Ames, Oakes, 25
Anachronism, 99
Angel Capital Association, 80
Angels, 74, 75, 80, 165
　groups, 80–82
　investor, 68
　super, 83–84
　syndicates, 80, 82
Anonymity, 112, 116–117, 123
Apple, 71, 149
Application (App), 1, 114
Applied Materials, Inc., 71
Arab Spring, 98, 102
ArtistShare, 154
As You Sow (non-profit foundation), 103
ASCII, 119
Asset(s), 16
　class, 70
　cryptocurrency, 170

　digital, 130, 130–131, 133, 138
　stripping, 102
Asymmetric cryptography, 119
Automated quotations (AQ), 89

Bain Capital, 94
Baltimore and Ohio Railroad (B&O), 26
　preferred stock proposal, 28–29
Band of Angels, 80
Bank of New York (BNY), 10, 15, 18
Banking corporations, 15
Barnett, Randy B., 94, 150
Base58, 119
Base64, 119
Beauty.com, 93
Behavioral costs, 58, 62
Benebit scandal, 135
Berkshire Hathaway, 27
Bill of Rights, 16
Binary digit (bit), 119
Bitcoin, 38, 112, 115–116, 118, 119, 120, 123–124, 130, 132, 133, 142, 147, 149, 170
　Genesis Block, 118
Bitcoin Cash, 130
Blockchain technology, 98, 112, 120, 122–123, 140, *See also* Cryptocurrencies
　hash problem, 122–123
　proof-of-work, 122
　solving double spend problem, 121
　startups, 134
Boston Stock Exchange (BSE), 33, 34
Bots, 91
Bounded rationality, 58
Brandeis, Louis Dembitz, 46
Brandeisian regulatory theory, 46–47
Breakeven, 72
Brokers, 13, 32, 33, 34, 38, 90, 107
Brown v. *Bullock* case, 63

Brown, Duncan, 104
Brute force hacking, 120
Bry, Charles, 118
Bucket shops, 7, 34–37, 38, 53, 54
Budd, Ted, 136, 138
Buffett, Warren, 28
Bulldog Investors, 102
Burr, Aaron, 15
Bush, George W, 93
Buttonwood Agreement, 7, 14
Buying on margin, 106–107
ByteDance Ltd, 88

Canadian Securities Exchange (CSE), 34
Cantor Arts Center, 25–26
Capital. *See also* Venture capital (VC)
   to entrepreneurs, 158
   formation for entrepreneurs in crowdfunding, 170–171
Capitalism, 1, 3, 7–8, 19, 31
Cardano blockchain platform, 130
Casey, John P., 34
Chesapeake & Ohio Canal Company (C&O), 26, 27
China Banking Regulatory Commission, 140
China Insurance Regulatory Commission, 140
China Securities Regulatory Commission, 140
Churchill, Winston, 134
Churning, 36
Cisco Systems, 71
Citizens United v. *Federal Election Commission* case, 144
Classic activism, 102
Clayton, Jay, 132
Clinton, George, 16
Coffey v. *Ripple Labs Inc.* case, 132
CoinMarketCap data, 144
Comcast Corporation, 141
Commodity Futures Trading Commission (CFTC), 130, 136, 137
   regulation of cryptocurrencies, 137–138
Compaq Computers, 71
Competitive regulation, 1, 3, 170
Compression, 119
Computational asymmetry, 51
Computational investing
   agency costs, 56–59, 62–63
   computer power, 59–61
   diversification, 54–56
   index fund, 61, 62
   information costs, 56
   Investment Advisers Act (IAA), 52–53
   Investment Company Act of 1940 (ICA), 52–53
   misaligned interests, 56–59

   mistakes, 63
   mutual funds, 53–54
   pre-regulation investment advice, 52
   transaction costs, 56
Computational technology, 64
Computer evolution, 67
Computer power, 59, 61
   ENIAC Project, 60
   Integrated Circuits (ICs), 60
   logarithmic increase in processing power, 61
   VFINX, 61
Contractual control rights, 10
Coolest Cooler, 154
Corporate
   direct democratization of corporate governance, 98
   externalities, 9
   fraud, 11–13
   gadflies, 103
   investors, 9–10
   limited liability, 8–9
   risk and reward, 10–11
Corporate America, 8
Corporate finance, 1, 3, 80, 153, *See also* Stock market
   crowdfunding and, 169
   and currency markets, 29
   development, 16
   future of, 189
   NYSE in, 15
   securities regulators, 170
   technological innovation in, 26
Corporation of Georgetown, 28
Corporations, 7–9, 22, 34, 78, 79, 96, 98, 133
   banking, 15–16
   for-profit, 15
   growth in America, 15–16
   issues with, 9
   nature of, 8
   payment for stockholders, 27
   reasons for failure, 10
   and Web 2.0, 98
Cost(s)
   agency, 36, 56–59, 62–63, 64, 159, 163
   behavioral, 58, 62
   information, 56
   opportunity, 12
   transaction, 56
Creative destruction. *See* Schumpeterian entrepreneurship
Crimean War, 21
Crowd science theory, 164
Crowdfunding, 151, 153
   avoiding crowd failures, 165

Index

care about, 169
crowd-lending, 155–156
crowdsourcing, 165
donative, 154
equity, 156
failure of, 157–159
fixing, 169
forming capital for entrepreneurs, 170–171
gamification, 167–169
investors, 163, 164
JOBS Act, 157
lack of resale options, 160–162
limited fundraising, 159
origins in dot-com era, 153
pre-purchase, 154–155
protecting investors, 169–170
rational apathy, 165–167
reputational effects, 167
rewards-based, 154
SPVs, 162
wisdom of crowd, 163–164
working strategy, 162–163
Crowd-lending, 155–156
Crowdsourcing, 65, 165, 168
Crypto Wars, 113
Cryptocurrencies, 2, 30, 119–120, 129, 130, 137, 145, *See also* Blockchain technology
   Bitcoin. *See* Bitcoin
   Commodity Futures Trading Commission (CFTC) regulation, 137–138
   congressional regulation, 136–137
   constitutional questions, 144
   Ethereum. *See* Ethereum
   Federal Bureau of Investigation (FBI) regulation, 137
   Federal Trade Commission (FTC) regulation, 138
   foreign governmental agencies (FGAs) regulation, 140
   and freedom from economic slavery, 150–151
   Internal Revenue Service (IRS) regulation, 138
   investing in, 123–124
   Litecoin. *See* Litecoin
   market share (2021), 115
   marketplace, 87–88
   markets, 112, 142–144
   mining, 139
   Office of the Comptroller of the Currency (OCC) regulation, 139
   private regulation, 140
   search and seizure, 147–148
   sovereign, 140
   white papers, 135
Cryptography, 112, 114, 147, 151
   asymmetric, 119
   Cypherpunks, 113–114
   and freedom from self-incrimination, 148–149
   and freedom not to speak, 144–145
   as natural right, 150
   origins of, 112
   regulation and freedom of association, 145–147
   symmetric, 119
Cyberspace, 147
Cypherpunks, 2, 113–114, 116
   intentions to use cryptocurrencies, 123
   Nakamoto's emails to, 118

Dark pools, 161
Data technology, 1
Davidson, Warren, 138
Dearie, Raymond, 135
Debt, 9, 26–27, 28
   crowdfunding model. *See* Crowd-lending
   investment, 156
   national, 17, 18
   obligations, 183
Debt Slavery, 102
Decacorn companies, 75, 88, 89
Decentralized Autonomous Organization (Ð), 170
Decryption, 113, 119
DeepFuckingValue, 106, 108
Defense Advanced Research Projects Agency (DARPA), 91
Defined-benefit plan system, 169
Delaware Bridge Company, 20
Demo days, 81
Democracy, 114
   shareholder, 98, 101, 103
Democratization
   of access to stock exchange information, 33
   direct democratization of corporate governance, 98
Digital assets, 138, *See also* Cryptocurrencies
   regulation, 130, 130–131
Digital wallet, 123
Disclosure, 48, 49, 52, 58, 64, 88, 93, 94, 100, 142, 157, 159
Distributed ledger, 121
Distribution Act (1836), 18
Diversification, 54–56, 68, 76
Dividend, 26, 28
Dodd-Frank Act (2010), 67
Dogecoin, 143
Donative crowdfunding, 154
Doriot, Georges, 69
Dot Com Bubble, 52, 70, 89, 91–93
   NASDAQ and, 89

Dot Com Bubble (cont.)
  penny stocks and, 89–91
  Sarbanes-Oxley Act (2002) and, 93–94
Double spend problem of digital currency, 121–123
Dow Jones Industrial Average (DJIA), 43, 54, 62
Dr. Suess, 93
Due diligence, 81

Early-stage financing, 71–72
E-commerce, 67, 92
Economic slavery, freedom from, 150–151
Economics, 11, 38
  Keynesian, 45
  trickle-down, 51
Edison, Thomas A., 32
Electric Boat Company, 54
Electron tunneling, 61
Electronic Arts, 71
Electronic Numerical Integrator and Computer (ENIAC), 60
Encryption, 113, 114, 119, 129, 147, 149, See also Cryptography
  patents, 118
  via cryptography, 146
Enhanced Surveillance Procedures, 146
Enron Corporation, 10, 92, 93, 162
Entrepreneur(ship), 68, 69, 151, 162–163, 170
  positive impact in social welfare, 171
Equity crowdfunding, 156, 157–159, 164–165
Ether, 133
Ethereum, 38, 130, 132, 142, 143, 170, 185
E*Trade Financial Corporation, 87, 142
Expansion stage financing, 72–73
External cost. See Negative externality
ExxonMobil, 101

Facebook, 80, 97, 99, 100, 102, 123, 171, 187
Farook, Syed Rizwan, 149
Federal Bureau of Investigation (FBI), 136, 141, 146
  regulation of cryptocurrencies, 137
Federal laws, 2
Federal Reserve, 169
  Regulation T, 107
Federal Trade Commission (FTC), 130, 136
  regulation of cryptocurrencies, 138
Female computer at Langley, 59
Fifth Amendment of U. S. Constitution, 147–149
Financial Crimes Enforcement Network (FinCEN), 138
Financial ecosystem, 51, 67
Financial Industry Regulatory Authority (FINRA), 158
Financial innovation, 14, 26, 53
  penny stocks, 89

  of preferred stock, 24, 26–28, 29
Financial law, 2
Financial markets, 1, 2, 157, See also Stock market
  evolution of, 67, 84, 129
  fraud in, 12
  social media impact in, 100
  technological innovation in, 61
Financial preferences, 28–29
Financial regulation, 1, 14, 131
Financial revolution, 1, 100
Financial Services Agency of Japan, 140
Financial Services Regulatory Authority (FSRA), 140
Financial technology (FinTech), 70, 143
Financing
  early-stage and seed-stage, 71–72
  expansion stage, 72–73
  later stage, 73
First Amendment of U.S. Constitution, 129, 145
Fix Crowdfunding Act, 159
Flash Crash, 63, 64
Foreign governmental agencies (FGAs), 130, 136
  regulation of cryptocurrencies, 140
Foreign Intelligence Surveillance Act (FISA), 146
Fourteenth Amendment of U.S. Constitution, 150–151
Fourth Amendment of U.S. Constitution, 147–148
Franklin Delano Roosevelt (FDR). See Roosevelt, Franklin Delano
Fraud, 11, 48
  bucket shop, 36
  consequences of, 12
  corporate, 11–13
  in financial markets, 12
  ICO, 135–136
  risk of, 11
Free banking era in American banking, 19–20
Free incorporation, 16–17, 19
Free riding, 100
Freedom of association, 145–147
Freenet, 153
Friends, family, and fools (FFF), 71
Funding portals, 157, 158

Gabbard, Tulsi, 138
Gambling on stock markets, 35, 38, 54
GameStock Short Squeeze, 108
GameStop Episode (GME), 105–106, 108
Gamification, 167–169
Gekko, Gordon, 51
General Electric Corporation (GE), 32
General Theory of Employment, Interest, and Money, The (Keynes), 45
Genesis Block, 118, See also Bitcoin

Genesis Investments Limited, 79
Gilmore, John, 113
Gnutella, 153
GoFundMe, 154
Gold standard, 29–30, 73, 88
Gold Standard Act (1900), 29
Golden Spike, 24–26, 67
   financial preferences, 28–29
   financing railroads, 26
   gold standard, 29–30
   preferred stock, 26–28
   replica of, 25
Goldstein, Phil, 102
Google, 71
Goose Chase, 167
Gottheimer, Josh, 138
Gottlieb, Mark, 102
Grassroots shareholder activism, 101–102, 103
Great Depression, 1, 2, 31, 44, 51, 53, 54, 64, 69
Great Recession (2008), 184
Greenbacks, 21, 29
Greylock Ventures, 70
Griswold v. *Connecticut* case, 148
Gut instinct, 62

Hamilton, Alexander, 10, 15, 16
Harrison, William Henry, 18
Hash function, 119
Hashing, 122
Hastings, Reed, 99
Hayes, Nick, 104
Hectocorn companies, 75, 88
Hells Fargo protests, 101–102
Henry, Patrick, 16
Herding, 164
Hewlett, William, 68
Hewlett-Packard (HP), 68–69
   garage in Palo Alto, 69
Hexadecimal digits, 119
Hitler, Adolph, 44
Hoover, Herbert, 44, 106
Howey Test, 131, 136, 143–144
Hughes Telegraph, 32
Hughes, Eric, 113
Human analysis, 62

Icahn, Carl, 100
Idiosyncratic risks, 54–55
Illiquidity discount asymmetry, 160, 161
Index funds, 51, 53, 62, 64, *See also* Mutual funds
   agency costs in, 62–63
   regulation of, 63–64
IndieGoGo, 154
Individual risks. *See* Idiosyncratic risks

Information, 7, 36, 99
   accessibility, 147
   asymmetry, 162
   asymptotic, 164
   cascade, 164
   costs, 56
   cryptography, 149
   decryption, 120
   democratic, 33
   digital, 122
   encryption, 113, 120, 147, 148
   exchange in bucket shops, 34–36
   financial, 31, 32, 33, 47, 97, 168
   limitations on dissemination of, 166
   networks, 171
   overload, 49
   sharing, 90, 96, 116, 121, 163
   stock exchange, 33
   in stock markets, 34
Initial Coin Offerings (ICOs), 132–135
   fraud, 135–136
Initial public offerings (IPOs), 67, 73, 88, 133
Instantaneous multilateral worldwide communication networks, 171
Integrated circuits (ICs), 60
Internal Revenue Service (IRS), 136, 148
   regulation of cryptocurrencies, 138
International government agencies (IGAs), 130
Internet, 1, 2, 67
   bubble. *See* Dot com Bubble
   development, 91
   shareholder voting, 98–99
   shopping. *See* E-commerce
Internet service provider (ISP), 91
Investment, 2, 17, 21, 36, 76
   advising, 52
   angel, 80
   automated, 53
   contract, 47, 143
   in cryptocurrency, 123–124
   early-stage, 72
   equity, 156
   in expansion phase, 73
   fever, 37–38
   later stage, 72
   in mutual funds, 62
   opportunities, 2
   as preferred stock, 82
   pools, 53, 62
   relatively safe, 169
   syndicate, 165
   Venture Capital, 70, 73, 75, 82–84
Investment Advisers Act (IAA), 43, 48, 52–53
   attempt to reduce agency, 58

Investment Advisers Act (IAA) (cont.)
    designed to resolve agency problems, 63
Investment Company Act (ICA), 43, 48, 52–53, 79
    attempt to reduce agency, 58
    designed to resolve agency problems, 63
Investors, 34, 35, 142, *See also* Accredited investors (AIs)
    activist, 100
    angels. *See* Angels
    corporate, 9–10
    crowdfunding, 163, 164, 169–170
    exotic and risky investments, 170
    long, 107
    margin, 43, 106, 107
    non-accredited, 75, 94, 158
    opportunities for, 87
    ordinary, 109, 163, 169, 170
    professional, 163
    share of, 10
    short, 107, 108
    startup, 162

Jackson, Andrew, 16, 17, 19, 29
Jay, John, 16
Jiaozi, 20
JPM Coin, 139
JPMorgan Chase, 15
Jumpstart Our Business Startups Act (JOBS Act), 153, 157–159, 165, 171
JUUL Labs, 88

Karpeles, Mark, 137
Keynes, John Maynard, 45, 46
Keynesian economic theory, 45–46
Kickstarter, 154
Kilby, Jack St. Clair, 60
King, Brayden, 103
King, Neal, 118
Kirzner, Israel, 171
Kirznerian entrepreneurship, 171
Kleiner Perkins Caufield & Byers, 71, 84
Kleiner-Sequoia model of staged investment, 73
Kodak (KODK), 96
    price spike, 97

Langley Memorial Aeronautical Laboratory, 59
Large private companies (LPCs), 87, 88
Later stage financing, 73
Layering, 63–64
Ledger, 121
Lee, Robert E., 22
Legal Tender Act (1862), 21–22
LendingClub company, 155–156
Leveraged investing, 17

LimeWire platform, 153
Limited fundraising, 159
Limited liability, 8–9
Limited liability companies (LLCs), 166
Liquidity events, 71, 73–75
Litecoin, 38, 130, 133, 142, 143
Lobbying, 12
Local regulation of cryptocurrencies, 139

Mac OS, 91
Madison, James, 16
Main Street investor, 34, 36
Malik, Tashkent, 149
Maloney, Carolyn, 157
Margin
    call, 17, 18, 107, 108
    investing, 17
    investors, 43, 106, 107
Massachusetts Investors Trust, 53
May, Timothy, 113
McFarland, Billy, 104
McKenry, Patrick, 157
Median market capitalization, 88
Mega rounds, 76
Melvin Capital, 108
Meme investing, 108–109
Meme stock, 108
Merger and acquisition event (M&A event), 73
Michigan's Act to Organize and Regulate Banking (1837), 19
Micro-celebrities. *See* Social media – influencers
Microsoft Corp. (MSFT), 143, 160
Miniaturized Electronic Circuits technology, 60
Mini-IPO, 157
Mint Act (1792, 1873), 29
Miranda v. Arizona case, 148
Miranda warning, 148
Misaligned interests, 56–59
Mochizuki, Shinichi, 118
Modern startup lifecycle, 83
Modern telegraph, 31
Modern venture capital, 75–77, *See also* Venture capital (VC)
Money Trust, 47
Moore, Gordon, 60
Moore's law, 61, 64
Morse code, 31
Morse, Samuel, 31
Mosaic web browser, 91
Mt. Gox, 137, 141
Multiplier factor, 45

Index

Munition, 113
Mutual funds, 53–54, 56, 58, 70, *See also* Index funds

Nakamoto, Satoshi, 113, 115, 116, 118, 121, *See also* Bitcoin
   emails, 118
Napster, 153
NASDAQ, 9, 89, 90, 133
   capital market, 90
   digital features, 90
National Association for Advancement of Colored People (NAACP), 145
National Association of Securities Dealers (NASD), 89
National Bank Act (1864), 21
National Banking Act (1863), 21–22
National Labor Relations Acts (1935), 43
National Quotation Bureau (NQB). *See* Pink OTC Markets
National Science Foundation (NSF), 91
National Security Agency (NSA), 141, 146
National Security Association. *See* National Security Agency (NSA)
Nat'l Ass'n for Advancement of Colored People v. State of Ala. ex rel. Patterson case, 145
Negative externality, 11
Nelson, Willie, 154
Netflix, 99, 100
Network effects in stock market, 33–34
New Deal, 43
   disclosure rules, 48–49
   Securities Exchange Act (1934), 47–48
   securities regulations, 47
New York and Mississippi Valley Printing Telegraph Company. *See* Western Union
New York Stock Exchange (NYSE), 2, 9, 15, 32, 33, 34, 51, 90, 133
   increasing membership, 43
   initial listing fee, 90
   loss of DJIA, 43
   origins of, 13–15
   purchasing seat on, 38
   regulations, 37
Ninth Amendment of U.S. Constitution, 150
Node(s), 118, 123, 163
Non-accredited investors, 75, 94, 158
Non-governmental organizations (NGOs), 103, 130
Nonymity, 116, 117
NSFNET, 91

Obama, Barrack, 157, 158, 171
Occupy Wall Street movement, 98, 101
Office of Comptroller of Currency (OCC), 136
   regulation of cryptocurrencies, 139

Office of Inspector General (OIG), 137
Ohio Life Insurance and Trust Company, 20–21
Oksman, Vladimir, 118
Open-source code, 114
Oppenheimer, Robert, 60
Opportunity cost, 12–13
Oracle, 71
Ordinary investors, 89, 90, 163
Other People's Money and How the Bankers Use It (Brandeis), 47
Over the counter (OTC), 89

Packard, David, 68
Palo Alto, 163
Panic of 1837 in US, 17–19, 22, 24
Patents, 7
Penny Stock Reform Act (1990), 90
Penny stocks, 89–91
People's Bank of China, 140
Perkins, Frances, 46
Perry, Scott, 138
Petro (₽) (sovereign cryptocurrency of Venezuela), 140
Pets.com, 92, 93
Petscore.com, 92
Philadelphia Stock Exchange (PHLX), 33, 34
Physical stock certificate, 160
Pink OTC Markets, 90
pink sheets, 89–90
Pink Sheets LLC. *See* Pink OTC Markets
Pitch, 81
Planned Parenthood of Se. Pennsylvania v. Casey case, 151
PlexCoin, 135
Ponzi schemes, 57
Porsche SE company, 107
Preferred stock, 24, 26–28, 29, 80, 82, 162
Pre-purchase crowdfunding, 154–155
Pre-regulation investment advice, 52
Principal, 27, 28, 57, 62
Privacy, 114, 115, 146, 148, 151
Private Financing's Safe Harbor. *See* Regulation D (Reg D)
Private keys, 119–120, 147, 149
Private regulation of cryptocurrencies, 140
PRNET, 91
Professional investors, 163
Proof-of-work, 121–123
Pseudonymity, 116, 117
Public Company Accounting Oversight Board, 94
Public corporation, 96, 98, 183
Public keys, 119–120
Public offering, 77
Public/private dichotomy, 87

Pullman Sleeping Car, 24
Pullman, George, 24

Qualified Institutional Buyers (QIBs), 161
Qualified purchases (QP), 78–79, 161
Quantum computers, 61, 120
Quantum Corporation, 71
Qume company, 71

Railroad Era, The, 24
Rational apathy, 80, 100, 165–167
Rational ignorance, 100
Ravikant, Naval, 80
Reddit, 97, 168
Regulation, 1, 14, 130, *See also* SEC regulation of crypto-securities
  competitive, 1, 3, 170
  of cryptocurrencies, 136–142
  of digital assets, 130, 130–131
  NMS, 63
  regulatory standards, 77
  T call, 107
Regulation Crowdfunding (Reg CF), 157, 158, 159, 165
Regulation D (Reg D), 83, *See also* Securities and Exchange Commission (SEC)
Regulation Fair Disclosure (Reg FD), 77–78, 96, 99–103
Relevance assessment, 168
Rent-seeking theory, 12, 13
Reputational effects, 57
  in crowdfunding, 163
Resale options, lack of, 160–162
Rewards-based crowdfunding, 154
Ripple, 88, 130, 132
Roaring Twenties, 43, 53, 68
RobinHood (free stock trading app), 88, 108, 142, 167, 168
Roe v. Wade case, 151
Roosevelt, Franklin Delano, 2, 43, 44, 93
Roulette game, 54
Rule, Ja, 104
Ryan, Harris, 68
Ryzen 7 3700X chip, 61

San Bernardino County Department of Public Health, 149
Sapien, Brendan, 38
Sarao, Navinder Singh, 63
Sarbanes-Oxley Act (2002), 67, 93–94, 182
SATNET, 91
Schumpeterian entrepreneurship, 171
Scytale, 112

SEC regulation of crypto-securities, 131, *See also* Cryptocurrencies; Securities and Exchange Commission (SEC)
  Coffey v. Ripple Labs Inc. case, 132
  ICO fraud, 135–136
  initial coin offerings, 132–135
  SEC v. Howey case, 131–132
Second-order effects, 37
Securities Act (1933), 43, 47, 52, 156, 158
  registration requirements, 77
Securities and Exchange Commission (SEC), 2, 43, 47, 48, 77, 130, *See also* SEC regulation of crypto-securities
  Regulation D Rule 501, 78
  Regulation D Rule 506(b), 78
  Regulation D Rule 506(c), 77, 157, 159, 165–166
  Rule 14a, 99
  SEC-mandated disclosure, 100
Securities Exchange Act (1934), 43, 47–48, 138
Security Tokens, 135
Seed valley of death, 72, 84
Seedfunding. *See* Seed-stage financing
Seed-stage financing, 71–72
Self-incrimination, freedom from, 148–149
Self-regulation, 34
  self-regulated stock markets, 13
Self-regulatory organizations (SROs), 14, 34
Sellers/selling, short, 106
Sequoia Capital, 71, 84
Sequoia Fund X, 79
Series A fundraising round, 83
Series AA. *See* Early-stage financing
Series Seed. *See* Early-stage financing
Shareholder(s), 11, *See also* Social media shareholder activism
  collective action, 99–103
  communication rules in SEC, 99
  democracy, 103
  direct democracy, 98
Shark Tank, 76, 171
Shelly, Mary, 116
Shirking, 57, 93
Short squeeze, 106–108
Silicon Valley, 2, 51, 87, 158, 170, 171
  AIs, 78–79
  angel groups, 80–82
  angels, 80
  early-stage financing, 71–72
  expansion stage financing, 72–73
  later stage financing, 73
  liquidity events, 73–75
  QP, 78–79
  Reg D, 77–78
  seed-stage financing, 71–72

startup model, 68–69
venture capital, 69–71, 75–77
venture capitalists, 82–84
Silk Road, 116, 137
Smith, Adam, 13
Social media, 96–8
  impact in financial landscape, 97
  influencers, 2, 104–105, 108
  investing, 109
  lending platform, 156
Social media shareholder activism. *See also*
    Shareholder(s)
  corporate gadflies, 103
  direct democratization of corporate governance,
    98–99
  GameStock Short Squeeze, 108
  GameStop Episode, 105–106
  internet shareholder voting, 98–99
  meme investing, 108–109
  Reg FD, 99–103
  shareholder collective action, 99–103
  short squeeze, 106–108
Social utility, 11–12
Solicitation
  for sale of stock, 156
  general, 78, 79
Song Dynasty of China, 20
Soto, Darren, 136, 138
Soulseek, 153
Sovereign cryptocurrency, 140
SOX. *See* Sarbanes-Oxley Act (2002)
Special purpose entities (SPEs), 167
Special Purpose Vehicles (SPVs), 159, 162, 166
Speculation, 52
Spoofing, 63–64
Stanford University, 67
Startup(s), 71, 72, 74, 88
  blockchain, 134
  Coolest Cooler, 155
  financing lifecycle, 83, 84, 88
  investing in, 81, 162
  Kickstarter, 154
  LendingClub, 155–156
  model, 68–69
  policy goal of democratization, 158
Statis Group, 135
Stellar, 130
Stock, 10
  earnings, 27
  manipulation schemes, 109
  portfolio, 53
  preferred, 26–29, 82
Stock market, 54, *See also* Corporate finance;
    Financial markets

BSE, 33, 34
bubbles, 89
bucket shops, 34–37
crash, 44–45
doldrums, 105
investment fever, 37–38
modern telegraph use, 31
network effects, 33–34
NYSE, 32, 33, 34
PHLX, 33, 34
SRO, 34
ticker technology, 31–33
wash sale technique, 37
Stockholders, 10, 27–28, 161
  securities regulations, 156
SPV, 162
traditional, 36
Stop Wells Fargo, 102
Stumpf, John, 102
Sub-prime mortgage crisis, 67
Sun Microsystems, 71
Super angels, 83–84
Supply-and-demand graph, 37
Symmetric cipher system, 113
Symmetric cryptography, 119

Tandem Computers, 71
Terman, Frederick, 68
Thiel, Peter, 80
Ticker technology, 31–33
TikTok app, 114
Token Taxonomy Act (2019), 138
Tokens
  digital, 121, 138
  Security, 135
  Tali, 121
  Utility, 135
  XRP, 132
Tor network, 116
Trading, 17
  algorithmic, 53, 59, 65, 67
  crypto-currency trading platforms, 38
  discretionary, 62
  electronic, 89, *See also* E-commerce
  fees, 36
  technology-driven trading schemes, 64
  volume, 33
Traditional Startup Financing Timeline, 74
Traditional startup lifecycle, 88
Transaction costs, 56
Transcontinental Railroad, 24, 25, 27
Transmission Control Protocol and Internet
    Protocol (TCP/IP), 91
Trevithick, Richard, 24

Trustless systems, 117
Twitter, 96, 100, 102
Two and Twenty formula (2 and 20 formula), 166, 167

U.S. Virtual Currency Market and Regulatory Competitiveness Act (VCMRCA), 136, 138, 140
Ultimate beneficial owners (UBOs), 79
Ultra-safe investments, 169
Unicorn companies, 75, 84, 88, 89
Union Pacific line, 25
United Stated Congress, 136
United States of America (USA), 7
  impact of Great Depression, 44–45
  panic of 1837, 17–19
  return to national banking, 20–22
  rise of corporations in, 15–16
United States v. *Gratkowski* case, 148
University of Pennsylvania, 60
Unlocking shareholder value, 103
USA Patriot Act, 146
Utility Tokens, 135

Van Buren, Martin, 18
Vanguard, 142
Vanguard 500 Index Fund (VFINX), 61
Venture, 68
Venture capital (VC)
  evolution, 70–71
  firms, 69–72, 73–74, 75–77, 78–79, 82, 83
  fundraising, 135
  investment, 70, 75, 82–83
  modern, 75–77
  origins of, 69–70
  transactions, 77

Venture capitalists (VCs), 75, 82–84, 163
Ver, Roger, 123
Virtual Asset Commission (VAC), 141
Virtual Currency Consumer Protection Act (VCCPA), 136, 137, 140
Voluminous prospectus, 134

Wall Street, 14, 34, 100
  investment opportunities, 36
  investors, 106
  stockbroker, 34
Wall Street Crash (1929), 44
Wash sale technique, 37
Washington v. *Gluckberg* case, 151
Web 2.0 technologies, 65, 97, 98
Webvan company, 71, 93
Wells Fargo annual shareholders meeting, 101
Western Union, 31
  Ticker Model, 32
White papers, 116, 134–135
Whitney, Richard, 43
Wikileaks, 96
Wildcat banks, 20
Wilson, Woodrow, 47
Windows, 91
Winklevoss twins, 123
WorldCom, 92, 93
WorldCom scandal (2002), 92

XRP tokens, 132, 143

YouTube, 106, 108, 164

Zero-sum game, 13, 55
Zietzke v. *United States* case, 148
Zillow (Z), 89

CPSIA information can be obtained
at www.ICGtesting.com
Printed in the USA
LVHW082020200922
728819LV00009B/395